The Masks of Society

THE CENTURY PHILOSOPHY SERIES

Sterling P. Lamprecht, *Editor*

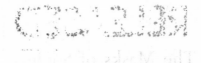

The Masks of Society

AN INQUIRY INTO

THE COVENANTS OF CIVILIZATION

JOHN F. A. TAYLOR

Michigan State University

NEW YORK

APPLETON-CENTURY-CROFTS

Division of Meredith Publishing Company

to

Betts, Ba, and Debbie
in gratitude for our covenant

Preface

This book is the exploration of a new path in social philosophy. The path is in fact as old as the books of the Hebrew prophets, as old as the tragedies of Greece and the *Politics* of Aristotle. But it must appear new for a generation whose memory is too narrow to recall its own covenants.

The foundations of consent upon which the human community is established may be permitted, in settled seasons of the world, to do their work in secret. In such seasons their proper work is disclosed not in the contemplations of philosophy but in the actions of men in the least exalted offices of ordinary life. Their proper function is not to provoke thought but to oblige conduct, to civilize our intercourse, to supply the common grounds of decency upon which we meet and frame normal expectations of one another in the peace of a human society. It is even, as I think, a mark of the vitality of social forms that men act for the greater part, as children act, with a spontaneous outwardness, doing without reflection and without awareness the things that are in fact essential to their community with one another. They act then out of the healthy condition of their institutions, accusing and excusing one another according to a law which is, as it were, in the old phrasing, written in their hearts.

It would be well for us all if the matter could be left there, left permanently there, in our mute habits of obedience. But in an unsettled season such as ours that absolution of the critical faculty which in better times is conferred by old and generous habit is precisely denied to us. The institutions which we have inherited and been taught in the sleep of innocence to revere are discovered in the contemporary moral arrest to be in conflict with each other. Our world is out of joint. We have lost the terms of animal peace. We are obliged, if we would have peace at all, to reconstitute its conditions, to study the terms of a new covenant under which, since paradise is lost, its benignity may be once again restored.

With sublime contempt, tart old Isaiah said of the Egyptians: "Their strength is to sit still." Their strength was their condemnation, and it may be ours. We are a sleeping Egypt. The power of science which sustains us cannot sustain itself, for the immunities that permit its free development depend on social conditions and political tolerances, in short, on human covenants, which not it but only we can renew.

We live afflictedly, we men of the twentieth century, in a rubble of broken faiths. Our buildings we have rebuilt. Our outward desolations we have mended or buried and concealed. We nevertheless leave untouched and unresolved the most profoundly urgent question of our social condition. The question is very simply stated. It is this:

What are the conditions essential to the dignity of persons in any form of human community?

That question is the burden of juristic philosophy. It is at last, when all is said, the sole topic of my inquiry, the inciting problem which has led me to reconsider, in the hard light of our times, all of the major covenants of civilized life—covenants of politics and law, of science and religion, of art and economy, of education and the moral life.

The idea of *covenant* is familiar enough in religious and political contexts. In religion the Hebrew prophets of the Old Testament, the evangelists and apostles of the New, in politics the signatories of the Mayflower Compact, the framers of the American Constitution—all alike have understood the moral fact of community as a relation of persons under covenant.

This fundamental notion of a community under covenant is capable of being generalized so that it may be seen to recur as a social constant in all of the major domains of human intercourse. Each of the domains of society has its proper ethic. Beneath each of them a covenant operates, latent and imperious, uncelebrated but always obligatory in consent.

Juristic philosophy is, as I believe, the path of a new science. It is perhaps too large an aspiration to have thought to do more than point to it. I have thought in part to transverse it, and it is my hope that the example I have given will make the path less lonely for another better equipped than I to move with a seasoned authority through its more intricate avenues. To my friends and colleagues who command such equipment and have generously shared it with me I have the greatest pleasure in acknowledging my indebtedness—to Herbert W. Schneider, who first encouraged me to believe the path worth taking, to Stanley J. Idzerda and Thomas F. Green, who allowed me to believe I had taken it, to my immediate colleagues—Harold T. Walsh, Paul M. Hurrell, Robert T. Anderson, Charles C. Cumberland and Ernest O. Melby, who have assisted me, to Jack Harrison, Paul Barru, and Truman Morrison, whom I found already on the way.

This study has been completed under the terms of a fellowship granted by the John Simon Guggenheim Memorial Foundation.

For permission to reprint materials which have appeared originally in journals I make grateful acknowledgement to the editors of the *Journal of Philosophy* (LIV:17; LV:12); the *Centennial Review of Arts and Science* (II:1; VI:1); the *Review of Metaphysics* (XIII:2); the *Harvard Business Review* (43:2); and the *Educational Forum*, a publication of Kappa Delta Pi (XXVI:4).

East Lansing, Michigan   J. F. A. T.

Contents

Part II
The Covenants of Civilization

Part III
The Reconstruction of the Human Covenant

I

The Juristic Foundations
of the Human Community

chapter I

Juristic Philosophy

1. Path and Covenant

In all settled seasons of society the principles men live by are
more stably secured by habit than by thought. The artist's craft,
the legislator's policy, the saint's conduct—all rest implicitly on
principles which a critical intelligence can discern. The discern-
ment of these principles is essential to our understanding of the
artist, the legislator, or the saint. Yet, for the actor himself, the
principle is apt to remain latent and unspoken, its presence betrayed only in the activity over which it presides. The legislator
enacts laws, not principles of legislation; the artist produces
works, not principles of art; the saint supplies examples for men
to imitate, not principles for them to study. Each addresses himself to the doing of his proper task in which principle is quietly
at work, but none suffers his doing to be postponed until the
naked principle has first been meditated by the bookish intellect.
Such is the uncalculated grace of all healthy moral natures. Their
rectitude is luxuriant. They perform their offices effortlessly, with
the same spontaneity with which a vine puts forth its tendril in
seeking for the light, so quietly intent upon its proper task that
it does not pause to reflect upon it or to study it, much less to
question it or to argue its defense.

All men behave with this tranquil assurance for a part of their
lives, and it is surely a sophistication of our moral career to suppose that it always begins, as reformations begin, with a defiant
nailing of theses on church doors. It does not. Men post theses

3

when they struggle with others; they reflect upon theses when they struggle with themselves. But for the rest, apart from struggle, principles are for use, not for declamation. There is in fact an essential wisdom in that provision of Lycurgus, the lawgiver of the Spartans, who strictly forbade that the fundamental laws of his people should be ever written. If you must write the law in order to remember it, the spirit of the law has been already forgotten; and if you must think the law in order to respect it, you confront the law as any mere stranger confronts it who is subject to it in an alien encounter. The only proper tablet of the law is the cultivated human soul. For law is secured among men not by tablets of stone but by habits of loyalty, by the settled habits of the citizen for whom the law has become, out of old and careful discipline, a simple echo of the soul.

A conscious preoccupation with principle is always, in human affairs, the sign of an unsettled season. It belongs typically to seasons of struggle, to seasons of revolution and moral crisis when the times are out of joint and habits are confused and all men are filled with the doubts and irresolutions of lost Eden. In general, first principles are reflected on only when they have been challenged. Unchallenged, they are simply illustrated in our quiet obedience. The supple mastery of a craft which informs an artist's hand, enabling it to respond sensitively to idea, needs no reflection to assist it, and for so long as it is equal to its commission it receives none. Its easy precision conceals the patient discipline in which its freedom has been prepared. The clay yields up our virtue as if our virtue were its own, and the unarrested spirit sings in the dull earth. It is only when the hand has been stopped, when its free mastery has suffered an arrest, that intellect will seek by an act of reflection to rediscover its sufficiency. Then, and then only, does the mind turn critically inward, take thought of its own limits, meditate principle.

The twentieth century is an age of such moral arrest. The crises of civilization have so multiplied that there is no major sphere of human activity, no sphere in which human community is at stake, whose foundations have not been challenged or rudely shaken. The result is that in our historical situation the search for principle is no longer the exercise of an intellectual option; it has be-

come, for all men of our times, an irrepressible moral necessity.
Such is the significance, historically, of those constitutions and
charters and declarations which men have produced in the effort
to frame the terms of peace and human dignity in this century.
When in solemn assembly the sovereign nations of the earth
joined each other in making a Universal Declaration of Human
Rights (December 10, 1948), no one, least of all the commission
which had drafted the instrument, was deluded into believing
that a mere declaration would be sufficient to dispel the cruelties,
to allay the fears, or to ease the wretchedness, of men in society.
Lion and lamb are in this respect entirely equal in their realism,
that each is the more persuaded of the virtues of civility when the
lion's belly is full. The only declaration which counts materially
for the lamb is a declaration which the lion will still be content
to honor at mealtime. And this requires, besides the declaration
of the lamb, the consent of the lion. In a world of law the fundamental rights of man must be in fact inalienable. That is the simple meaning of a world of law, a world in which the rights of
persons are honored, and civility is preserved, in the general consent of all who are party to the legal order. It does not follow that
we have such a world, or, if we had it, that the citizens of this
world are immune to the invasions of the enemy beyond the walls
or of the enemy within the walls or even of the permanent barbarian within each of themselves. We live in a lawless world, and
the establishment of a comprehensive peace is, with all of us, a
matter rather of aspiration than of actuality. Why then should the
Declaration excite anything more than the passing concern of a
serious man who has some little awareness of the ways of the
world? The Declaration has this permanent claim upon our respect. It is a perfectly clear-headed recognition of the fact that
as the rights of man are not nature's gift but man's institution, the
critical preservation of our covenants with one another is on all
occasions the proper business of mankind. The first sentence of
the charter of UNESCO reads: "Since wars are made in the minds
of men, it is in the minds of men that the foundations of peace
must be constructed." In that simple sentence is expressed, with
an admirable brevity, the practical challenge to social philosophy
in our day.

In every society there are dead morals and living moral issues. The dead are the lore of anthropologists, the part of the moral world which the past has settled and which now persists as congealed habit of mind, nowhere critically defended, nowhere vitally reflected on, for the reason that it is everywhere passively inherited. Such passive inheritance is possible so long as the pattern of custom is internally harmonious. But when custom quarrels with itself, when old, consecrated, and inviolate forms fall into conflict with each other and the immemorial harmony of tradition is destroyed, then a society is thrust rudely back upon itself. Its ancient garment is torn which hid the natural nakedness of men, and men in society suffer an estrangement from one another, find strangers where formerly neighbors were. If custom will not king it for men, who then shall be king? That becomes a living moral issue which, habit failing, the living must decide.

All such questions concerning the foundations of human society will be found to fall naturally into two kinds. They will be questions of Path, or they will be questions of Covenant. Questions of Path are questions concerning the limits which nature has imposed upon our acts. They are the province of technology, of science technically applied to the pursuit of human purposes. Questions of Covenant are, on the contrary, questions of obligation, questions concerning the limits which we impose upon ourselves. All that is distinctively human in our lives—in language, in art, in science, in religion, law, and logic—falls among them. These questions of Covenant are the special province of the critical disciplines, of the branches of history and philosophy which I describe as "humanities," as *studia humanitatis, studia humaniora.*

In our day, in political science, in economics, in sociology, the questions of Path are very assiduously cultivated. The questions of Covenant remain untouched. They remain untouched not because their seriousness is not felt and everywhere admitted, but because the covenants of human community do not admit of the kind of confirmation which we are accustomed to requiring for matters of fact. Matters of fact are capable of being confirmed by the ordinary methods of empirical proof. But what kind of proof is it possible to give, or in propriety to demand, by way of demonstrating the authority of the rules of a game, or the rules of order in a deliberative assembly, or the articles of the American Constitution? Let the particular problem be, for instance, to account for the authority of the Charter of the United Nations in relation to its signatories. The juristic argument which will suffice to deduce the obligations of the member nations to one another and to the international organization is evidently not supplied by pointing to the historical occasion of the signing of the charter at San Francisco (June 26, 1945) or to the subsequent acts of ratification by the nations each according to its own constitutional processes. For the juristic fact which challenges our understanding is not the physical event but the moral engagement, not the fact of the signing on that occasion but the solemn obligation there begun, which binds the parties to the covenant from that time forward to honor rights in each other and duties in themselves. The charter does not profess to describe a fact of nature. It defines a norm of history, and the authority of the norm is presumed to extend beyond the acts by which it has been constituted and even beyond the infractions by which, from time to time, it has been breached.

Such juristic covenants are the despair of our positivist generation. They are indispensable to any understanding of the historical structures which we occupy; they are nevertheless not amenable to what we ordinarily understand by proof. The positive sciences are therefore unequal to conferring upon us an understanding of the objective foundations of our moral community. Those foundations have been presumed to fall beyond the reach of any rational justification or to be at best the outward and delusive expressions of the power relationships on which they rest. In the dogmatic scepticism which has become the intellectual fashion of our day all human covenants are without discrimination viewed as our merely arbitrary conventions, the fictions of estranged actors who are condemned in hatefulness to walk a common stage and admit there no authority beyond the authority which force exacts or fraud steals or fear allows.

The decline of the questions of Covenant, even among the best and most nobly cultivated minds of our times, is the scandal of modern philosophy, and I conceive that there is no single enterprise of the understanding which is theoretically so essential or practically so urgent as to restore the questions of Covenant to their rightful place in the economy of the modern mind.

2. *Juristic Philosophy and the Covenants of Civilization*

All of the positive sciences have this in common, that they are without exception addressed to problems of *description*. They have but one aim, to describe on grounds of observation the *de facto* order of nature or of human society. All alike proceed upon the assumption that if we are able to discover uniformities in the observed behavior of men or things, we shall be able to predict behavior, and therefore to govern it, according to our interest.

It requires therefore an enlargement of our conception of science to see that in the perfectly practical matter of working at the forms of human society the most urgent problems of social theory are not problems of description. They are problems of *justification*, or, as I shall say, problems of *criticism*. The interest is not to describe a fact but to apply a standard. Criticism attempts on a consideration of evidence to judge whether fact conforms to the standards by which we have agreed to measure it. Its aim is not to predict but to adjudicate, not to establish fact but to study legitimacy.

In any argument over claims jurists are accustomed to distinguishing between two types of issues. As a point of orderly procedure they will distinguish between an issue of fact (*quid facti*) and an issue of law (*quid iuris*). Until issues of fact have been, settled, the court will forbid the issue of law to be heard. Therefore the issue of law must be argued separately and remains still to be determined even when all issues of fact have been disposed of. For it may always be asked (the facts of the case being now admitted) by what right the facts are warranted, or in what respects they need amendment if the justice of our moral community is to be preserved.

All of the great moral and political conflicts of our century are grounded in men's fateful oppositions over issues of this sort. They raise issues of law, not issues of fact. They propose problems which are not open to resolution by the simple exercise of a nicer observation or a more subtle analysis. They require of us not an additional fact-finding but a taking of sides, a deliberate suspension of our moral neutrality in confronting fact, an alliance under principle. In a word, they raise questions of the radical variety which I call *juristic*. By this description I do not intend to convey that the questions raised are restricted in any narrow sense to questions of the lawcourt, or that the rights at issue fall clearly in all cases within any formally established jurisdiction, or that there is any power which stands ready with sword and fasces to compel obedience if rights should be abridged. On the contrary, the questions which I describe as juristic are those which in political life we meditate as the precarious questions of war and peace. The great interest of juristic questions is precisely that they appear on the moral frontier, as Truman Morrison would say, "at history's growing edge." The contests concerning them are waged in the silence of law or precedent, beyond the formal limits of any positively declared legal covenants. They have to do not with inherited patterns of conduct, but with the moral problems of men whose inherited patterns have (for want of coherence or consistency or relevance) failed. Men who have experienced the radical dislocations of a social revolution will know how desperately at such times the need for principle is felt. In the contexts where principle is most needed, tradition affords no principle, at least none which is adequate or fully believed in. Therefore, for a painful interval, men are without rule to guide them and are required, by giving rules to themselves, creatively to lay the foundations of such moral community as they permit themselves to have.

We are so used to conceiving the traditions of society upon the physical analogy of a mere sediment borne in time's stream that we leave unnoticed the normative structure of every historical civilization. The inheritance of a society, what it receives and transmits as its tradition, is never the merely physical object—the building, the document, the relic sherd—which it preserves out of the past. A society's tradition does not consist of things; it consists of *obligations,* of the forms and institutions and styles of mind in relation to which obedience and disobedience are first possible. Thomas Masaryk once said: "Tradition is not the dead hand of the past laid upon a people. Tradition is the covenant of fathers and sons." Human society is, in short, as Masaryk saw, a juristic phenomenon, a matter of the peace of men who stand in relations of covenant with one another. In every society there will be found a variety of such covenants. There will be found in fact as many covenants as there are domains of civilization, covenants not merely of politics and law but of art and science and religion and economy and language.

I entitle the study of the covenants of civilization *juristic philosophy*. By juristic philosophy I do not understand the enterprise of jurisprudence. Jurisprudence is simply the philosophy of law, the philosophy of the law formally adjudicated in the courts. The term suggests a narrowly legal interest, a formal and casuistical as distinct from the broadly moral meaning which I in fact intend. By juristic philosophy I understand, on the contrary, an inquiry into the phenomenon of obligation in each of the several domains of civilized activity. Thus, I shall speak of the obligations of persons in political community. But I shall speak also and equally of the obligations which attach to persons as a condition of their membership in the scientific community, or as a condition of their membership in the community of the market. All of these are juristic communities; all of them exhibit persons obligated under covenant. But only the political community conforms to the kind of covenant which is considered in what is ordinarily understood by jurisprudence. In my extended usage an inquiry will be said to be juristic if its purpose is to exhibit the covenant of any form of human community—the constitution of a political order, the parliamentary law of a deliberative assembly, the rules of exchange in a market, the method of a science, the creed of a religion, the conventions of a language, or the style of an art. If such an extension of the ordinary range of the term "juristic" seems at this juncture strained, I can only ask for patience in a new undertaking in which language must be bent to new uses. Language has not been framed for enterprises of the kind of generality which must interest us in traversing all of the major covenants of civilization. I am content therefore, for the moment, to go begging, to borrow unashamedly from one precinct of civilization a notion which I propose to generalize and use in another. By "juristic philosophy" I shall understand the general inquiry into covenants, an examination of the conditions of peace under law in whatever branch of human activity we chance to study it. It is well in introducing these matters not to begin with the sanctities of society. Consider the juristic conditions of a simple game such as chess. The game is a deliberate piece of artifice. It matters not at all that its object is simply the activity itself, that it is without ulterior interest, that in the web of our larger purposes it matters not at all. The rules of chess are a form of covenant. They are the obligations which all who are party to the game must consent to regard as binding upon themselves. None consents to the fiction? Then the game is unplayed; historically, there is no game. But let two consent. Then those two who consent stand with respect to each other in juristic relations which they do not share with any beyond their number. They are, with respect to the game which is their common undertaking, set apart in the peace of a society which is their new creation in the earth. The singular fact is, that they are at peace even in spite of the circumstance that they are divided in competition. For they compete not beyond rule, but in obedience to a rule commonly admitted which transcends their division. They compete under covenant, and the covenant has civilized their opposition.

This transformation of the meaning of competition, which has been effected by the simple artifice of placing the competitors under a commonly admitted law of their own making, has for serious men the profoundest philosophical interest. Whether men shall play chess is plainly their free option; but whether, if they play, they shall play according to rule, is not their option. The great question is not whether there is any game which all mankind is constrained, on pain of extinction, to play. In our world, politically, that is in process of becoming true. But I am not for the moment concerned with the constraints of civilization. I am concerned with its covenants, with the obligations which men have in the exercise of human freedom historically undertaken and maintained. With respect to such covenants juristic philosophy poses the question, Whether there are any rules which belong to games as such, rules so profoundly essential that without them there could be no game at all?

3. Covenant and Ideology

Let us for the moment abstract from any special form of association, from any peculiarity which belongs to a community by reason of the circumstance that it is, say, a political or a religious community, or a linguistic or an economic or a scientific community. The possible forms are manifold, and the differences among them—the differences between a nation and a church, or between a market and a university—these differences, which set communities apart, dividing men from one another, sometimes against one another and sometimes even against themselves, must occupy us eventually. But for the moment let these differences be set aside. I may then formulate our larger problem in its simplest terms, thus: What is the fundamental covenant of human community in any of its forms?

Or, to put the same question in different words: What conditions are essential if men are to stand in the dignity of persons in each other's presence?

In so limited a phrasing I do not expect the full burden of that question to make itself felt. This, however, the question will suffice to make clear, that the solution of it does not depend upon our being able to exhibit a neighborhood in which community has been perfectly achieved, in which community has become, in inward fact as in outward ritual, a literal communion. Walt Whitman once said of democracy that its history remains unwritten for the reason that its history has yet to be enacted. It is just so with human community. Its history has yet to be enacted. There is no city of men which is not in part deserted, even when all of its inhabitants are physically at hand. The perfect sufficiency of human community may be nowhere realized, nowhere actual in fact, nowhere available for observation or description. The conditions essential to it are nevertheless the very matters at issue whenever we discuss the idea of a free society in a society which is imperfectly free, or the meaning of human rights in a world in which rights are denied, or the possibility of peace among men in a century which wakes to war and sleeps to a hostile truce.

Karl Marx was accustomed to marking a radical distinction between science and ideology. The primary recommendation of his scientific materialism was, as he conceived, its capacity to expose the ideological dimension of all historical currents of social thought. The real and consequential divisions in society, the divisions which fatefully preside over our labors and make unacknowledged differences in our reflections, are divisions of classes, of economic estates, in the class struggle. Ideologies mirror these divisions. An ideology appears wherever one speaks out of the partisanship of a class. At bottom it is simply this partisanship become articulate. If power were to attempt to justify itself in a social system, what would it say? What it would say is inevitably, in Marx's view, ideological, that is, argumentative, interested, undetached. An ideology can never claim the disinterestedness of scientific truth. Truth is not its purpose. Its purpose is practice, not knowledge; survival, not theory. The real motive of an ideology is never to confer understanding or an unprejudiced vision of what is the case, but to form and enforce the attitudes which are essential in the minds of men if their class is to preserve itself athwart the stream of history.

An ideology is the creed of a partisanship. Like all class-consciousness the first stage of its development is militant; all subsequent stages are defensive, intolerant, jealous of prerogative. Let an ideology at any stage admit the least moiety of doubt concerning the authority of its own premises, it is already in part dead. Historically, it is in process of being displaced. For the power of an ideology does not lie in its capacity to resist the critical challenges of a freely inquiring mind. Its power lies in its capacity to induce assent, and having induced it, to insulate it from the competition of other options.

At the present juncture of human affairs, when ideologies everywhere divide the world, the great temptation is to suppose that all partisanships are thus arbitrary. The temptation is to protest that all rectitude is myth, and every justification a concealment; that beyond the brute dispensations of power in human affairs there is no objective ground for preferring one partisanship to another; that since in nature no partisanship is justified, therefore in history all partisanships are equal. Such is our absurd modern capacity for desperation, disbelief, and monstrous paradox. We have made humanity itself an ideology, a conception as arbitrary in the human world as it is inconsequent in the infinite moral silence of the physical universe.

But suppose it were possible to show that there are juristic conditions which are essential to any moral community whatever, conditions without which men could not claim to have community at all or to stand even in the least degree related to each other in the dignity of persons. Then whether we should decide to have community or not would be open to our choice, just as civilization or barbarism is always in fact open to our choice. But whether, if we decided in favor of community, these conditions should be admitted, would be open to no choice. They would be the objective and perfectly inviolable requirements of any form of community, objective and inviolable not in the sense that they belong to nature apart from our interests but in the sense that they are *juristically necessary*, that is, indispensable to any community of persons whatever.

One of the most luminous concepts which comes to us out of the ancient world is the Stoic idea of *humanitas*. By *humanitas* the Stoic philosopher understood a moral estate, not a biological species. He intended what we should understand by "human brotherhood" or "the family of man." Essentially, *humanitas* signified the moral community to which all human beings are by the exercise of right reason capable of belonging but to which no one belongs by the mere passion of heredity. Membership in the species *homo sapiens* is a relationship which a human being acquires by the simple adventure of being born. But membership in the moral estate of *humanitas* is not to be thus passively acquired. This membership is the measure of our moral achievement; it is the condition of our moral relapse. For as only by commission do we gain admission into it, so only by commission do we preserve our place there. We may not preserve it. We may fall out of it, lose our estate and extinguish our privilege, relapse to mere thinghood, biologically living but morally dead, in the brute catalogue of things.

It is the perilous fashion of our day to treat that conception as a piece of ideology, as if it were on a par with other accidents of partisanship, neither better nor worse, neither more nor less worthy of philosophic interest, than the patterns of culture which are discovered among modern nations or primitive tribes. But that fashion is one of the most cancelling sophistications of modern belief. For it destroys the serious significance of all inquiry into the foundations of human society. It is, in effect, a denial of the root-problem of political and social theory, to discover the real conditions under which men may move as persons, as subjects of rights and as subjects of duties, in community with one another. Nothing is so healthy as the contempt of modern men for Utopia, for any speculation which is by fraud of sentiment or intellect divorced from a serious concern with the actual conditions of our society. But neither is anything so contemptible as the modern affectation of realism which has made its peace with actuality, which is willing to settle for it, to excuse its omissions and to dignify its insufficiencies. "The ideal," said Goethe, "is the spirit of the actual." It is just so. The ideal is not the actuality but the spirit implicit in it. That is why, at the present stage of our understanding of the human domain, history is more philosophical in its burden than our positive sciences of society. For the latter describe only the letter of the actuality. History, on the contrary, is the source of our sustaining awareness, in confronting the actuality of the human condition, of the deprivation in it, of the relevance of the ideal which the actuality has incompletely liberated.

That is why we cannot afford to dispense with the historical sciences if we would understand the setting of our proper act, not the indifferent order of nature in which distinctions of good and evil are suspended, but the order of freedom, of what Rabelais described through the mouth of Gargantua as our "second nature" which is man.

4. The Juristic Mode of Encounter

It is said of the historian Michelet that his method was to climb inside his subject, to see history not in its desiccated aftermath but in the mode of actuality, as it were through the eyes of those who lived it. Inherited documents preserve only the letter of the old thing done; the task of the historian is to restore the young spirit of the doing which produced it.

To view the human scene after that fashion is to view it *dramatically*, to view it as the dramatist views it who knows how to recapture in imagination the intimate inward sense of an act not his own.

The dramatist seeks by a free imagination to construct a world; the historian by a bound imagination only to reconstruct one. That is their difference, and a profound difference it is. Historian and dramatist are nevertheless allied in the art of imaginative construction, and it is just the achievement of the dramatic mode which at last distinguishes the observation of a historian from that of any other scientific observer of human affairs. Ordinary observation, the observation of overt behavior which we commonly describe as the ground of positive science, is precisely undramatic. Ordinary observation is by systematic intention alien to the thing seen. Therefore invariably it fails in the presence of *persons*. It fails wherever the relations of persons, precisely those relations which I call obligations, are the facts at issue. Blind to persons, blind to their modes of encounter, blind to the distinctiveness of their moral community with one another, ordinary observation discloses the relations only of *things*. It affords sight, not insight.[1] It is the vision not of the prince who regrets poor Yorick but of the gravedigger whose spade has disturbed an animal skull. The prince describes a moral encounter, the gravedigger only a hollow piece of the earth in which the memory of Yorick has been reduced to a present offense in the nostril. If I were asked to indicate what I take to be the historian's special virtue and endowment, I should point to Michelet's capacity for objective sympathy, for entering vicariously into the part of another, for resurrecting into life, out of old forms, the spirit of the dead.

The historian's accomplishment is to see human behavior not

---

[1] This phrasing agrees with the very useful distinction which Richard E. Sullivan draws between the hindsight of the chronicler, the foresight of the scientist, and the insight of the historian.

stipulate formally what it will accept as an outward evidence of
the obligation, it will never be guilty in the manner of the behavioral sciences of confusing the fact of the obligation with the
proof of it. The obligation is the *ratio essendi* of the contract; the
handshake is but the *ratio cognoscendi*. The loss of that distinction has estranged us from any genuine understanding of the
foundations of peace in our civilization.

Civilization is a juristic phenomenon, and any proper study of
civilization will assume a perspective, a standpoint of observation,
suited to its topic. Juristic philosophy adopts the point of view of
the participant, not of the external spectator. It employs the historian's mode of encounter, not because the phenomenon is past
(it is not), but because the phenomenon is juristic and is therefore visible only from the point of view of the actor.

Historically, the most sustained critical reflection upon the
ends of civilization appears in the body of belief and affirmation which we are accustomed to identify as "the Western tradition." The Western tradition is very complex. It has, as one comes
to see, very little to do with the points on the compass or with the
hemispheres of the earth. Its development is spread over more
than 2500 years of evolution, and there is every evidence that it
is still evolving, that it remains at this day, in the Near and Far
East as in Europe and the Americas, the most revolutionary tradition of society in all the world. The Western tradition is surcharged with internal tensions, fragmented by oppositions and
schisms and counterclaims, interrupted, hurt, abused, betrayed,
at times almost extinguished by the unresolved and in some respects unresolvable conflicts of its parts with one another. In its
mode of execution it is filled with strains. Yet nevertheless in its
deep its unity is sufficiently assured. Thus, when men say
of Hitler's Third Reich that it was a desecration and betrayal of
Western tradition, they are understood not merely to have
voiced a fact of geography or narrative but to have voiced a moral
judgment, perhaps in social terms the profoundest criticism that
man is so far capable of. By the Western tradition I intend

merely as an external spectator sees it, who sees in the act only
the thing done, but as the participant sees it, who has insight into
the obligation which it honors or betrays, who sees therefore, besides the thing done, the thing that requires doing but may be
left undone or left wrongly done.

> For that which I do I allow not: for what I would, that do I not; but
> what I hate, that do I. If then I do that which I would not, I consent
> unto the law that it is good.[2]

It is regrettable that modern readers apprehend only the saint in
Saint Paul. He is, besides being a churchman, one of the world's
great writers on jurisprudence, and it is from his capacity as ju-
rist, as down-to-earth lawyer, that one gains the scalding awareness of the discrepance which every historical civilization has
drawn between its moral actuality and its moral ideal, between
its fact and its covenant.

It is this covenant which the historian's mode of encounter
seizes, which it alone can seize or enable us to seize. A generation
ago his mode of encounter would have been described as a species of *empathy*. Etymologically, for the purpose of conveying the
singularity of the dramatic mode, the term empathy had much to
recommend it. For it suggested, or appeared at least to suggest,
exactly the matter that needed insisting on, namely, the feeling
oneself into the role of another, the adoption of a point of view
distinct from one's own. The phenomenon which by this phrasing
men sought to describe underlies all knowledge of social relations
whatever, and the last generation's manner of describing it would
still recommend itself if it were not for the fundamental ambiguity which attaches, and has always attached, to the term empathy itself. Empathy has come in ordinary usage to signify not
a way of knowing but a mode of illusion, what in other connections we would identify as a pathetic fallacy. Thus, into the taut
contrapposto of Michelangelo's sculpture, into the mute thing of
stone, I project the awareness of my own muscular adjustments,
an awareness of the bodily tensions which are part of my imitative

[2] *Romans* 7: 15-16. Compare Ovid, *Metamorphoses*, VII, 19-20: "Video
meliora proboque, deteriora sequor." Also Epictetus, *Discourses*, II, xxvi:
"Every error implies conflict; for since he who errs does not wish to go
wrong but to go right, plainly he is not doing what he wishes."

response to the contemplated form. In empathetic response, by a systematic illusion, I impute to the object the feelings of tension which belong only to me. Such objectification of the observer's own responses is precisely forbidden to anyone who is seriously engaged in the historical enterprise. By the historian's dramatic mode of encounter I would be understood to mean, on the contrary, the singularity of a special and distinctive *way of knowing,* the tentative adoption of a point of view distinct from my own, an awareness not of a content which I have arbitrarily read into a form but of the real meaning which I have critically read out of it. What would it be to see the world as Caesar saw it or as Christ saw it? What would it be to encounter society as an Athenian encountered it or as a Hebrew encountered it or as a Massachusetts Yankee encountered it? What is the difference between the worlds of Aristotle and Darwin, or of Rousseau and Hume, or of Roosevelt and Ghandi? It is these differences, not differences of things but in our ways of relating ourselves to things and to each other, which the historian aspires to study, enabling us to understand, in the face of all of the alternatives of covenant in the human condition, the meaning of the human freedom and the possibilities of moral community among men.

The dramatic mode of encounter is the historian's distinctive and illimitably precious contribution to science. In our day it is in process of becoming a lost art. "Not all audiences are gifted," the actor Jouvet used to say. We are, in spite of our profound concern for social studies, an audience of very narrow gifts. For, past or present, the human world speaks only to those who know how to listen for it; it is visible only to those who come prepared to see.

I remember my loss when as a child I learned that the sound I heard in a seashell was not after all the echo of the sea. I cast the shell aside as a vain thing without meaning. For I was the perfect primitive, disposed to people all the world with persons, to see all effects as I saw my own, as effects intended, from which, if one had but the wit for it, one might read all the secrets of animated nature. I was of course in this matter quickly disabused. The young of my generation were taught to thank God that our century was not given to vain superstitions, and in the brief interval of my life the advance of the behavioral sciences has, I am

assured, succeeded in making even thanks superfluous. was laid upon my fantasy. But this restraint upon fan was proper and warranted with respect to seashells. generation incontinently extended to human affairs generation taught that human affairs, that is, the doi like you and me which did actually proceed from tention, were also to be treated as the seashell, chanical facts of nature, not as moral facts of hist

We labor in a dry season. We labor in a season point of method disciplined itself to the role of e Therefore we are not prepared to hear the irony ing that art and life are very much alike, exce dialogue is so poor. We hear no dialogue. We as alien seashells, all things, even the human th and *res gerundae* which concern us most ferently of a kind, part of the world's poo which the eye meets in a listless vacant e persons, we content ourselves, or at least selves, with things—with the fossil, with t empty shell, and the dry leaf. So far a Michelet's art of climbing inside our subj efforts are made to the end of getting o the intellectual disaster of our century, zation from the subject-matter of its s

Consider a simple contract for the s fact, the objective circumstance which apprehend, is the moral bond which themselves, the one consenting to del goods at the price agreed upon. But tion, which is the objective social to an external spectator invisible. T observer sees is the written instr the poor handshake. A court of evidence. But a court of law wi behavioral sciences have made. dence which is seen with the witnessed through it. In a cou not the handshake but the o

the intellectual and moral premises which enable that criticism to be understood.

There are certain emphases which are clearly and by universal consent essential to the Western tradition wherever it is thus understood. First, the emphasis upon covenant, upon a community of consent, which is drawn from the prophetic tradition of the Hebrew world and from its Judaeo-Christian developments. Second, the emphasis upon the dignity of the free moral agent moving as a person in the community of his equals, the bequest of the classical tradition, especially of Greek philosophy and Roman law.

To the sources of these two emphases we now turn. A former generation permitted itself to speak of "eternal verities." But I am very impatient of such verities. I am content with historical verities. I have sign enough without miracle. For I seek only to describe the part of love that falls within understanding.

chapter II

The Covenant of History

5. *The Hebrew Tradition*

When at the beginning of our epoch Christianity was carried abroad from Palestine, it was carried first to cities. Not the countryside but the cities—Ephesus and Corinth, Philippi and Thessalonika, Alexandria and Athens and Rome—were the places in which the Gospel was first heard. It is our custom, as it was the custom of the early Christians, to attribute the irresistibleness of the torrent which overran the Gentile nations to the operations of the Holy Spirit. And it may be so. But for a practical missionary—for a Saint Paul who traveled the rough road—the torrent which should one day sweep forward unarrested and carry all things before it was nowhere to be found. He moved in the dust of the drouth. He moved among strange peoples and strange gods in a pagan world which knew not Joseph. He moved pregnant in the barren land and solitary in the peopled sea. Therefore, necessarily, he moved to the cities. For in the cities he could find what the sea and the land could not afford, a branch of the vine to which he himself belonged and whose last best fruit he professed himself to bear.

In the cities were the Hebrews of the *diaspora*, the Jewish communities of the dispersion, the remnants of Israel congregated in the Jewish quarters into which they separated themselves, there preserving out of the moil and license of the Gentile city an insularity as perfect, and an identity as unabridged, as any that could be claimed by those who foregathered in Judaea in the

22

face of Zion's holy mount. If a Jew like Simon of Cyrene jour-
neyed to Jerusalem in order to worship in the temple of his
fathers, he set out with no view of remaining there. He did but
exercise a privilege which belonged to all of the scattered children of the covenant, nor had he any reason to believe that his
bond of brotherhood was a ligature less real that he celebrated
it normally, in his everyday act, from afar in a Jewish assembly
set on a shore of Africa which neither patriarch nor prophet had
ever visited. For if the bond of the covenant is in the remnant
of Israel, shall it not be thought equally in a remnant of the
remnant?

Without such communities Christianity might have been
spoken, but without them it would never have been heard. And
if the letters of Paul despair of the Jews to whom the covenant
was given, it is as a Jew that he despairs. He is simply repeating
to them their own discovery as a nation, the identical witness
which the Old Testament prophets from Amos to Jeremiah had
spoken before him, that their community with one another is not
heritable in the blood of the fathers, or in the observance of
an outward ritual, or in the possession of a precinct here or
there. It is heritable in the promise which they perpetually renew, binding themselves even when they are free to walk unbound, obliging themselves even when another sees no obligation, consecrating themselves even when they kneel single and
uncompelled, unseen and in secret, each in the privacy of his own
closet.

Job says (29:14): "I put on justice, and it clothed me." In that
simple sentence is the whole burden of the Hebrew's sense of
history: in community, he is clothed; cut off, he is naked; and there
is no other nakedness.

There are acts of men's solitude which wear the character of
parable. Quite unpremeditatedly they distil a larger meaning
than they were ever intended to declare, and the spirit dilates in
their simple presence. They have the felicity, and all of the simple
directness of expression, of the touch of a child's hand laid unreflectively in your own. So light and revelatory are they, yet so
clean of irrelevance and accident and distraction, that if they
were thought to be addressed to another, we should suspect a

calculation and impute their eloquence to art. But they are un-addressed, and their unaffectedness is their perfect charm. Their significance runs beyond themselves, and we discover in them the uncontrived revelation of the human encounter, the world in the microcosm.

In some measure, if one but had the eye to see it, all historical events have this character of revelation: the connection of event with meaning is what we intend in describing them as historical. The outward event, which is seen, is the revelation of an inward meaning, which is not seen but imputed and reflected on. Thus, the erosion of a stone is no part of the historical order; but the erosion of the pyramid of Chephren is the disappointment of a man's pathetic aspiration after eternal life. These outward registrations of meaning, when they are intended, appear in letters and monuments; when they are unintended, they appear in potsherds and ashes and erosions. But, intended or unintended, they are nevertheless in this alike, that behind the thing, which is the object seen in nature, is the person, who is the subject acting in history.

Of all revelations of men the most incontrovertibly reliable are those produced in seclusion, out of the solitude of an individual or the solitude of a nation, the word spoken only to oneself in a soliloquy which makes no argument to another and therefore can invite none. The Hebrew writings are of this order. Addressed to the Hebrew people, they are the naked reflection of a nation on its own commission, produced in seclusion and intended only for itself. Of all human confessions they are the most absolute in their inwardness, and that is the impregnating virtue which other men or nations of men, who have dared solitude, have always discovered in them. They are the most sustained tragic awareness of a people concerning its own historical commission in the whole history of the world.

But it must be confessed that we see only as much as we permit ourselves to see. We see the root out of the dry ground. The Hebrew tradition comes to us as a history of the religious life of a nation. For an age which conceals its own myth that is a very serious limitation. For we suppose that in rejecting the Hebrew cult we reject equally the conception of human community which sponsored it. In this is our great loss, for the religious element of Hebraism is instructive not because it reveals the god of a cult, but because it reveals the juristic meaning of a nation, the meaning of a community which has put itself under judgment. I say, the meaning of a community which has *put itself* under judgment, not merely one which has been put there. If the Hebrew covenant were solely the act of God, it would have the trivial interest of an earthquake, or of a hurricane, or of a bolt of lightning, which is also, as some say, an act of God, unilateral and punitive. But the Hebrew covenant was no such thing. The Hebrew put on justice, and he was clothed. And it is not indecent that men who are naked should take account of him.

The Hebrew history has this singularity, that it records the history of a nation as the nation sees itself. The bare fact of history as others saw it—the wandering of a Shemitic people loosed from a bondage in Egypt, ranging abroad in the peninsula of Sinai, and coming at last in the thirteenth century before our era in blood and fire upon the land of Canaan—that fact existed for the Hebrews too. But its juristic meaning, the sense of the fact as it was felt by those who enacted it, was not this circumstance, outward and manifest, which others equally could see. For an unimplicated observer the fact has many parallels; for the implicated observer, who participated in the event, it had none. The event was unique, unexampled, heavy with a meaning which was a new creation in the earth.

I must ask you to attend to this distinction between the implicated and the unimplicated observer, between the point of view of the participant and the point of view of the external spectator.

An American will speak five times of his standard of living before he speaks once of his standard of life. Therefore for those who are accustomed to attending, after our discreet positivist fashion, rather to performance than to performers, it inevitably appears that the primary article of American life is the pursuit of an economic affluence. There is some justice in that proposition, for the American has typically from the beginnings of his history refused to put his life and his living into opposition, as if the pursuit of the one and the pursuit of the other were jointly incompatible. On the contrary, the American has always held, with an intractableness which is the perfect despair of all sellers of locusts and wild honey, that poverty, deprivation, any want of the means of living on the part of any member of society, is a social defect which he is under obligation to remedy. The correction may be postponed to the fullness of time. But the demand for it is never questioned. The American finds in poverty a painful discrepance between society's fact and society's promise, and the social remedy concerns him not because he believes material affluence a sufficient pursuit but because the want of sufficient means cancels a man's office in every other pursuit. It is therefore always easy in the American scene to suppose that the outward life which alone is manifest is the only life, and that there is no inward life, latent, imperious, and consequent, which commands the moral allegiance of the citizen and supplies the last motives of the man.

This illusion of the unimplicated has formed the conception of the American character among all peoples who view the American actuality from abroad. And if the image very poorly coincides with the way the American conceives himself, his ordinary act does nothing to mend it. In seasons of tranquillity he confuses peace with privacy, wealth with commonwealth. He distrusts all government and trusts least of all the government he has named. He is as little disposed to brook an interference with his private act as by ordinary habit he is equipped to formulate the principle which could justify it. Principle nevertheless there is, and its implicit force becomes overt and visible in the moment that the conditions of his privacy are threatened. The threat transfigures the whole outward habit of his life. The society of which in periods of security he is so sublimely careless becomes in time of war or social arrest his manifest concern. He makes society his calling. He regards himself as party to its commission and will suffer it to command his last obedience, conscripting his powers, using his substance, exacting his blood and bone. For at that time he marks the distinction which silently underlies the offices of American life at all times. He recognizes the permanent moral gap between the American actuality and the American promise. The actuality may be sordid or corrupt or profane; the promise is luminous and sacrosanct. It is his one invincible affirmation that if America be not yet the city of God, the fault, whatever it may be, wherever it may lie, whether in him or in another, at all events does never lie in the constitution of his society. The constitution is his soul's last covenant. He inhabits a covenant community, and the covenant he holds beyond reproach even if reproach must fall upon himself, accusing his omissions and condemning in him the betrayal of a trust which is his last calling and election among all men and nations.

That is precisely the Hebrew pattern in American life. The Hebrew, like the American, conceived his nation to be engaged in the performance of a covenant. Indirectly, as member to the nation, he was accessory to this covenant, capable by his individual act of offending against the obligations which it laid upon him in his relations with other members of the covenant community. But the principals, the parties directly related in solemn compact, were properly God and the community itself—God and the corporate person Israel. Thus the individual was born into the community, and he died in it: the covenant remained steadfast and intact in the face of his coming and his going. It overarched his generations and bound them all together in the life of one people, supplying to them as the children of Israel such community and continuity as they ever professed to claim. Let the child depart, the nation is preserved. Let the children be scattered, the nation is still preserved. For the nation is wherever its law is, wherever its law is treated as obligatory in the lives of men. But let the nation desert its covenant, its community dissolves. The children are stripped of their patrimony, left naked, bewildered, beyond election and beyond history in nature. In the desuetude of the law, even though the children be gathered, even though the blood remains pure and all the citadels of place and time intact, their moral community has lapsed: they have renounced their historical identity as a people and in renouncing it have suffered themselves to be mingled without distinction in the bare round of nature.

Such, to the Hebrew, was the absolute terribleness of that rejection in Hosea: "Call his name Lo-ammi: for ye are not my people, and I will not be your God." Between history and mere nature this gulf was fixed: history was the order of covenant, nature the order beyond it, and over the life of the nation presided the peril of a relapse from the condition of covenant, the moral death beyond community which was the soul's last condemnation, the Hebrew Sheol.

The belief in Israel's covenant with God carried with it this most extraordinary consequence, that the nation, the nation itself, was under judgment. The Hebrew was prepared for the sake of community to draw that consequence without flinching. He was prepared to draw it even though it must follow that the iniquity of the fathers would be visited upon the children unto the third and fourth generation. If the children must suffer, it is the nation that is judged, and the suffering is redemptive because it is for the nation's sake.

That awareness was proper to the Hebrew's tragic view of life, part of its moral grandeur. No claim to separateness was ever allowed to diminish the individual's responsibility for the nation's guilt or glory. If the Hebrew is complete only in community, he must share the burden of responsibility for every respect in which the community itself is incomplete. Men live with their fathers' ghosts as the American lives with his negro ghetto and his slum; they inherit their fathers' penalties as the American inherits the dustbowl in his nostril; they pass to posterity their guilt as the American passes to posterity the memory of Hiroshima. It is unjust that it should be so? Not more unjust than that they should inherit the benignities of the past for which they are as little answerable. We are born for individual dignity, but dignity carries with it the obligations as well as the privileges, the duties as well as the rights, of the community which nurtures it. The moral community has its costs, and the children's teeth shall be set on edge for so long as any part of its price remains unpaid.

Yet though the Hebrew claimed no authentic individuality apart from the moral life of the nation, it was only the moral nation, the nation equal to its covenant, that he venerated. For in reality there were two nations. The Hebrew belonged at one and the same time to the nation of fact and the nation of promise. And he was like the perennially afflicted American: the promise of his society always exceeded its actuality. The nation of fact was no less than the nation of promise a nation under covenant. Israel was nation at all only because it acknowledged the obligations of the law which governed it. But the nation of fact was forever unequal to the demands which the covenant laid upon it. The covenant laid upon it the obligation to become the nation of promise, a just nation which should bear a light to all other nations, setting judgment in the earth and in all the isles that waited for its law.

And Israel, alas, was never that. Neither did the Hebrew believe it was. In no other nation has a people been content with such absolute remorselessness to condemn its own performance, to preserve the penitential awareness of its own ignominious failures and omissions, to heap such bitter scorn upon itself that no assault of alien contumely should ever be quite equal to its own. The Hebrew forbade himself, even in the flush awareness of the triumphant hour of David's kingdom, to exalt the nation or to deify the state. The view which we tolerate with equanimity, that the state or the nation can do no wrong, that the church or corporation which is elected to bear the covenant is beyond judgment, that the folk is sinned against but never sinning, that the voice of the people is at every count of egotisms the voice of God —any such view would have struck the Hebrew as an idolatry, an abomination practiced by god-makers in a society which has vacated its commission, created its lawless despot, and made a scandal of its own ideals.

The moral grandeur of Israel consists in its magnificent refusals, and neither Judaism nor Christianity has been quite equal to it.

> And if some of the branches be broken off, and thou, being a wild olive tree, wert graffed in among them, and with them partakest of the root and fatness of the olive tree; boast not against the branches. But if thou boast, thou bearest not the root, but the root thee.[1]

Mercilessly Israel rejected every attempt to confound its moral possibility with its actual moral achievement. The Hebrew is the first protestant in the life of men and nations, and whatever is valid in Christianity is valid because his example has been kept.

Doctrinal Christianity insists upon the advent into actuality, on one historical occasion, of the pure image of love. The purity of

[1] *Romans* 11:17-18.

that image shall be never questioned. But Christianity is a betrayal of the genius of the prophetic tradition in the moment that its claim upon belief is made to depend upon such a publication of a sign. Let any historical event, even so luminous an event as the life of Jesus of Nazareth, be treated as an assurance, you make justification by faith a justification by fatality. Which is to say, you have made faith superfluous and justification unnecessary. You have suspended your covenant, for you have suspended your office under it. You abase the love of God from a historical allegiance which you have actively embraced to a fact of nature which you have mutely endured. For my part, if I may love God only because he forgives, then though he forgives me, I am unable to forgive him. His grace is as ruthless as his wrath, and his forgiveness as despotic. For he permits me to love only on grounds of interest which I despise, and which Jesus equally despised, who taught by surrender of self the path to selfhood. Jesus is closer to Hillel than to Paul. For Hillel at least maintained a bilateral covenant in which the dignity of the moral agent was preserved. The sanctity of the member was forbidden to disappear in the corporate entity—in the nation, the church, or the synagogue—which he sanctified. "If I am not for myself, who will be for me? And if I am only for myself, what am I?"

To live for others is to gain life, not to lose it—to respect the worth of persons wherever it is found, in oneself as in another. For a Christian community is a community of selves, not of ciphers. If selfhood were despicable, then to love one's neighbor as oneself would be to despise one's neighbor.

Doctrinal Christianity makes man the object of grace; the Hebrew makes him its subject. The suffering servant of the second Isaiah is elect not because he suffers, neither because he serves, but because he consents to suffer in order to serve. And that is Judaism's, as it is Christianity's, loftiest conception, which the Hebrew tradition expressed in the idea of an objective covenant of the human community.

6. The Order of Fact and the Order of Obligation

The objectivity of its covenant is what the Hebrew nation intended in saying that Israel's covenant was with God. The manner of speaking is alien to the modern idiom, and men accustomed to the modern idiom immediately suppose that the meaning hangs or falls on the question of God's existence. For, as it is thought, unless the existence of God can be certified, the covenant must be subject to the same suspicion of nudity which attaches to its major party.

I have no objection to that way of putting the matter, provided only that its meaning is understood, as the Hebrew understood it, juristically. But for most moderns the juristic meaning is, so far from being understood, not even guessed at. The significant opposition for the Hebrew is not between God and man, but between history and nature, between the order of covenant and the order of fact.

The moral freedom of the human agent is the profound problem of all Hebrew reflection. And the Hebrew discovers the meaning of freedom not in miracle, not in an escape from the conditions of nature, but in obligation, in the instituted structures by which, historically and creatively, he has confined his own path, giving laws to himself where nature sets no law, respecting the conditions of his own community with others in the face of nature's appalling indifference to his exaltation or abasement. He refuses to sanctify in himself the license which nature indifferently allows to him. The opinion proposed in Greek antiquity by the Cynic philosopher Antisthenes and repeated with vulgarity in modern times by Jean Jacques Rousseau, that man is by nature good but made corrupt by his own institutions, is a literal inversion of our juristic circumstance and a denial of our moral problem. It compasses the dignity of the individual at cost of putting his community beyond his care. It treats our community with one another as an accident superfluous to our need, inessential to our happiness, and improper to our hermitage.[2]

2 "To live according to nature" becomes the fundamental tenet of the philosophy of the Stoics, for whom the term "nature" is a normative concept. "To live according to nature" implies for the Stoic the positive affirmation of a higher law, the affirmation of a law superior in authority and sanctity to any man-made law. That idea is dissipated in the transformation given to the term "nature" by Rousseau. Rousseau's conception of nature is perfectly negative: he sought here as elsewhere not to affirm a superior obligation, but to escape obligation itself, whether the obligation were of nature or of merely human convention. For the normative conception of nature, see Chapter III, 9: "The Greek Tradition."

For the Hebrew it is a confusion of thought to prescribe a return to nature to the human animal who has never been absent from it. The only serious prescription, the only prescription which can enlist the voluntary and permanent consent of the free moral agent, is to *realize community*—to realize community in spite of the natural circumstance in which we find ourselves inextricably to be placed. For by nature man is neither good nor bad. In nature he is without distinction and without privilege, caught up indifferently in the universal web which mixes him with things, in mute thinghood, as an organism interacting with an environment. Thinghood he has by submission to the conditions which nature has set for him; selfhood, moral personality, he can have only by obedience to conditions which he has set for himself. Only by his institutions in community shall he be exalted; only by his institutions in community shall he ever be abased. For, juristically, he is as his institutions make him, and as he has made them. You would be person? Be then obliged in the bonds of community. You would be thing? Walk then estranged, beyond community, in nature. For there is no freedom except of persons, and no person except in the justice by which we clothe ourselves.

That is why they mistake who suppose that the Hebrew's search for God was the search for an alien object in nature. His search for God was the search for the objective conditions of his own moral identity in history.

The Hebrew's revelation was in his history, not before it or beyond it. The only supernature which he ever sought to affirm was history. But he viewed history more seriously than we view it, who see in it only an extension of the moral vacuity of nature, a merely physical encounter, the overt displacements of power in which, out of shattered egotisms, the moral silence of nature is maintained. We are so distrustful of interpreting nature *ex analogia hominis* that we interpret history *ex analogia naturae*. Therefore the real conditions of our moral community are forbidden to appear, and history's brooding revelation is as if it were not. We affect to study the human drama; we attend in fact only to the limits set by the indifferent stage upon which the play is cast; and we allow our children to believe that upon that stage there can be no distinction made between a good play and a bad one. But that distinction which eludes us was precisely the revelation which the Hebrew nation labored to decipher. The Hebrew refused to allow the juristic fact to be obscured by the power struggle. He affirmed its centrality as steadfastly as we affirm its futility in the contexts of power. And one must confess judicially, observing his result and ours, that his indomitableness comes better off. Armed with all of the instruments of power, we are captive to nature. He, sufficient in his great surmise, in spite of all of the monstrous outward desolations which his nation suffered, took self-knowledge from his servitude and redemption even from the hand that plucked his beard.

The Hebrew saw community as his calling, and he had made the discovery that there are objective conditions of history just as there are objective conditions of nature. There are conditions, juristic conditions, which are necessary if men are to have community at all. The moral precariousness of those conditions, the possibility that we may fail to realize them even though we preserve all of the manifest outward signs of society, dividing our labors, producing and consuming, harvesting utility, begetting progeny—this tragic possibility is history's immanent revelation. It excited in the Hebrew's vision of his life a tragic awareness of unparalleled intensity. For beyond the uniformity of nature he had discovered the liability of man.

The conditions of nature are fixed by nature. They are usable by our intelligence, but they are not alterable by our act. Therefore the question whether they shall be obeyed can never arise, since it is impossible that they should in any single detail be disobeyed. They are part of the fatality of our lot: we are constrained to submit to them or perish. But the conditions of community are of a radically different order. They are obligations which owe their authority to our consent. We are party to their authority, and apart from our consent they can oblige us not at all. Therefore, with respect to these obligations which our consent has instituted, our obedience or disobedience is precisely in question. For as, having consented to them, we may honor them, so also, having consented, we may fail to honor them. The conditions of community are so little a part of fatality that a man is capable of being without community. Naturally, he lives; historically, he is dead. He lives as Cain lived, exile in the alien earth, quick in the web of things but decedent in the web of persons.

Nothing in nature forbids that relapse to mere nature. Only men in community can forbid it, governing themselves according to the objective requirements of a moral peace of which nature knows nothing. For the requirements of human community are simply the requirements of peace among persons. Juristically, those requirements are as real and intelligible as, naturally, they are voidable. That is the profound inward fact of our moral condition: as community can be established only by those who are party to it, so it can be violated only by those who are party to it. No external power can limit it or alter its conditions, for its conditions are simply the limits which we have laid upon ourselves, who acknowledge obligations to one another for its sake. In the order of things, those obligations are arbitrary; in the order of persons, they are not. For they are not cancellable as custom is cancellable; they are not capricious as ordinary conventions may be capricious; they are not rescissible by government as the statutes of government may be rescinded. They are objective exactly in the measure that our affirmation of community is objective, and real exactly in the measure that our desire for peace is serious.

We sanctify nature; the Hebrew chose rather to sanctify the community which made possible his own sanctity.

Yet, as there were two nations—the nation of fact and the nation of promise, the Hebrew needed terms in which their difference could be defined, terms which would enable him to express the critical tension under which at last all Hebrew life was led. He called the one nation the kingdom of man; he called the other the kingdom of God; and the tension between the two—between the community achieved and the community aspired after, between the letter and the spirit of his law, between the legalism and the justice of his society—this tension was the primordial fact of his awareness of himself as a historical being.

In all of his intercourse—in getting and spending, in making exchanges, in contracting engagements—he confronted other members of his community as equals. Distinctions of wealth or power or social estate might conceal, but were forbidden ever to cancel, his awareness that they were met in equality of membership in the one national life; and the oneness of that life, which sheltered the Hebrew's generations and gave to him an identity apart from the life of Philistine or Moabite or Amalekite, he personified as Israel.

Descriptively, as a fact of nature, the person Israel was without reality; juristically, as a fact of history, it was the prime reality of his moral being. Israel was at least as real as the Israelite, as real as he was, who was history's creature as well as nature's denizen, and if nature be thought to exclude this amphibium of two worlds, then reality must be thought to include him, and it is not he, but nature, that is demoted. For Israel made claims upon him, excited his loyalty, exacted his allegiance, as truly as he made claims upon it, contracting his relations with his fellows according to the norm of expectations which it made possible. Israel was the structure of relations which he and they made animate. It nevertheless presided with an impassive perduring artifice of its own over his conception and his birth and his leavetaking, independent of his individual adventure as the womb of woman is independent of the child which on any one occasion it protects. The relations he contracted with his fellows were his private institutions; the relations he acknowledged with Israel were not. They were in the public domain, and kept him there. They were institutable as they were alterable, not by the man but only by the member. Others could take his place; nothing could take the place of Israel. He related himself to Israel not as to an ordinary person with whom he had, or at least might claim, equality, but by subordination, as an agent is related to a principal who commands his obedience and sets his calling.

But alas, poor Israel, if thou wouldst be a people that the children may know justice in their relations with one another, shall nothing be required of thee that thou shouldst be thought holy, and reverable, and deserving of obedience? If the child be capable of fault, shall the womb be capable of no fault? Israel is kingdom, but what election is in that? Have not Philistine and Amalekite and Moabite a kingdom as well? If the bare having of a kingdom suffices, then Israel is without distinction, and a despotism is as justified as a benignity.

The kingdom of man is a positive phenomenon, a phenomenon

describable in terms of the laws which men have positively enacted. What then can be meant by the kingdom of God? Simply
this, which is the crowning insight of the prophetic tradition, that
the kingdom of man is on any historical occasion *criticizable,*
amenable to a standard of justice as inflexible in its demands
upon nations as nations are inflexible in their demands upon men.

The Roman emperors on occasion allowed private persons to
press claims which ran against the state. They proceeded in such
instances on the maxim, *Legibus soluti legibus vivimus,* "We who
are not bound by the law nevertheless submit to it."[3] The maxim
has the most extraordinary interest. In public law the state is invariably obliged to be judge in its own cause. The consequence
would therefore seem to be that the state is beyond judgment,
that the justice which it demands of the subject cannot be demanded of the sovereign. The maxim civilizes the process by a
distinction: the interest which is permitted to the state in its role
as litigant is forbidden to the state in its role as judge. That submission of power to a self-imposed restraint is, though it comes
from a different world, precisely the Hebrew principle. The *res
publica* respects rights, not ordinations, even when one of the ordinations is its own custodian. In Roman law as in American the
employment of the maxim is discretionary. The Hebrew treats it
as the indispensable mandate of public justice in any free community.

"Shall I count them pure with the wicked balances, and with
the bag of deceitful weights?" says Micah (6:11) with unassuaged contempt for the opinion, not entirely without its contemporary celebrants, that so you measure a thing, you have
dignified it. What is wanted in exchange is not a measure, but a
measure commonly consented to by all who are party to the ex-

---

[3] *Institutes,* ii, 17.8. Before the institution in 1855 of a Court of Claims,
the maxim of American law, that "the State, being a Sovereign, cannot be
sued," operated with inflexible rigor. Every private claim against the United
States required a legislative action of Congress in order to be admitted.
Crusty old James Wilson, then Justice in the Supreme Court, protested in
1793: "On general principles of right, shall the State, when summoned to
answer the fair demands of its creditors, be permitted, Proteus-like, to assume a new appearance, and to insult him and justice by declaring 'I am a
Sovereign State'? Surely not." Quoted in T. E. Holland, *Jurisprudence,* 13th
ed. (Oxford: Clarendon Press, 1924), 133n.

change. And in the life of nations, if men would assess the strength of their bond with society, what is wanted is not a standard merely, but a just standard, a standard capable of eliciting the free consent of men, who measure justice in its terms not because they have no other option, but because, having another option, they discover still in it the conditions of such individual dignity as they may ever profess to own.

7. Juristic Article and Juristic Act

In any community which places itself under law a distinction will appear between the part of law whose authority is original and the part of law whose authority is derived. The law of original authority is described in juristic terms as the *constitution;* the derived law, which depends for its authority on the constitution, is described as *statutory.*

The law of original authority among the Hebrews, their constitution, is the part of their law which the prophetic tradition invariably intends by the word "covenant" (*berith, diatheke, testamentum*). The Hebrew covenant was the fundamental engagement whereby the Hebrews became, in the eyes of those who were party to the engagement, a corporate entity, a nation. It was to the Hebrews what the American Constitution is to Americans, the solemn original agreement by consent to which individuals and families of individuals otherwise dispersed in the face of nature gathered themselves into the moral alliance of one community under law. Let the law of original authority be granted in the initial consent, the authority of all other law may be seen to follow from it as explicative or applicative, as a statutory elaboration of its meaning in relation to the detail of conduct.

When Jesus enunciates the summation of the law in the two commandments,

> Thou shalt love the Lord thy God with all thy heart, and with all thy soul, and with all thy mind,

and

> Thou shalt love thy neighbor as thyself,

he is in fact marking this distinction.[4] All other commandments are to be regarded as statutory, these only as constitutional: "On these two commandments hang all the law and the prophets."

Juristically, that reduction of the Hebrew law to principle is the profoundest positive insight into the conditions of human community which humanity has been heir to. But I do not, at least I do not now, ask assent to that proposition. I ask only that it be seen as a feat of generalization, a generalization of the Hebrew law as perfectly extraordinary in its context as was the code of Justinian, whose *Institutes* effected the same kind of simplification for the Roman law. That manner of simplification, and it alone, is for the moment in question, and it is a matter of last consequence, especially for those who take the act of Jesus seriously, that its positive genius not be obscured by attending to the holiness of the proponent.[5]

The term "covenant" has, like the term "constitution," a dual meaning: it refers to the articles of agreement to which consent is given; it refers to the giving of consent, to the juristic act, whereby the parties to the covenant place themselves under obligation to govern their conduct according to the articles agreed upon.

Thus, in the American *Constitution,* the articles of agreement are announced in the body of the instrument; the juristic act is announced in its preamble: "We, the people of the United States, . . . do ordain and establish this constitution for the United States of America."

The Hebrew covenant contains the same elements. The articles of the Mosaic covenant appear in the Ten Commandments conveyed to the people and entered into by them at Sinai; they are reduced in number, but preserved in effect, in Jesus' summa-

---

[4] *Matthew* 22:34-40; *Mark* 12:28-34; *Luke* 10:25-28.

[5] Hillel performed the same act. Jesus' first commandment may be found in *Deuteronomy* (6:4-5), the Hebrew Shema, which has been the fundamental confession of Judaism in all ages. The second commandment may be found in *Leviticus* (19:18). Asked to condense the law into its briefest distillation, Hillel paraphrased *Leviticus:* "Whatever is hateful unto thee, do it not unto thy fellow: this is the whole Torah; the rest is explanation." Quoted in *The Pentateuch and Haftorahs, Hebrew Text, English Translation and Commentary,* 2nd ed., edited by J. H. Hertz (London: Soncino Press, 1960), 502, 564.

tion of the law. The juristic act whereby their authority was constituted as binding upon the parties by consent is recorded in *Exodus* (19:5-8):

> *Now therefore, if ye will obey my voice indeed, and keep my covenant, then ye shall be a peculiar treasure unto me above all people: for all the earth is mine. And ye shall be unto me a kingdom of priests and an holy nation.* These are the words which thou shalt speak unto the children of Israel.

> And Moses came and called for the elders of the people, and laid before their faces all these words which the Lord commanded him. And the people answered together, and said, *All that the Lord hath spoken we will do.* And Moses returned the words of the people unto the Lord.

In short, the Hebrew covenant, for those who were party to it, was a deliberate convention made in the face of nature, a consensual act jointly undertaken and bilateral in its force. The covenant acquires its authority, and the people their status under it, not by a despotic imposition which subjects the people to a law not their own. On the contrary the law is theirs. They have put on justice, and they are clothed: *they are bound by the law because they are party to it.* Their consent confers upon the law its authority, and the dependence of the law upon their willingness to be obliged by it insulates their community from the annulments of any alien assault. Babylon may compel their outward submission; it is powerless to compel their inward allegiance. In that contrast between servitude and obligation, between physical conformity and moral obedience, lies the whole meaning of Israel's sense of election among nations.

Israel is elect not because God has stipulated the articles of community, but because Israel has consented to regard those articles as obligatory. Israel's concurrence is essential to its own election, and without that concurrence there can be no election.

> . . . And I will say to them which were not my people, *Thou art my people;* and they shall say, *Thou art my God.*[6]

We moderns are for a variety of reasons indisposed to that phrasing. But the meaning is graver than its vehicle, and the de-

---

[6] *Hosea* 2:23b.

cline of social theory in the modern world is measured exactly by our inability to translate that meaning into terms whose relevance can be apprehended.

The meaning is twofold. First, the articles under which men are capable of standing in permanent and voluntary relations of peace with one another are neither capricious nor arbitrary, but fixed by the conditions which are essential to any juristic community whatever. If we are to stand related to each other not as thing to thing, nor as person to thing, but as person to person, as *I* and *thou,* the subjects of rights and duties allied in the mutuality of one society, then there are certain demonstrable obligations which must necessarily be admitted by all parties to our community.

Second, the meaning is, that the conditions which are juristically necessary if men are to have community compel no one to have it. Our community is our care, not our condemnation, and it shall not be had without our care. For community is not the social datum which we have; it is the moral possibility which we labor after. If there are conditions of the human drama which are independent of our idioms, then the goodness of the drama will depend upon our observing those conditions. But the play is not the performance. The performance of the play will depend upon there being actors who are content to limit their idioms for its sake, who consent to oblige themselves each according to the demands of his part. For the simple goodness of the play does not assure that it will be acted, or if acted, that it will be acted well. It assures only that the act of anyone who affects to perform it is capable of being criticized according to a standard which the actor himself confesses.

Look therefore to the significance of that juristic act of the Hebrews. Outwardly, in terms of their natural circumstance, the act has left the Hebrew people unchanged; inwardly, juristically, they have been transformed. For though visibly they are after the covenant precisely as they were before it, yet nevertheless, as they conceive their own circumstance who are implicated in it, they have become, by virtue of their voluntary engagement, one people, unitary, indivisible, and perduring, for so long as the terms of the covenant are kept. They are no longer a natural aggregation assembled by the accident of contiguity and the stupor of instinct; they are a juristic corporation of persons gathered under obligation, "a kingdom of priests and an holy nation."

No one who restricts himself to the point of view of the unimplicated observer shall ever apprehend the singularity of that transformation. Nor does the reason lie in the circumstance that Israel conceived God among the covenanters. An unimplicated observer shall as little apprehend the transformation which followed from the juristic act establishing the union of Americans. For the singularity as seen from the point of view of the implicated participant consists precisely in the creation of a moral bond which is not outwardly declared. It consists in the creation of a status which nature does not afford. Men acquire in community a privilege of status which they are forbidden to have beyond it. Naked, they have been clothed, and they stand as persons in each other's presence.

8. Community and Communion: Relations of Contract and Relations of Covenant

Sir Henry Maine describes the advance of civilization from ancient to modern times as a progress from a condition of status to a condition of contract.[7] The sense of that distinction has occupied the industry of great and learned men since it was first proposed. For the whole meaning of civilization would appear to be implicit in that passage from status to contract, and to understand it would seem to provide a clue to civilization's last secret.

I do not diminish those labors. But it has always seemed to me that they were better turned, for the purposes of a philosophical jurisprudence, to the understanding of the lesser rather than the greater of the two terms. The secret of civilization is more properly sought in status than in contract. For the burden of civilized activity lies not in the progress from a simpler form of status to a more complicated form, but in the acquisition of status in any form, in the primitive fact of status itself. The philosophically interesting contrast is found in the opposition between the privilege

[7] *Ancient Law* (London: Dent, 1861 [1954]), 99-100.

of men in the most rudimentary community and their unprivileged nakedness in nature.

The idea of men in a state of nature appears in one form and another in all theories which have sought to understand the foundations of society in a social contract. It has therefore always been assumed by historians that the theory of social contract is sufficiently disproved by a showing of history, by the showing that as a matter of record the state of nature is a pure conjecture without grounds in historical evidence. That negative showing is, I think, doubtful. But even if it be admitted, it is certain that the attempt to counter the theory of social contract on this ground is mistaken. The idea of a state of nature is, like the idea of a shadow, a privative concept. The idea of a shadow refers not to the presence of something new in the world, but simply to the absence of something old. A shadow is not a positive existent like light. It is on the contrary the name for the privation of light, the name for light debarred and withheld. In the same way, in the theory of the social contract, the idea of a state of nature is a privative concept, the name for an order of relations among men from which all relations of obligation have been systematically excluded. Let all man-made law, all law positively enacted by human institution, be conceived to be at one stroke suspended, men will then stand beyond the pale of any positive legal community in the uncontaminated innocence or barbarism of mere nature. Nature is simply the shadow of law.

The question is, not whether men are ever in fact found in this condition (nations, as old Hobbes tartly observed, certainly are), but how to understand the difference between that condition and the condition in which we do actually find ourselves.

That question is real enough. There are, however, real and very serious objections to the theory of society as founded on relations of contract, and it is well to make clear with a degree of precision what those objections are.

If in a simple barter I contract with another for an exchange of goods, we, the parties to the contract, institute for the purposes of that exchange a limited community. The community begins with the engagement into which we enter; it dissolves in the moment that the exchange has been completed. The community, such as it is, has no other purpose except to effect that exchange. It therefore deceases as soon as its purpose has been fulfilled according to the terms agreed upon. Yet nevertheless, in that simple transaction, we have realized the typical achievement of all civilization whatever. We stand momentarily opposite to each other in a bond which is our own creation. We enjoy, with respect to that exchange, a temporary privilege of status which is not shared by anyone not party to the engagement.

The momentariness of the bond in this instance conceals its originality. For its originality resides not in the fact that goods have changed hands (the physical transfer of possession may not yet have occurred), but in the fact that, by the common admission of both parties, rights have been redistributed. Each party to the exchange acquires a right to what formerly belonged to the other, and that feature of exchange will appear declaratively where, as in the more ordinary sense of contract, the performance of one of the parties is, for an interval of time agreed upon, postponed. Thus, if I borrow money of another, I engage to pay him, for the use of the money now extended, principal and interest according to a schedule agreed upon. The transaction is still one of exchange: we exchange the use of money for the interest to be paid for its use. But in such a case the debitor of whom the future performance is required is said to be obliged to a duty of performance, and the creditor to whom the future performance is due is said to be entitled with a right to demand it. The contract has created an obligation where none was, and the parties to the obligation constitute with respect to that relationship a community apart, each bound to the other as person to person—the one the subject of a right, the other the subject of a duty—in a ligature of their own making.

But such a contract can occur only within an already constituted order, within an order which exists already before the exchange and continues to exist still after it. The contract may not once allude to this order. The contract nevertheless always tacitly presupposes it. Goods may pass between hands independently of this order; but rights can pass between persons only within it. Rights can be transferred between persons only if they are already admitted to be vested in persons. Every contract presupposes an order in which rights have been already distributed, in which things, the objects of rights, are admitted already to be owned, held as property, by persons who are the subjects of rights. The whole meaning of contract consists in making an orderly redistribution of these rights, such that the equilibrium between persons which subsists before the contract shall also subsist after it.

The preservation of such an equilibrium of persons is the objective meaning of justice in any society. It is the basic restriction which society lays upon all private acts; it is the basic affirmation which the society contemplates in all public ones. Whatever preserves this equilibrium of persons is just; whatever offends against it is unjust. The demand of justice to preserve this equilibrium where it is had, and to restore it where it is lost, is the measure of real community in any society of men or nations.

The Romans described this basic equilibrium of the juristic order as *res publica*. We have from it our word "republic." The Romans intended by *res publica* the primary constitutive fact of any legal community. Apart from it all private associations, all communities instituted by contract, are delusive. For a contract is always and at best a merely statutory, never a constitutional, act. All, for example, that a contract of exchange ever envisages is a transfer of rights between persons, so that what was admitted independently of contract to be *mine* becomes *thine,* and what was admitted independently of contract to be *thine* becomes *mine.* Unless we who are parties to the contract were admitted to have the status of persons independently, the contract would be superfluous and without motive. I should eat of your substance directly without attention to the fact that it was yours, and you of mine directly without attention to the fact that it was mine. Each of us would take of the other without affirmation of any basic community, take simply beyond community, as the bird takes which eats of the fruit of the vine, as the vine takes which eats of the decay of its own generations, as the generations take which eat of the light of the sun.

Let the basic order of persons which is presupposed by contract be called the *latent community,* or *community of covenant;*

and let the statutory community which presupposes it be called the *manifest community,* or *community of contract.*

Then it will immediately appear that every relation of persons in manifest community is in fact grounded on a relation of persons in latent community; and that apart from a community of covenant there can be no such thing as status.

In the ordinary intercourse of a society those relationships may not always be explicitly witnessed. They are in fact in any society only intermittently attended to. For all men live the unchallenged part of their lives in the manifest relations of contract. That is why no American can read Jefferson, that is why no American can read Lincoln, with comfort. For both of them are in fact, as an American hears them, prophetic voices, voices strangely and deeply moving, filled with grave resonances sounded out of strange depths, surcharged as no other voices ever quite succeed in being in equal measure. The one spoke in the revolution in which the republic was born; the other spoke in the revolution in which the republic was preserved. Both spoke to challenges in which the normal expectations and securities of the manifest life of America were tragically at stake. And both excite the same renewal of awareness, that the challenges are not of a season, that the same stakes are always permanently at wager, and that unattended to they may be lost.

I ask you to attend to that impression not because it is American, not because it is patriotic, but because it illustrates a social fact, the prime social fact which may be witnessed from the point of view of the implicated participant in the life of any society. To have status is not merely to stand; it is to take a stand.

The individual who walks within the articulate structures of a society, the more particularly as he has been born into them and, being unobliged to constitute, is permitted simply to inherit his status in an already settled order—such an individual may live out his entire life without ever once reflecting upon the latent human artifice which confers upon him the dignity of his status. He uses his status; he makes no problem of it. He confounds history with nature. He exercises the privileges of his inherited place in society as if they were, like the properties of his natural species, a natural bequest, which makes no demands upon him, which requires no affirmation of him, which he enjoys by gratuity, effortlessly and without cost, as the bird draws utility from the vine, and the vine from its generations, and its generations from the sun. He treats society as the economist treats land, as a pure natural resource, part of the unsolicited bounty of the earth, had without labor for the simple taking, like the air he breathes.

Every society in all the world is subject to that illusion. The basic institutions of a society, once fashioned in perilous revolution, won by taut struggle in the last tragic efforts of the unliberated human soul, are inherited in pure passivity, the simple gift of an unwon security, by the later generations. The old fierce obligation, unrenewed, is forgotten. The whole of life is passed in the manifest relations of statutory intercourse; the latent community, which actually sustains it, lapses from memory and from instant moral surmise.

Americans have community. The manifest society of America exhibits all of the external behavior of a community under law. The courts sit, actions are pleaded, due process is after the fashion or default of American justice rendered. All of this occurs, in theory, under the implicit guidance of a written constitution. And for the great majority of cases there can be no question that the theory represents the American circumstance accurately enough. For the great majority of cases are, in America as elsewhere, routine instances, novel in the life of the litigant but redundant in the life of the law. The only matter at issue is a matter not of principle but of fact. Therefore, once the fact has been established, the court stands ready to rule upon it, since the principle of decision has been long since established in written law or in precedent.

Yet on occasion there will arise for the court's decision a case for which there is neither an explicit reckoning in the written law nor any clear anticipation in former judicial decisions. Such a case is described as a case *primae impressionis,* and it is to such cases that the Supreme Court, on appeal, judicially addresses itself. The Supreme Court performs a merely statutory act. It is the creature of the Constitution. By the separation of the powers of government it is forbidden to make law, and so far as it acts within its competency it professes simply to explicate the law already written in the constitution. Yet, in spite of the most solemn conservatism in the exercise of its delegated office, the Court makes law. To interpret the law is inevitably to make it. Woodrow Wilson said of the Supreme Court that it was "a kind of Constitutional Convention in continuous session."[8] In every case of first impression the Court gives forth a decision in which one of the litigants must suffer defeat by *ex post facto* condemnation, the society being ignorant of the law until the Court has acted. By what law of original authority is the Court guided? We say, By the *Constitution*, meaning the written document, whereby we suppose the constitution of the American people to lie in the letter of the written document. But that is of course, as every litigant condemned in the first instance learns, a pretense. If the letter of the written document is to be treated as final, the prohibition against *ex post facto* legislation (Article I, Section ix, Paragraph 3) is more literal than any decision taken in the silence of the letter can ever be. Justice Holmes, with an ambiguous candor unbecoming in the greatest legal genius of his generation, described the knowledge of the law as a capacity to predict the behavior of judges. But the proposition is more distinguished for its shock than for its relevance. For the question is, not how to predict the judge when he acts in the idiom of his private capacity, but how to predict him when he acts beyond idiom in his public capacity. From Holmes I am content with cynical acid; from the Justice I am not content with it, and neither in fact was Holmes himself. What, then, in the silence of the letter, guides the court's decision when, acting in its public capacity and putting aside the caprice of men, it attempts to make law govern? If, for example, it is a question of determining at what point the exercise of freedom of speech becomes an abuse of freedom, in Holmes' phrase "a clear and present danger" to the public safety, the ground of decision must be Jefferson's principle of tolerating error so long as reason is free to combat it. The test must be to decide whether the time between the utterance and its predictable effects is sufficient to permit the public to be informed concerning the danger of those

[8] Quoted in Edward S. Corwin, *The Constitution and What It Means Today* (Princeton, N.J.: Princeton University Press, 1948), 3.

effects to itself.[9] What must guide the court in the silence of the letter of the law? The spirit of the law. That simply, the spirit of the fundamental covenant which is forever beyond the written article, which guided once the framers and must guide us still in the part of the labor of community which they left undone.

What would American society be if it were to realize, in its manifest outward act, the latent community which is its calling, if it were ever to realize the spirit of its fundamental covenant? We have no word for it. Let it be called *communion*. The Hebrews called it the kingdom of God, "the Holy One in the midst of thee." But the sense is for them and for us the same, identically the sense of communion, the demand that every relation of contract be assimilated to a relation of covenant. That is not what we have. It is what we labor at. Nor is it even approximated by the phrase which some, too immersed in the statutory commerce of American life, describe as "the system of free enterprise." America is not a system except in its outward semblance. Inwardly and properly, America is an aspiration after covenant relations made visible in our every day's most quiet act.

Thomas Carlyle once declared that if he had a sermon to make, it would consist of no more than this: "All you people know what you ought to do; well, go and do it." His mother, who sat by, replied quietly: "Aye, Tammas; and will ye tell them how?"

That precisely is the question. Knowing our duty, how to do it? For the letter, it must be confessed, does never suffice; or if it suffices, it suffices only to the legalism, which is not what we mean by the doing of our duty. And if, in order to mark the difference between the legalism and the larger obligation, we distinguish between the letter and the spirit of the law, it is that spirit and not the letter which is the real constitution of our society, the spirit which guides the judge when he acts in his public capacity, the spirit prophetically witnessed by Jefferson and by Lincoln when they bare forth, out of the depths of our manifest community, the latent community, the communion, which presides imperious but unseen beneath it.

---

[9] *Per* Brandeis, *Whitney* v *California* (1927), 274 U.S. 357. Jefferson's phrasing of the principle occurs in his first Inaugural Address: ". . . error of opinion may be tolerated where reason is left free to combat it."

Greek marks the distinction between Greek and barbarian, he does not meditate the difference between one form of the human condition and another. He intends the contrast between a condition which is human and a condition which is not. He treats humanity as the Greek achievement, as a moral distinction which challenges affirmation. Humanity was not for him, as it is for us, a biological category, a designation of the bare estate conferred by accident of birth into the species *homo sapiens*. Humanity is task, not gift, or if it is inheritance, it is the inheritance of a vocation of which germ-jelly is innocent. The indifferent character which we own by birth, open to every possibility, committed to none, is part only of the passion of being human. That dissoluteness of status is precisely what the Greek intends by barbarism, by the lapse from the moral condition of humankind or the failure to attain to it. The Scythian is a barbarian. He is to the Greeks what Ishmael was to the Hebrews, the man beyond covenant: "And he will be a wild man; his hand will be against every man, and every man's hand against him; and he shall dwell in the presence of his brethren." But there is a barbarian that lurks in each of us, the unconversant Cyclops who lives lawless, stranger to justice and to all society, "like a wooded peak of the towering hills, which stands out apart and alone from others." This barbarism is the common liability of us all. It is the liability which makes humanity eligible. For our humanity is not the thing we have but the thing we labor at, the moral community which we receive in ust and transmit in patrimony, as a second birth and our proper w creation. The vision of Er is a distillation of the Greek con... of its sense of covenant

usness, the prophetic affirmation...
h Lethe has covered over:

us saith the maiden Lachesis, the daughter of Necessity. . . r destiny shall not be allotted to you, but you shall choose it f selves. . . . Virtue owns no master: he who honors her sh more of her, and he who slights her, less. The responsibility he chooser. Heaven is guiltless.[2]

mbarrassment which we experience on discoverin Ethics that the slave, though he wears the ext ublic of Plato, translated by John Llewelyn Davies and an (London: Macmillan, 1929), 366 (617b).

---

chapter III

The Covenant of Nature

9. The Greek Tradition

It is customary in Western thought to interpret the contribution of the Hebrews to the Western tradition in the terms supplied by Greek philosophy. That is not without its advantage if one knows in the Greek tradition where to seek advantage. But I choose a contrary and less familiar path. I propose for once to interpret the Greek contribution in the terms supplied by the Hebrews. I propose to look at it juristically, to look at it with a view to preserving in the foreground the latent covenant which is implicit but never fully acknowledged in the Greek philosophical tradition.[1]

For this by no means ordinary course I make no excuse except that it enables us to see an element of the Greek genius which our habit has obscured. For those who do not see that element, the profit is excuse enough; for those who see it already, no excuse is necessary.

The genius of the Hebrews was the affirmation of their historical covenant. They asked, addressing themselves to God: "What is man, that thou art mindful of him?" The Greeks asked the same question, addressing only themselves. Their genius was the affirmation of nature.

The dictum of Protagoras, that man is the measure of all things, announces the tragic motive of Greek philosophy. For it signifies

[1] The tragic writers acknowledge it. It is the very substance of Greek tragedy. It lies at the root of what Plato described as "the ancient quarrel of poetry and philosophy" (*Republic*, 607b). See Section 10.

that nature is known only mediately through forms which history supplies; nature is history's prime artifact, shaped to the measure of her artificer, which is man.

Greek philosophy could neither live with that perception nor ever perfectly renounce it. Socrates' whole life of thought is a remonstrance against it, yet neither he nor his successors found it possible to dispense with the distinction which the example of Protagoras made necessary, the distinction between *physis* and *thesis*, between what belongs to nature and what belongs only to history and to human convention.

The concept of nature is the central article of the Greek historical covenant. The Greek covenant is so imprescriptible a part of the Western mind that we fail to see it for what it is. It is not the discovery of a new fact. It is the discovery of *criticism*, a confession of our obligation in the pursuit of fact. Nature was to Socrates what the voice out of the whirlwind was to Job, a release from the contingency and arbitrariness of every human act which falls beyond covenant. The idea of an objective order of reality, independent of all caprice of judgment or opinion, is not the product of critical inquiry; it is the condition of it. For unless the authority of a common ground of belief is assumed, every claim to truth must be allowed to be equal to every other, and no opposition among claims is capable of objective resolution. The rationality of Greek philosophy is not expressible, and has never been expressible, in terms merely of its respect for the demands of logic; its rationality consists in its respect for the demands of a *community of inquiry*. That is rational which preserves the community of inquiry; that is irrational which does not. The will to believe is not in question. Only the *right* to believe is ever in question, and the right is not arguable unless the idea of nature be invoked.

The implicit awareness of this circumstance is the Socratic element in Greek philosophy, and the Socratic covenant is Greek philosophy's most astonishing paradox. To Protagoras' belief that all knowledge, all social forms, all institutions of economy and law and justice are man's historical conventions Socrates lodged a sublime historical dissent. The Athenian agora is the Greek Horeb. I contempt of "History's bare Was," opposite to all historical co

ventions, Socrates put nature. History supplies no measure. Nature alone can supply a measure, it alone can function as the proper object of knowledge, since it alone is constant, equal to exacting obedience and the consent of a free mind, beneath all vacant human vicissitude. The rest is a tedium of error and poor anecdote, the thing made with hands, the product of unlicensed human acts, subject to the variations which men discover, in a pained arrest of faith, in human laws and institutions—in mutations of politics and morals, of art and language, of economy and religion. Where then, unless in nature—in Antigone's unwritten laws of heaven or in the form of the Good which is beyond God and heaven too—shall one seek the proper destiny of man or find the permanent and ineffaceable conditions of dignity to which all merely human conventions must be made to conform?

There, in Greek philosophy's tragic pause, Socrates perform for the free spirit of Greece the protestant task of philosoph all times. He marks the difference at any stage of the human between the human and the merely human, between huma an obligation and humanity as a fact. In the preservatio distinction Socrates divined a historical commission m than any root of hemlock. He is the most prophetic Greek world.

If that description appears strange as applied fault is, like all contemporary poverty, in ourselv tradition is unrecollected in our world, and w for a banality the generous old meaning whic once conveyed. The Hebrew prophet was n to come. He was the bearer of a witness, who spoke with such plenitude and assu most need of men of his own day tha an intimation of their own, heard i intimate sense of being in the world and inarticulate in themselves, ou the articles of a covenant by w separations and divisions, one ing to the bond which he laid Just so Socrates concentr hat Greece ever succeed

demeanor of a man, is after all mere thing, a "living tool" excluded from the privilege of moral estate, is experienced not at all by Aristotle. The slave is party to the species. He is party to the neighborhood. He is not party to the moral community. The Greek speaks out of the same profound sense of exclusiveness and election which belongs to the Hebrew, who regards the separation of Jew from Gentile as a consequence not of race or tribe, or even of a token circumcision, but of moral commission.

As the Hebrew nation was not at last a matter of geographic location or of blood, but of consent to covenant, to a rule of life, to a sacred obligation which set it apart, so the Greek nation (if I may for a moment be allowed that expression) was at last, and for the same reason, sacramental. The seed of Abraham was a moral seed; so also was the fire of Prometheus. What matter that the covenant of the one was given of heaven and the covenant of the other stolen from it? On the part of the beneficiaries the demand for obedience was the same, and the sense of election was felt with the same invincible assurance by both. Pericles speaks without constraint of Athens as the education of all Hellas. He admits the Greek in the Spartan as he would refuse to admit it in the Persian who a generation since had walked brute, predatory, and idiotic in the land. For Hellas, the nation, is not a political but a moral category. It includes not only Athens but Sparta as well. It includes them both even in the martial hour in which they were at each other's throats and in process of extinguishing their political possibility. Pericles thinks Athens is closer to the fundamental covenant of Hellas than Sparta. Therefore she alone can educate since that is what an education is, an obedience neither to the habit of Athens nor to the habit of Sparta but to our last calling, to a last calling which is superior to us both, and embraces us all, and remains steadfast in nature even in the face of our divisions.

That prophetic vision of a nature which remains steadfast beneath all vagrant historical conventions is Socrates' bequest to Western philosophy. The Socratic testament is at the root of all that we mean by the Greek dispensation. Socrates speaks in dialogue. He makes no soliloquy. It is Hellas that soliloquizes in him. He is, as Erasmus described Plato, "the Attic Moses," and nothing so testifies to the poverty of modern opinion concerning him as our disposition to make of him, after our own image, another Hamlet. He is an authentically tragic figure, tragic in the severe primal sense in which the Greeks understood tragedy. But the tragedy he enacts is not the tragedy of intellect. In his encounter with Protagoras he experienced a stark moral arrest—an arrest not of the scrupulous intellect before what is found logically absurd, but of the moral allegiance to scruple itself. And that is what in modern terms we have to rediscover, who have lost his capacity for radicalness.

Protagoras held the unexceptionably modern opinion, that every human obligation is a merely *de facto* convention, without authority except as men have instituted its authority. On purely formal grounds that opinion is without fault. It is so far from being logically repugnant that it recurs in every season of the human story and appears in our season as the fundamental persuasion of the positivist mentality. Why then should Socrates have discovered in it a tragic doubt? The reason is clear, but it is almost lost on our world which cultivates, besides the vision of positivism, its blindness as well. Protagoras' opinion is not logically absurd. Its absurdity is *juristic:* to hold that opinion is to destroy the grounds for any justification of its claim to truth.

The nemesis of the positive intellect is the positive intellect itself. Its fault has never been that it is too radical; its fault is precisely that it is not radical enough.

Inevitably positivism sets itself a problem which it forbids itself to answer. Its great and unquestionable virtue is its demand for evidence, and if there is any mark of sober merit for which positivism deserves to be venerated, it lies exactly in the critical requirement that knowledge must be put beyond the caprice of judgment of those who seek it. The rule of method which is to govern the admission of evidence into inquiry may be debatable; the need for having such a rule, if there is to be any community of inquiry, is beyond all debate. The demand to respect evidence is an obligation which we incur in seeking to know at all. Therefore it must transcend all of the partisanships of philosophies and schools. Let every other human obligation be treated as a merely *de facto* convention, this obligation, if it be indeed a convention, is at all events not a convention of the same sort, merely covenient or arbitrary, contingent or abridgeable. The obligation to respect evidence is the radical covenant, the constitution, of any community of inquiry whatever. It supplies the indispensably necessary ground which enables criticism to be practiced, belief to be corrected, and knowledge to be claimed.

What is the status of this demand which enables Socrates and Protagoras to dispute, and not merely to dispute but to dispute significantly, concerning the rectitude of any human belief? Shall it be thought simply another of the beliefs which one discovers abroad in the world, as one discovers Scythian and Persian, Athenian and Spartan, abroad in the world? No, it cannot be so. For whatever one may say of Scythia and Persia, or of Sparta and Athens, the community of inquiry which discovers them and permits them to be ranged side by side for comparison in "History's bare Was," is grounded in a latent covenant which obliges all men who would seek to know at all.

The first question of philosophy is a question of civilization not of nature, a question of obligation not of fact. For the pursuit of knowledge is always at last a matter of adjudicating claims. In the order of knowing, nature is not the determinant of belief; on the contrary it is the matter to be determined out of the critical concert of our beliefs. Nature's circumstance is invariably the thing problematic in inquiry, the thing to be known which it is the business of inquiry to disclose. To make belief conformable to nature is no doubt the object of all inquiry, and if nature were known independently of belief, it would be possible to speak of knowledge as the achievement of that simple conformation. But if nature is not known but requires on the contrary to be sought out, if we are obliged to begin not with it but only with our professions concerning it, then the problem of knowledge becomes a matter of discriminating among our professions, of placating our oppositions of opinion, of civilizing the contest in which our claims and counterclaims are pressed.

How, out of the ignorance that covers us, if every opinion is a claim upon belief, shall any opinion be thought to have a greater dignity or authority than any other? How shall we who are powerless to bind nature justify our claims to know her? We do it by binding ourselves, by placing ourselves under covenant, by submitting ourselves to a common rule which unites us in one community of inquiry. We consent to refer every opinion and every claim to a ground of evidence commonly agreed upon. The consent to be bound by the decision of evidence is the constitution of our community of inquiry, the bond which unites us, in spite of our manifest divisions, in a common pursuit. Without it there can be no knowledge, but only your claim and mine, or your claim on one occasion and your claim on another. For unless some claims may be regarded as privileged, there can be no justification of any claim, and every claim is barbarous. The civilization of inquiry is the minimal condition of any profession of knowledge. The covenant of our scientific community is not a fact which we discover by inquiry, but an obligation which we honor for its sake. And that obligation at least, which is the condition of all objective inquiry, cannot be supposed to be its product.

When the youthful Socrates protests that unless virtue be knowledge it cannot be taught, that is his simple meaning. The thrust of his argument is juristic. Protagoras is obliged to admit the necessity of any truth which is essential in order that his own act should be justified. If teaching is possible, then knowledge must be possible; and if knowledge is possible, then we are under covenant and are forbidden to treat the community of inquiry as merely contingent.

A man denies the positivist predicament in the moment that he argues in its favor; he affirms the juristic predicament in the moment that he argues against it.

Yet by what right do we hold that this covenant which we institute in the face of nature and in ignorance of her habit confers upon us a knowledge of nature? By no right at all, but by a primary act of civilization. The primary acts of civilization are not themselves civilized. They hang abjectly upon the affirmation of our community with one another, upon our consent to comply with the fundamental obligations which are essential to our having community at all. In science as in law the constitution of a society may provide for its own amendment, and the amendment becomes by due process an addition to the fundamental law. But the constitution which defines due process is not itself achieved by due process. It is achieved by an act which the sleep of barbarism leaves permanently undone. Civilization is the waking of the man in the barbarian, the act whereby from barbarism he lifts himself into the relations of covenant in a law community.

Knowledge is the civilized achievement which proceeds from the constitution of a community of inquiry. What we intend by its objectivity is the civilized release from the contingency and arbitrariness of your opinion or of mine, the consent on the part of those who seek knowledge to a rule of neutrality which they institute and hold inviolate in order that they may have community, and revere inquiry, and walk corrigible in the face of error.

Juristically, the obligation to neutrality in inquiry can never be permitted to become as other covenants may become, merely alien, part of the inconsequent residue of things, the buried wisdom or the buried folly which we preserve in recollection of what men have said and done, or in observation of what now they say and do. I who know Persian and Spartan walk unimplicated in the covenant of either, and I describe as fact what they experienced as instant duty. I may know the covenant of Persian or Spartan without being party to it. But I may know the covenant of inquiry only by being party to it. For as men would have community of belief there must be such a covenant; and as they would claim knowledge as distinct from opinion there can be but one such covenant.

That is the juristic predicament which is implicit in the simplest act of any man who would profess to seek knowledge. He stands allied to all inquirers in one law community, and can walk beyond those relations only at cost of suspending his profession. He admits himself to be under a judgment not private to himself, and will admit it still, even though he walks alone, as a Socrates or a Galileo once obliged himself to walk alone. Though every man in the world were of opinion contrary to his, the question still would remain which of them, they or he, was under the covenant which could permanently command the free allegiance of the whole of mankind. Whether men have such a community in fact is a question of fact. But that is not the Socratic question. The critical concern of philosophy is not to decide whether there is such a community, but to show what is essential if there is to be one.

Such was the force of that strange proposition of Socrates, that unless virtue be knowledge it cannot be taught. It was not his aspiration to make Athenian gentlemen of us all. He had confronted with an eye appalled a barbarism which is beyond all gentility, the unlicensed barbarism tempered neither by a Lycurgus nor even by a Solon, which it is philosophy's function in all seasons to hold off.

Men may reject the covenants of Athens; they may reject the covenants of Sparta. They can reject their status as covenanters only under peril of being without their human occupation. For the establishment of community under covenant *is* the human occupation. Therefore in the Greek affirmation whatever is necessary to the making of a covenant must be natural. That at least can be no fiction, though Athens is our fiction, and even Sparta too. By irresponsible artifice men have detached themselves from their natural estate, created among them distinctions and conditions of which nature knows nothing, and shut from the light, as worm shuts itself in chrysalis of its own contrivance, the nature which it is reason's task to rediscover and unfold.

10. Greek Philosophy and Greek Tragic Awareness

What I have described as the Socratic covenant I have described with a view to understanding the Greek historical achievement. But the Greeks were temperamentally too extrovert to think of themselves in these terms. They pursued their vision; they did not question it. They pursued their vision as an artist pursues his, self-forgetful in conquest of the outward form which he seeks to liberate in Pentelic stone. Therefore of their part in the covenant of nature they were only partially aware. They expounded the articles of their covenant, never their own juristic act in relation to it. And since the articles were not arbitrary but essential to their community of inquiry, they imputed the articles to nature, putting them beyond the adventures of mere history.

Accordingly the human task, if one would know how to live, is to conform to nature, to conform to the covenant which nature has written and humanity is obliged to accommodate.

The Greek genius was, in comparison to the Hebrew, childlike —spontaneous, inquisitive, directed always outward beyond itself. It was perfectly unvexed by any of the hesitations or misgivings which invariably beset a developed historical awareness. I do not diminish it by this description. On the contrary I regard the childlikeness of the Hellenic point of view as the prime signature of its health. Its childlikeness is its objectivity, without any question the tonic property which all who venerate it and have learned richly from it prize most. But the Hellenic innocence is like all innocence which is unaware of itself defenseless against assault, and nothing so imperils the Hellenic spirit in the Western tradition as our repetition of its delusion, the delusion that innocence is by right of nature impregnable.

Er sleeps, and wakes in forgetfulness. He wakes ignorant of the fateful words of Lachesis, that man's destiny shall not be allotted to him but must be chosen for himself. The Hebrew, who experienced the same tragic intimation, refuses to wake if to wake is to forget. Therefore, beside the Greek, the Hebrew spirit must always appear a waking dream, as, beside the Hebrew, the Greek spirit must always appear a sleeping innocence.

The historical precariousness of the human community was the discovery not of the Greek philosophers but of the Greek tragic writers. Tragedy was the singular mold in which Greece cast its reflections on the cancellableness of man's place in the moral order.

Greek philosophy apprehended the reality of the tragedians only at a second remove. It could never discover the poignancy which a modern inevitably experiences in the Platonic image of the cave.[3] For a modern the cave is the image of the human condition in time; for Plato it is but a shadow world of illusion. The inciting problem of Greek philosophy was to discover a basis of permanent order in the midst of change. Its object was not the cave but the sunlight, and having found the sun, the cave and its shackles could appear to it only an illusion of the unwise. Reality was gained, it was gainable, only by being freed from process: changeless itself, it explained all change, or that part of change which alone was capable of being known. Time—the felt flux which was actually lived through—was therefore set impenitently aside as the domain of the unphilosophic.

[3] *Republic*, VII, 514.

For this womb of becoming was beyond the grasp of knowledge properly so-called. It is possible to know of any event—of the *Parthenon*, or a falling star—only that in it which is capable of recurring, of occurring again, in another part of space or another part of time. The condition of its occurrence, the spatio-temporal matrix in which its character as an event can alone be realized, is incapable of being known, since in the very act of knowledge one seizes not upon the bare happening which is sensible and unique, but solely upon the character which is intelligible and shared. The particularity of the event therefore eludes all categories of intellectual knowledge, and becomes in Platonic philosophy the vast illimitable ocean in which eternity is mirrored by a perpetual illusion, as clouds reflect themselves in the ocean's face. Icarus is splendid as he soars aloft; he is tragic only as he plummets to the sea.

European philosophy has shaped itself within this scheme, and history has remained, both as a fact and as a form of discourse, a vexatious embarrassment within it. For history is the extended and incomplete parable of the cave. The study of history attempts to gain knowledge and wisdom of life within the conditions of life as it is actually lived. Self-knowledge, if it exhibits in part this free contemplative act of spirit moving among ideal forms, exhibits also the struggle of the creature, tangled in time and space, shackled darkling in a cave, and forced to regard these shadows, if they be *sub specie aeternitatis* unreal, as at least *sub specie temporis* the sole reality which things living have the luxury of confronting.

Greek philosophy could never take the cave quite seriously: its genius was to gain inevitably the pattern, its fault was to lose inevitably the gut, of circumstance. It did not forbid itself the opportunity of finding in sensuous immediacy the forms which it had intellectually elevated. This precisely was the function of art as Greek philosophy came finally to conceive it, the bodying forth of an ideal character in sensible form. So the sculptor Kresilas, in representing Pericles, impregnates stone with the image not of the man but of the statesman, not of the individual but of the type. Greek art is the ideal adumbration of the typical. In the plastic representation of the human nude it invariably generalizes its subject, seizes upon the perfect proportions which are approximated to in all men but are realized in none. The idiosyncrasy of the individual man, the particular trait which is merely accidental to the type, is eliminated as inappropriate to the norm which it is the business of art to impose upon life. Thus Aristotle writes of the distinction between history and art:

> . . . It consists really in this, that [the historian] describes the thing that has been, and [the poet] a kind of thing that might be. Hence poetry is something more philosophic and of graver import than history, since its statements are of the nature rather of universals, whereas those of history are singulars. By a universal statement I mean one as to what such and such a man will probably say or do . . . ; by a singular statement, one as to what, say, Alcibiades did or had done to him.[4]

The passage is the sheerest revelation of the Greek conception of art; it is, besides, the final assessment of Greek philosophy on the historical enterprise.

Beyond this sensuous immediacy of forms in art there exists, for Greek awareness, the realm of the accidental and the contingent, the realm of the merely historical. Greek history itself rejects it. The oration of Pericles, which the paragon of Greek historians has recorded, is an essence distilled by Thucydides himself, the record not of what the statesman actually spoke but of what his genius must be assumed to have thought; in short, the substance which enabled genius to command in speaking. Thucydides' consideration of the Peloponnesian War has the character of a concrete reflection on an intellectual issue and constitutes, besides a record of events, an essay in political theory. It could therefore be presented, as indeed he chose to present it, as an "everlasting possession," more perennial than brass, though, in the collision of Greek powers, he tragically perceived the decline of his own world, in which Athens and Sparta, too, must sink defeated in time's dark backward and abysm.

If Greek philosophy were anywhere to have grasped the meaning of the cave, it must have sought it in the analysis of life and

---

[4] *Poetics* 1451a-1451b: *The Basic Works of Aristotle*, edited and with an introduction by Richard McKeon (New York: Random House, 1941), 1463-1464.

growth. Yet even Aristotle's analysis withdraws itself from the fluid incessance of raw time. In any concrete analysis of life the real problem is not to detect a potential pattern of development, but to preserve the vital impulse of its expansion. To discover potency, real but not yet actual, in a germinating seed is simply to divorce a pattern of development from the development which makes it actual. Aristotle plucks movement out of nature and describes not this dynamic life becoming, but only a formal fact not yet become. The static formal pattern, which represents the recurrent cycle of birth, growth, and reproduction, alone is preserved. The prime miracle of the living, that the cycle preserves itself in time, in spite of time, that the organism endures from within a destiny which an observation from without can never grasp—this miracle eludes the causes of Aristotle's metaphysic. As the analysis of the structure of a wheel, which marks the relation of rim to spoke and of spoke to axle, discovers nothing of the wheel's mobility, so the analysis of growth, which grasps its pattern only, discovers nothing of its special quality of incipience, of expansion, of tendency. The potentiality in the seed, the actuality in the tree, are after all but one and the same thing, which time has accidentally sundered. The temporal transition between them, the process of actualization, which to the unfolding organism is experienced as the inheritance and destiny of living, is therefore, on these premises, only an idle bondage by which accident afflicts life, but from which, so long as life lasts, there can be no deliverance.

The special property of living things, which causes them to be held together as of a kind, consists in the circumstance, that a living organism, while it exists indivorcibly in an environment, nevertheless delimits itself as an intelligible unit within the environment. Only within an environment can the pattern of an organism's life be realized; but the organism contains within itself an active tendency which remains constant even as the environment changes. The environment may cancel out its life, extinguish it, but so long as the environment permits its survival, the organism will preserve its immanent destiny. It contains, in the phrase of the ancients, its own end, and it is the imperturbable fixity of this end which ancient philosophy excerpts from the natural process. The end survives the individual organism by being illustrated in its progeny; the singularity of the individual remains unappropriated. The individual organism exists for Greek science only in its universal aspect, by what is repeated in it and by what shall be repeated after it. The rest belongs only to the awful contingency and insensate waste of time.

For this reason history, which consists of unredundant singulars, could never become, in ancient philosophy, a matter of philosophic consequence. For in history not merely individuals but ends also are subject to cancellation, and if ends be cancelled, the intelligible tissue of process has been dissolved. The process can be nothing but a vacant succession of particulars, a slag of episodes relating, in Aristotle's phrase, to the singularity of what Alcibiades, for example, "did and had done to him."

The idea of a succession of cultures, of a process of civilization in which social and political and economic structures engage and supplant one another in time, in which languages and religions and arts evolve and respond creatively to the emergent needs of men—this idea could acquire no tenancy in the philosophy of ancient Greece. It is nevertheless the stern intimation of Greek tragic awareness, and of the tragic awareness of all peoples who have reflected upon the historical condition of men.

It is the power of Greek tragedy to exhibit in man the capacity, by his own act, to cancel the pattern which makes his life intelligible to himself. Time is the essential condition of every tragic fact; for what is indispensable to the idea of tragedy is an inherited structure of moral relations which is capable of being displaced, and is in fact imperilled, by the act of a protagonist.

In the last of the plays of Sophocles, the *Oedipus at Colonus*, Oedipus, blind wanderer, reflects upon the principle of evil, the source of sin in himself (*hamartia*). Murderer of his father, husband to his mother, brother to his children, he claims fairly to have sinned by no choice of his own, but involuntarily without choice, in ignorance of the identity of the man he has slain or of the woman upon whose body he has begotten his own pollution. Yet even Oedipus regards himself as contaminated by his act of incest and of parricide. Ignorance of circumstance may permit him to disavow malice; it does nothing to extenuate the offense.

The moral law is binding, the moral order must be preserved, even though he must suffer to preserve it. The gravity of his career therefore transcends him. Not he alone, but the moral economy which, though his act offends against it, he nevertheless affirms as the very substance of his moral nature, is placed in danger. It is easy enough for Oedipus to suffer extinction, but that the moral world should die too in him, that the basis in which his moral identity is sustained should be destroyed, this is the origin of the tragic qualm, as it has been called, and of the moral revulsion which causes him to despair. The tragedy is not in the suffering, which is merely pathetic, but in the consent to suffering, which is heroic. The tragic protagonist discovers in himself a destiny which has singled him out, of all men, as one who must suffer to preserve inviolate the law which sustains the community of all men. He is forbidden merely to die as an animal dies, in inconsequent solitude. He is obliged even by death itself to affirm the justice of the order which afflicts him. His death gains therefore a heroic eminence, an exemplary character, which others have not, or have but obscurely. The order of obligations survives even though the life which inhabits it be cancelled. Not Oedipus, but what Oedipus affirms as the reality of his nature, remains triumphant over time and becomes the inherited destiny of others than himself. This is the primordial datum of historical awareness, that the order of obligations which man is heir to exists perilously in time neither by fate nor by the will of God, but by the present consent of the living, because men actively affirm it and identify themselves with it.

11. Descriptive and Prescriptive Law: Order and Rules of Order

A people which has been taught to regard itself as a kingdom of priests and a holy nation is apt to visit with contempt the Greek description of man as *zoon politikon,* "the political animal." In the same way, if not for the same reason, a modern stumbles at the opinion of Aristotle, that the state is a "natural institution." For nothing appears so unimpeachably evident to the modern as to the Hebrew mind as that the political condition of mankind is a historical institution, and that the state, so far from being found in nature, is a declarative work of artifice which man has implanted there. Men make laws, they do not find them; they establish government, they are not merely governed.

Aristotle's phrasings are nevertheless, in the sense in which he understands them, profoundly instructive, and if we experience an arrest before them, the arrest is occasioned not by any want of sense in Aristotle, but by an ambiguity of the term "politics" in modern use.

Aristotle intends simply this, that to be human is to exhibit a basic disposition to the ordering of one's society according to rule. Society is not our sufferance but our act. The disposition to engage in the relations of an ordered society is as real in the life of a social insect, in the life of the bee or the termite, as it is real in the life of man. But while insect and man are both alike committed by nature to a social estate, they exhibit this great difference, that the form of the insect society is fixed by nature, the form of the human society is not. As the capacity for speech prepares the human animal for the symbolical activity of language but leaves undetermined whether the language shall be English or French or Italian, so the capacity for social relations prepares the human animal for a social estate but leaves undetermined what the form of his society shall be.

Man's political disposition marks that indeterminacy. The form of the bee society is a natural dispensation: functions are distributed according to the complementarities of anatomy, as male or female or neuter. In a human mating the biological function of man and woman is determined as silently and with the same sufficiency. But in human society the complementarities of gender do not suffice to define the domain of social relations. The bee society has *order;* the human society has, besides order, *rules of order.* And the capacity in man to institute such rules, and to oblige himself to obedience to the rules he has instituted, is his political disposition. The state is natural in this sense, that it is an actualization of this disposition, of this natural capacity, in ourselves. The state is a realization in men of the capacity to constitute, and having constituted to maintain, the form of their own society. The disciplined exercise of that capacity is an art, the art of the statesman; and the instrumentalities of that art, the tools of the statesman, are what we mean by *law*.

The distinction between order and rules of order is indispensable to any significant discourse concerning human society. The term "law" is unfortunately employed to refer to both—both to order and to rules of order. It is employed descriptively to signalize any observed uniformity of behavior; it is employed prescriptively to signalize a required uniformity of behavior, whether or not behavior of the kind required is observed.

Thus, the law of diminishing returns describes an observed uniformity. It describes a condition of the bee economy as well as ours. For it states an inescapable condition of any productive activity whatever—a fact of the world, not of human legislation. Man has not stipulated that condition; neither can he abolish it or mitigate it or evade it. It limits his activity in economy as inflexibly and impassively as the laws of motion limit his physical movement. That law which the science of economics has discovered does not concern our obedience or disobedience to the demands of economy; it concerns only the conditions within which economy can be practiced. The demand for economy—the imperative to *maximize utility*, the fundamental law by which the person economizing governs his conduct—is, therefore, a law of a different sort. It does not profess to describe anything. It is not a prediction that anyone will in fact economize. On the contrary, its force is prescriptive. It is for the economic actor a rule of order. It is not a description of what *is*, but a prescription of what *ought to be*, a prescription of that ideal distribution of his resources which he is obliged to make real if he would economize at all.

Let the meaning of law which refers to an observed uniformity of behavior be entitled the *theoretical conception of law*, or *descriptive law*. And let the meaning of law which signalizes a required uniformity of behavior (whether or not behavior of the kind required is in fact observed) be entitled the *practical conception of law*, or *prescriptive law*.

Then it will immediately appear that the kind of law which is sought after in the modern sciences—in physics, in chemistry, in biology, in economics—is descriptive law; and the kind of law which is sought after in the art of the statesman, the kind of law which is enacted, for example, in a legislature, is prescriptive law. The first relates to the *is*, the second to the *ought;* the one to the possible, the other to the obligatory; descriptive law to order, prescriptive law to rules of order.

That the two conceptions of law are distinct will be evident from the circumstance that when a theoretical law fails to conform with fact, fault is imputed to the law; when a practical law fails to conform with fact, fault is imputed to the fact. If fact is meant to control law, the law is descriptive; if law is meant to control fact, the law is prescriptive.[5]

The nineteenth century still maintained a division of what nowadays we describe as the behavioral sciences into natural philosophy and moral philosophy. Natural philosophy was the study of order, moral philosophy the study of rules of order. Thus, according to this division, Kepler was a natural philosopher: his object was order, though he believed the order he found to have been laid down by a geometer God. Grotius was a moral philosopher: his object was rules of order, though he thought the laws of peace and war to be established in nature. The whole tendency of positive science in the latter half of the nineteenth century and in our own has been to draw the tooth of that distinction. In an effort to assimilate the sciences of society to the sciences of nature we have, by a covert enactment of method, restricted all observation which we call scientific to the point of view of Kepler, to the point of view of the external spectator. We have suspended Grotius' point of view, which is the point of view of the participant. Therefore we have suspended our capacity to see the imperativeness of the obligations which Grotius reflected on. The consequence is the scientific disaster of our century. For we are no longer able to mark a distinction of kind between the insect society and our own. We have effaced the difference between nature and history, between force and freedom, between Buchenwald and community.

An implicated observer will view a rule of order as a claim upon conduct; an unimplicated observer will view it simply as an

[5] Compare Quincy Wright, *Contemporary International Law,* rev. ed. (New York: Random House, 1955), 54.

element of order, a limit upon behavior real in the measure that it is enforced by the external sanctions of government or of popular sentiment, unreal in the measure that government and popular sentiment are unprepared to enforce it. An obligation is thought to be positive if power sustains it, whether or not the person constrained regards the constraint as justified. Without the support of power an obligation is considered to be without incidence, null and void, even if the person who escapes constraint condemns his own performance. The question of moral philosophy, the question which most exercised the critical reflections of the Greek and Hebrew worlds, whether there be any rules of order which are so perfectly indispensable, so perfectly beyond the caprice of men and nations, that without them no relations of moral community are possible, must therefore, on these premises, appear to be empty of meaning. Jurisprudence has been made into a study of the monopoly of violence in the body politic; political science into a study of the principles of power equilibrium. Both have become studies in ecology. That proposition is so fundamental to this critical part of our study that I must ask for a moment to dwell upon it.

Suppose a balance-arm to be so placed upon a fulcrum that the arm, sustaining only its own weight, will hold stably, as in the image of blind Justice, at the horizontal. Those two elements, thus brought together in the monstrous frame of nature, form a simple mechanical system, singularly delicate, even exquisite, for an eye not blunted to look past it. The singularity of that effect must be admitted to be an accident of nature. For if I abstract from its relation to the sensitivity which encounters it and prizes it, those elements are as perfectly indifferent to that structure as they are indifferent to me. The pattern which they insensately realize is but one of the patterns of which, in the moral absolution of mechanics, they are capable. Were balance-arm to be removed from fulcrum and laid beside it on the soil, I should then meditate an alternative equilibrium, an equilibrium as real but less perspicuously visible, one of an infinite number of static alternatives which nature equally and indifferently permits. Those elements—balance-arm and fulcrum—endure passively in mute sufferance whatever happens to them in blind nature's dispensation; but always, in any of their vicissitudes, they will be found to figure at last in an equilibrium. Always, mutely and inevitably, they will gravitate to some settled distribution of elements, a static equilibrium in which, once realized, there is no further tendency on the part of any element to change.

Meditate it, then, that simple horizontal rod at its precariously temporary rest in space, unsupported, save at a single point, in midair. Suspended thus in equilibrium, it is compact of all the stresses that refuse to sleep within it. It is at rest. There is no stress, in that relation of its members, which is not for the moment perfectly neutralized, perfectly met and compensated for, so that, despite all the forces antagonized within it, it appears to float passively in space, visibly inactive, and betrays no further tendency to movement, though a grain of dust, intruded from without, would make it topple and destroy in a moment its clean perspicuous economy.

I call it—those members in that relation—a simple mechanical system. By which I do not mean to dissever it from the prodigious residuum of nature, including that dust-grain, which lies beyond it. On the contrary, its systematic properties depend quite abjectly on those relations and on their effective constancy. Cancel those relations to nature beyond it, you cancel it. For such unity as I impute to it in calling it a system consists not in its separateness from nature, but precisely in the visibly equal distribution which it realizes, subject to the constant forces that impinge upon it, in the midst of nature. The system is not those gross physical members, but the economy of stresses which they signalize, the concert of compressions and of tensions which they make visible.

Well, that is as a city of men is, if you view it for its order, and omit to view it for its rules of order. A city has the same kind of silent immersion in the world. To the eye of an external spectator, if he restricts himself exclusively to the merely outward aspects of its behavior, forbidding himself to project into it any perception of the meanings which course through it and qualify its texture, it must appear, like balance-arm and fulcrum, a mechanical system, an equilibrium of elements in nature, which from their relations to each other and to the world beyond comprise a settled economy, an internally stabilized order of elements which preserves itself, *vis à vis* the world, as an island in space. Inwardly, it may be filled with stresses; outwardly, it appears at peace with itself, somehow one, a collectivity, despite the manifoldness of its parts.

That is what a Kepler sees. In the life of a city, for one who views it with the detachment of an astronomer from abroad, there is exhibited a gross behavior which is, despite the babel of men's voices and the collisions of men's pursuits, somehow unitary. Out of all of the diffuse purposes which agitate the will and act of individual men, a pattern is realized, and presides over their common life, large, recurrent, perfectly unpremeditated, the chief external feature which gives to a city, for anyone who stands apart and sees it as alien, its distinctive character and coloration.

For such a one Boston or San Francisco, New York or Chicago, Birmingham or Topeka, is simply at last the name for the inter-wovenness of the actions and passions of men, the product which collects their habit and images their concert and their divisions. A participant in the life of a city, who inhabits it as its denizen, is always in some measure aware of that pattern which implicates him. He accommodates his life to it, he draws his anticipations from it, he discovers his proper virtue in it or in spite of it, beneath a smoke of anthracite or incense. But always, beyond his deliberation and his act, there is a part of the pattern which escapes his conscious design, as the dumb, unwilled respiration of the metropolis escapes it, which inhales its busy multitudes in the sublime tumult of the traffic from its suburbs of a morning, and exhales them spent at night, like the ancient Aeolus, who loosed his chained winds that they might recuperate in untamed separateness, before he assembled them again to confuse the east and west and south.

Into that pattern of the city men are born, out of it they die, and in the little interval between they take from it their external identity, as they take from it their external condition, in riches as in poverty, in sickness as in health, in cleanliness as in filth, according to the dispensations which it affords. The child who sits at table and repeats the benediction has not willed the number of mouths which the porringer must feed, that he should be filled or rise empty still. So, as little wittingly, has the man of the city willed, in begetting the child, that the spasm of his body should affect in a determinable measure the wealth or poverty of a nation. But it is so, and the external spectator of a city of men may know it to be so. For out of these multiplied individual acts of men whose destinies are mingled there emerges a gross effect of mechanical equilibrium which works most fateful consequences for them all.

I call this gross effect of natural equilibrium which Kepler sees the *ecological fact* in the life of the city. The ecological fact is not necessarily a public value. The equilibrium had is not necessarily the equilibrium wanted. It is simply the brute result which circumstantially exhibits itself as the consequence of that unpremeditated concert or conflict of wills. Of its value or disvalue, whether men shall find within it the plenitude of the heart's desire or an annihilation of all prospect of selfhood, only those who move within it can ever know, or for that matter are ever competent to decide. It is the ecological fact not because it is good, neither because it is evil, but because it is the joint product of those whom it affects. Given the forces that are assembled and the order of their aggregation, that product is inescapable, and must in benignity as in cruelty be endured.

It is the aspiration of all statesmen, and the exercise of all scholars, to understand the descriptive laws of this unpremeditated part of a city's life, that, the forces being known and their effects predictable, government should be able, in the group's behalf and for its sake, to control those consequences—to produce by the prescriptions of the laws which it frames, out of all of the possible patterns of which the group is capable, that pattern in which society's good is found most abundantly to lie, as the governed see that good. Not that the governed shall, either now or in any predictable future, be thought to understand in detail the total effects of those laws which they institute through government. An individual immersed in society never experiences that total effect directly. He experiences it only distributively as it affects himself or those near to him, as he feels the pinch of it or a release by means of it, in his ordinary private act. The taxation of a society, if it be graded according to men's ability to pay, is in fact a redistribution of society's wealth. Nor need the man whose tax is least be presumed to like it any more than the man whose tax is greatest. Neither the one nor the other may celebrate it. Nevertheless its total effect may be to guarantee, in the life of that society, a degree of permanent well-being which neither could have had without it. And that is the justification of that tax-law, and the only justification of it, as of any other prescriptive law, that it conduces to the permanency of their voluntary association with each other. For, while neither would will the tax which falls upon himself, yet both alike will the conditions of their permanent association, and when they cease to will those conditions, not merely government but society itself dissolves.

A civil war is the clearest of all betrayals of our positivist illusion. Men who stand beside each other discover themselves in pained surprise to belong actually to two cities, each claiming occupancy of one space. Grotius sees a rupture of the human covenant; Kepler only another piece of ecology.

That is why the fact of civilization in human life, though it is everywhere hedged by ecology, is never explicable in its terms. Men may continue, even in the absence of any affirmed community, to live side by side without outward offense, each enduring the other's presence because, as their labors are divided, without each other they cannot live. But where they do, they form no longer a city, but only an aggregate, eating out of men as they eat out of other dust of the land.

The descriptive laws of ecology describe the range of real possibility in a city's life. But it is an illusion of the unimplicated to suppose that they describe a city as the city sees itself. They do not. The flow of traffic in a metropolis is a city's achievement —the product not of a bare ecology but of contractual relations among all traffickers, who govern themselves according to laws of their own making for the sake of their community of endeavor. The descriptive laws of ecology are as tolerant of the disorder which arrests the flow of traffic as of the order which sets it free. The prescriptive laws of a city, its rules of order, have no such tolerance. Into the silence of nature they introduce limits of which nature knows nothing. Within the range of real possibility which nature has delimited a city sets its own pattern which delimits it further, and a city is in fact free to pursue its own purposes only in the measure that it institutes such limits and consents to preserve them. So, by design, in statute and in covenant, men assembled in community attempt to realize out of the range of possible equilibria the equilibrium which they consent to regard as obligatory, as normative. That normative equilibrium is what they will describe as the justice of their society. All significant reflection on the terms of civilized community must therefore proceed within this juristic tension, the tension experienced by all human beings between a merely ecological and a normative equilibrium.

In Parts II and III, I propose to inquire into the normative equilibrium which appears in each of the major domains of civilized activity—in politics and law, in the economy of the market, in the science of the university, in the arts of expression, and in the education of a citizen.

II

The Covenants of Civilization

chapter IV

The Masks of Society: Law

12. *The Masks of the Law*

The organized societies into which human beings are born have a manner of existence which is not granted to human beings themselves. Within their structures men live and die; the societies endure. The enduring thing, which is the society, is nothing apart from the individuals out of whose dust its life is formed. It nevertheless retains its identity as the same society though all the individuals who compose it have changed. Its identity is in the structure which they animate, and such identity as they have, in their coming and going, they acquire by animating it, taking their character from the relations which it supplies.

The Latin word *persona* preserves still in its juristic use the sense implicit in its dramatic origin. In the drama of the ancients it signified the "mask" worn by the tragic actor. The masks of the drama, *personae dramatis,* declare the roles out of which the action is evolved. The actor acquires his dramatic personality, he wears the mask of Oedipus or Agamemnon, by virtue of the relationships he sustains within the purview of the drama. His mask identifies his station in the play, and it is only by occupying a station, by enacting the role annexed to it, that he is party to the play at all. His existence as a natural individual is of dramatic consequence because the mask unworn, through which no lines are sounded (*per-sonare*), is not a person, but a dead prop. It requires, in the performance of the drama, to be animated. Yet the identity of the individual who animates it is submerged and neutralized in the relations it prescribes. The mask is but the physical token of these relationships. Provided the relationships be observed, it may be dispensed with, as the drama has in fact dispensed with it. The knave remains a knave even though he don a kingly crown; the king a king even though he wear no crown at all. The meaning of the mask is in the role; and in the role alone is to be found such personality as the actor can aspire to have within the compass of the play. The antic mask may break, the rhapsodist may die, the part endures, if men may still be found to acknowledge it as real and to reanimate it in the living scene.

So, in the law, the legal person is distinguished from the natural individual as the dramatic role is distinguished from the actor. Legal personality can belong only to a subject of rights. It is therefore denied to those natural individuals who have neither the status for holding nor the capacity for exercising rights. A slave, having no status before the law, has no legal personality. A man banished, or one who renounces his allegiance, relinquishes his person though he retains his life. The personality of an individual who suffers imprisonment for life, or who enters a monastery, may be by statute extinguished (*mort civil*): actually he lives, civilly he is dead, and his property is distributed as if his death had in fact occurred. A child, born to legal persons, acquires its personality not by being born, but by the circumstances of its birth. Its personality is conferred upon it by the relations into which it is thrust. Yet these relations, which define for the child its legal estate in society, have no residence in nature. Nature supplies only the actor, the law supplies the role. The child finds itself already implicated in a play in which its natural nakedness is masked. It exists from the moment of its birth, or even *en ventre sa mère*, in a personality prepared in advance to receive it. The relations of the law are distinguished from the relations of the drama not because the ones are artificial, the others not. Both are artificial, artificial in the same degree and for the same reason, that nature, which provides the actor, leaves undetermined the role to which he shall be committed. "Cover your heads," says deposed Richard,

> Cover your heads, and mock not flesh and blood
> With solemn reverence; throw away respect,

Tradition, form, and ceremonious duty;
For you have but mistook me all this while:
I live with bread like you, feel want,
Taste grief, need friends:—subjected thus,
How can you say to me, I am a king?[1]

The difference between dramatic and legal person consists in this circumstance: for the one the real consequences of acts performed are mercifully withheld from the actor, they impinge only in semblance on the wearer of the mask; for the other the actor both lives and dies in the mask and has no personal existence outside it. Yet, in law as in play, the mask is so far separable from the wearer that it may be worn vicariously. In inheritance it is the mask, not the identity of the wearer, that is transmitted. Even where the legal personality of a child is assured, it may be incomplete: during the child's nonage the capacity to exercise its rights may be reserved to the discretion of another, who is then said to act "in its person," i.e., to wear its mask. The legal principle *respondeat superior* employs the same artifice: it imputes responsibility for the acts of an agent to his principal; which is to say, that the agent has acted not in his own person, but in the person of another. The same natural individual may be clothed with more than one personality. A magistrate performs the duties of his office in his person as a public functionary, he sells land in his person as a private proprietor, he marks a ballot in his person as a citizen. In articles of incorporation the law gives the status of a legal person to an artificial entity which it has itself created. A corporation corresponds to no entity in nature; it joins together, as the members of a group, individuals who in nature exist separately. The group is nevertheless, in its corporate capacity, capable of act and policy. The corporation is therefore regarded, for the purposes of the law, as a single person, the proper subject of legal rights as of legal duties. The law itself affects to distinguish between artificial and natural persons. It regards only the corpora-

---

[1] *Richard II*, III, ii, 172-178. Compare *King Lear*, III, iv: "Thou owest the worm no silk, the beast no hide, the sheep no wool, the cat no perfume. . . . Thou art the thing itself: unaccommodated man is no more but such a poor, bare, forkt animal as thou art.—Off, off, you lendings!—come, unbutton here."

tion as its fiction; the person which coincides with a single natural individual it regards as a "natural person." But a natural person is, like the corporation, the creature not of nature, but of law.[2] The vicissitudes in nature, which affect the natural individual, do not affect the natural person. Richard II in his prison is the same natural individual as Richard II on his throne: it is his person only that has been usurped; the natural individual remains—alas, poor Richard—to regret its loss. A legal fiction marks a legal distinction. But the practice of absolute fictions describes the whole content of the law.

It thus arises that all agency before the law is personal agency, the action not of men but of maskers. The context of legal relations into which the natural individual is born confers upon him the sole personality which he may claim by right. He may not extricate himself from the masks of society; it is given to him only to exchange masks within society. To be without a mask, to wear no mask at all, is, in human society, to exist without personality and without title, to suffer the condition of having no status, to be slave or outcast beyond the pale of the law, which requires that every legal relation be a relation between persons and will suffer with equanimity any desecration of men, so it be not done to the masks the law is designed to protect and men are predestined to wear.

That nature is the stage of all human acts, that society itself is the natural condition of men, as indelible a fact of nature as the organisms out of which it is composed—these truths no man can question. But the admission of these truths is not equivalent to

[2] The natural object to which personality is imputed need not be human or even animate. It may be a fund, such as a charitable endowment, or a bankrupt's estate, before administrators have been appointed. Compare G. W. Paton, *Jurisprudence* (New York: Oxford University Press, 1951), 316n: "Animals have been regarded as legal personalities in some systems. In Germany during the Middle Ages, a cock was tried for contumacious crowing, and, in 1508, in Provence, the caterpillars of Contes were condemned for ravaging the fields." Demosthenes, *Oration against Aristocrates,* translated by J. H. Vince, in Loeb Classical Library (Cambridge, Mass.: Harvard University Press, 1955), 267: "There is also a fourth tribunal, that of the Prytaneum. Its function is that, if a man is struck by a stone, or a piece of wood or iron, or anything of that sort, falling upon him, and if someone, without knowing who threw it, knows and possesses the implement of homicide, he takes proceedings against these implements in that court."

admitting that the proper study of mankind and of human society is exhausted in a reflection upon the natural conditions with which man and society comply. It still remains that all that is distinctive in the human condition—in economy as in law, in science as in religion, in art as in language—is a function not of men's relations in nature, but of the web of artifice which men impose upon nature as the determinate texture of their activities in society. Men are born for society, but it is part of the fatality of nature that the positive form which human society shall take remains completely undetermined. Respecting everything which men regard as properly humane nature simply equivocates. For the dispensations of nature are without exception merely negative. Nature makes no decision in regard to the patterns which men may realize in society; it stipulates only that there are some patterns which cannot be realized in itself. Nature legislates, in short, by prohibition alone. It supplies the bare stage to whose dimensions any scene that men aspire to realize must be accommodated. It eliminates alternatives but selects none. It proscribes without prescribing. The limits which nature imposes on human actions are absolute and beyond appeal. No scene may exceed these limits. But within the limits which nature still allows there remain the most prodigal variety of alternatives which, nature failing, men must choose. The scene of their choices is what men call history. Where nature fails, conventions are contrived to take its place. Whether there shall be a play it is not granted to men to choose: that is a need which nature gives its creatures. But the play itself is a historical structure which nature knows not of.

13. Nature and Law

In describing actions within a legal community jurists make the useful distinction between a power which is exercised *de facto* and a power which is exercised *de iure*. Wherever men are met in civil community, the goods which the community affords are distributed among its members as *mine* and *thine*. Each member of the community is the bearer of rights which the society authorizes him to exercise and acknowledges as his before the law. The rights which belong to the individual in his status as a legal person demarcate the sphere within which he is free to move without interference as it pleases him to move, subject indeed to the community itself by whose forbearance all rights are held, but independent of the private will of any of its members. That is mine *de facto* which I can by my own powers, by natural sinew or by cunning, get and keep. That is mine *de iure* which, independently of my natural powers, society will assist me in getting, and having gotten, in keeping. I own a dwelling by right; that is to say, as the law interprets property, there are grounds, admitted before the law, whereby I am empowered to exclude others from the use of the dwelling. I may have no interest in making that exclusion. The right is mine independently of my interest. I may want, in my natural capacity, the might to make the exclusion effective. But the right is mine independently of my natural capacity. My might failing, I may, provided the right can be confirmed, invoke the might of the body politic to assure its free exercise. How shall the right be confirmed if another claim it too? By an exhibition of title. By grounds admitted according to a rule which binds us both.

A man who acts by lawful title will be sustained by the law; he who acts without title will not. Justice, in the venerable language of the *Institutes* (I, 1), is the set and constant purpose of rendering unto each that which is his due (*constans et perpetua voluntas suum cuique tribuendi*). What is due a man, his *suum*, is that to which he holds title. He therefore who acts according to his rights acts from title, *de iure*. The operation of the law thus invariably presupposes that each man has already his *suum*, that titles are already distributed, and the effect of the law is to preserve this distribution, each man being guaranteed, in relation to his neighbors, what he may rightfully claim as his due.

Whether the distribution itself be just the law does not inquire, for the law is not the judge of the norm which it defines. In this circumstance lies the immemorial objection which all reformers of society have to the law of society. The law preserves to Lazarus that which is Lazarus', and to Dives that which is Dives'. Yet the law of a reformed society would remain necessarily, even as in society unreformed, profoundly conservative, the one as insistent on conserving proportion as the other is insistent on con-

serving disproportion, the one as solicitous of equality as the
other is solicitous of inequality, the one as mechanically bent on
freedom as the other is bent on tyranny. For the law is the blind
tool of those who fashion it, and it is sometimes fashioned by the
blind. Yet whether the eyes of those who fashion the law be quick
or dead, the law will inevitably operate, if it operates at all, to
conserve the pattern of society which they have chosen.

The pattern which the law defines consists, for good or evil, in
a distribution; and the defined distribution will function as the
normative equilibrium of the society which that law governs. Let
the *normative equilibrium* of a society be defined as that state in
which each man has his due. That state is the justice of that society. Lazarus may reject this justice, he may denounce it as unjust. He does so by appealing to some higher law, a law of nature
or of reason or of heaven, unwritten and inalienable, the law of
God's kingdom into which he may enter and Dives may not. But
this law will be found as inflexible in its exclusions and inclusions
as the law he rejects. It may be better law, law more equitable
and humane, but it is describable as better or worse only according to the ends it serves, not according to the function it performs
in serving these ends. A knife is made to cut; it does not itself
decide whether it shall be used to wound. The juristic equilibrium
is the norm which those who legislate for a society—the makers
and interpreters of its laws—have chosen. It is what they have
stipulated as the normal condition of society, which they would
by law preserve, and if it be lost, by law restore.

In the equilibrium of a society, the power to perform an act
and the right to perform it are conjoined the one to the other, so
that where the right is held, the power is held with it. It is the
function of the law to preserve this coincidence in society. Every
infraction of the law may be found actually to have disturbed it.
A person's goods are stolen: his rights are invaded. Which is to
say, the exercise of a power has been separated from the person in
whom the right of exercise inheres. The right *de iure* remains still
assigned as it formerly was. The invasion succeeds only in dis-
rupting the *de facto* power from its proper agent. In a civil order
of society, if the law is invoked, the effect of its operation will be
to restore to each that which is his own, to correct the disbalance

by taking from the injurer what he has unlawfully appropriated and restoring to the injured what belongs to him by law.

A legal government normally exercises over the people it governs a *de facto* as well as a *de iure* authority; that is, it is competent not merely to make policy, but to execute it. It has the power to get its will done, it commands the sanctions whereby its decisions may be made effectual. But this power, which belongs to it by law, may on occasion, in revolution, be unlawfully usurped, assumed without right, by another body. The usurping body then appropriates to itself all of the functions which were formerly exercised by its predecessor. It will act, it will makes laws, it will govern; and men voiceless, like sheep whose herdsmen change, will do and suffer according to its dictates. It exercises a visible authority. It has not merely the power to issue commands, it has the power to exact submission. Circumstantially, it rules, though in relation to the law it abrogates, its rule is illegal. It exists not by that law, but beyond it, in spite of it, by conquest over it.

The government expelled is not therefore dead. It continues, though dispossessed, to press its claim. In court of nations it appeals to the distinction between an authority *de facto*, which it lacks, and an authority *de iure*, which it professes to retain. The two kinds of authority, which normally are conjoined, have in revolution been divorced, so that for a time all authority is equivocal: there exist two governments over the same people, one of which has the power to govern but not the right, the other of which has the right but not the power. Though in the life of the society from which it has been extruded, the displaced government wants the power to get its will done, it claims still that in its will resides the sole legitimate authority. The legal authority it carries with it beyond the seas; only from the circumstantial authority has it been estranged. The latter alone remains behind, temporarily relinquished but still watched in dumb impotence, in the defensive fastnesses of some wretched Formosa, until by force equal or superior it may be regained.

For so long as its legal claim is recognized, either among the people from whose effective destinies it has been separated or among the nations in whose concert it shares, the expelled government retains its place, poor spectre, ineffectual but potentially effective, in history. But should people or nations decide at last to take from it its claim, to recognize brute fact, to dignify incivility by placing the legitimacy where actually the power lies, then the revolution is complete. The old claim lapses with the law which guaranteed it. The recognition is in fact an acknowledgement of the legitimacy of the *de facto* order, which becomes, by consequence of recognition, also the order *de iure*. Thenceforth the law is redefined, and with it the incidence of all claims which can be sustained within the law.

In the affairs of nations the granting of recognition has the profound consequence of a constitutional act. It is in effect, upon the international scene, a treaty of peace, in which a government is admitted to parity of status in the community of nations. Henceforth, the usurping government acquires what hitherto it had wanted, the enabling right not merely to act, but to act in the mask, the person, of a people. It exercises its role, *vis à vis* the other nations of the earth, within an established order, not by the forbearance of its equals, but by their consent, from which now even they can depart only by war, by an act of revolution like its own.

The recognition which is extended has therefore the effect of constituting a new international order, of establishing a new norm, in which legal relationships may be contracted, maintained, and at least theoretically enforced. The physical relationships of the contracting nations are in no wise altered. The factual distribution of power remains after the act of recognition as it was before. But the political scene, among the nations who are party to the recognition, has been radically transformed. The recognition constitutes a legal community where formerly none was, or another was. Every relationship within the legal community acquires a normative character, becomes a factor in the equilibrium which the community covenants among its members to maintain. The privilege of status which has been conferred may, if disturbed, be claimed again by right, and where no other redress is found, may be seized legitimately by force. The same force, which prior to recognition was lawless, is by recognition made lawful.

Throughout this transaction nature has remained serenely impassive. It is not merely neutral, partisan to no claims; it is indifferent, vacant of all norms.[3] It acknowledges any distribution of power as equally legitimate, which is to say, it acknowledges no legitimacy whatever. The notion of a juristic equilibrium is foreign to it, and foreign to discourse about it. In the sense of law in which men are said to govern themselves by law, nature is lawless, abjectly and totally indifferent to any and every condition which men may contrive for themselves. There is in nature no distribution of powers which *ought to be,* which is written in the stars as inalienable or legal or just. There are only distributions which *are.* Nature contains no *ought,* no obligation, for the reason that it leaves to its creatures no room for disobedience to itself. It simply *is,* and they are as it would have them be. You would injure another: there is nothing in nature which forbids it. You would love another: there is nothing in nature which commands it. The stone gravitates, the streams combine their burden of silt and salt into the ancient sea, the tree puts forth leaf and fruit, the lamb feeds, multiplies, and is fed upon, the man lives and labors and perishes. That is the pathos, the sufferance, of the natural condition. But the norm which men legislate for themselves is not their sufferance. It is their act, what they have for better or worse made for themselves, constituted within the indifference of mere nature, which is content that they should live or die, eat or be eaten, gain happiness or be afflicted, enslave themselves or make themselves free, so long only as they do each of these things within the conditions which it disposes.

Every norm to which men subscribe inevitably marks a distinction between what is and what ought to be, between an order of relations which is merely *de facto* and an order which is *de iure.* It is this merely *de facto* order which men commonly call "nature." Nature is the order of indifference, the order of mere circumstance, which men find, or by default allow, to vary inde-

[3] Neutrality, where nations struggle, is a positive legal act, in which a nation, its own status being secure or its advantage not yet clear, premeditatedly detaches itself from any share in the tipping of the scale. But that is the prime characteristic of nature, that its detachment is unpremeditated, there is no scale to tip. Nature participates in no decision, it performs no act at all, its indifference is complete.

pendently of human prescription.[4] The *de facto* order may on occasion coincide with the order *de iure*. In the perfect equilibrium of a society the two orders *must* coincide, for in this state each member of society will circumstantially exercise the powers which belong to him by right. But this actuality of the norm, which is the perfect consummation of the law, is, like the norm itself, inessential to nature. Nature permits the coincidence of the two orders, it permits equally their discrepance: it is partial to neither. That is why the concept of natural selection, which biology employs, is so remarkable a metaphor. For it is precisely the consequence of the theory of natural selection that nature is indifferent to the issues at stake within it. It selects only negatively by failing to eliminate. The selection which circumstantially occurs in nature occurs not by the design of those individuals which exhibit adaptation to the demands of the environment, but by the extinction of those which do not. Nature selects only by default of the weak. The strong of the earth inherit the earth not because nature finds virtue in strength but because, nature finding virtue in nothing, the weak are destroyed. The strong survive and the weak perish: that is the *de facto* circumstance which biology discloses. The theory of natural selection discovers no norm in nature; it discovers only the circumstance, that for nature's creatures norms can operate only under the conditions which nature sets.

When human beings legislate for themselves, they do not abate the consequences of their natural condition. They do but choose some consequences in nature which they approve out of the range of consequences which it allows. To the production of these approved effects, since nature promises no rewards, they attach artificial rewards—honor, privilege, position; to the production of effects disapproved, since nature metes no punishments, they attach artificial punishments—obloquy, fine, loss of freedom or of life.

----

[4] The principle of Giordano Bruno, that nature is everywhere the same (*indifferenza della natura*), signifies that the same laws which describe terrestrial occurrences are indifferently operative throughout the total universe of nature, in the heavens as well as on earth. This principle is not in question. The contrast is not between heaven and earth, between one part of nature and another, but between nature and history, between order of fact and order of obligation.

Why, when nature takes no side, should men so persecute themselves? Because in this exercise of artifice, whereby they dedicate themselves to ends of their own choosing, they first enact their peculiar function as human beings. They constitute the order of *de iure* relations in which alone it is possible to be human. That order, the order of obligations self-imposed, is the sphere of all distinctively human activity. It sketches upon the face of nature the limits within which men's acts become the domain of history, the episodes of a drama no longer merely natural, but historical as well, in which the actor, whom nature owns, enacts a role of which nature is improvident. For the setting of limits, which nature does not provide, is not nature's act, but man's. Humanity is discovered in an effort which aspires to generate a species, not in a torpor which is content to inherit one; in a wager which tempers the indifference of nature, not in a default which, in the Stoic inversion, makes a norm of indifference itself. To be human is to pursue ends which not nature, but men, have set. It is therefore to observe obligations which not nature, but men only, can suspend. To be committed to no end, or to be committed otherwise than by themselves, is to be, in the order of humanity, nothing:

> Rolled round in earth's diurnal course,
> With rocks, and stones, and trees.

The laws of any society are the instruments of its commitment, and in such commitment is the justification of all laws.

14. Obligation

Society is man's *de facto* circumstance: he is spawned in it, and it regenerates itself in him. Both belong physically, and inextricably, to the order of mere nature: they ripple its surface, they squat upon its soil, like insects of a summer whose swarm the wind blows. But just for that reason, because the dispensation which nature provides supplies none of the distinctions which their life requires, they supply by artifice what nature has omitted. The society belongs to nature; the form of society does not. Its structure and its limits men contrive. They mark out within nature a normative order of relations which binds not nature but only themselves. It binds them because they consent to be bound by it and ally themselves together in the concert of function which is fashioned to maintain it. It is for them the legal order, the equilibrium, to which, as they choose to live together, they consent to make their actions conform.

No merely descriptive account of nature will discover this "ought" within it. As Adam's was the first disobedience, so mine is ever the last, and to describe his act or mine, as if in what was done nothing were left undone, is precisely to omit that character of the act which is, to him who performs it, its essential quality, that it deserts the real obligation by which he owns himself to be bound. The fault alone is actual. Yet this which is actual takes its character from that which is not. That is the simple meaning of the dictum: *Nullum crimen sine lege.* As an event in nature, the eating of forbidden fruit is not different from the eating of fruit unforbidden. The physical act which the eye sees is in either case the same, and were there no prohibition which had been disobeyed, the two acts must be indiscriminable. Yet this prohibition which makes of the one act a transgression is what the transgressing act does not itself betray: it is transgression not because of what it is, but because of what it fails to be. Just so, the complete conformation of a society to the legal order, which is required for the equilibrium of the society, may in no single occasion of the society's existence be observably actual, so that in no single occasion is it available for description. The real possibility then remains permanently ideal. Yet, for the members of the society, who even in delinquency acknowledge the relevance of the norm, this order which is not actual is incomparably more real than the order which is. Nature is no partisan: it cannot therefore be disobeyed. The form which men give to human society exists by partisanship: obedience and disobedience first become possible within it, for only within it does there appear the distinction between an order *de iure,* which is possible, and an order merely *de facto,* which is equally possible but forbidden.

In any age or political circumstance the law is dedicated to securing a pattern of social relations, and as any pattern of social relations can be justified only by its capacity to serve interests which men hold, the question, Whose interest shall be served?

is invariably the fundamental question of political philosophy. Over Cain's query, "Am I my brother's keeper?" the law itself permits no hesitation. For each man in community must build his expectations upon the behavior of others, and apart from a settled order of relations in which behavior is circumscribed, in which each is willing to abide and be predicted, there is no virtue in community either for keeper or for kept. As I elect to live in community with others, I implicitly subscribe to making myself the keeper of others; I subscribe also to being kept by others. That is the imperious demand of society itself, without which there could be no society at all. The prime question of political philosophy is not, therefore, whether I shall be my brother's keeper, but who shall be regarded as my brother? The blood-tie that unites Cain with Abel is the only tie supplied by nature: it is not sufficient to restrain the hand of Cain. The tie which alone will suffice to bind Cain is a tie which he consents to acknowledge as binding upon him. He acknowledges none? Then he is bound by none. But he must then be content to accept the consequence, which is his defenseless isolation in nature. For he will be punished, in the society to which he opposes his valor, independently of his acknowledgement or consent. As he is bound by no tie to others, so no other is bound to him, to respect the status which he acquires. What he gains by talon, he may lose by claw; what is his by tooth is another's by fang. He is "outlaw" because he excludes himself from any order of prescriptible relations. He excludes himself, therefore, from the mutuality of status which these relations confer. Brother to no one, he is estranged from everyone. He exists in an utterly precarious solitude, alone in the midst of nature, where he must find the company of those who place themselves beyond the law no less hazardous than the company of those who abide within it. A bee separated from the hive, though it be supplied with every nourishment necessary to its subsistence, will die. A man separated from society will not. His destiny is not so merciful. He suffers only the desolation of being able neither to die quietly as an animal nor to live obediently as a man. Unless a man keep his brother, he shall not be kept. But who shall be regarded as his brother? Upon so radical a point nature has rendered no decision.

A decision is nevertheless made. Men, in being born into society, are born also into the masks of society. The child newborn
has adjudicated the one part of its circumstance as little as the
other. He has inherited both—his natural dependency upon others
as well as the masks which relate him to others. Passively, with
the same innocence by which he has inherited his natural species,
he is committed to his social role. In neither the one nor the other
has his consent been solicited. He discovers himself already immersed in the texture of relations, some natural, some juristic, for
which society destines him. The obligations which circumscribe
his acts and define his status in the economy of the moral community or legal corporation are, with respect to any act or decision of his own, as blindly endured as his animal hungers. The
obligations attach to the role to which he has been born; they
would attach still to the role even had he not been born. But in
belonging to the role, they belong also, though indirectly, to him.
so long as he enacts the role. Who, then, shall be regarded as his
brother? Even those are his brothers to whom he stands obliged.
His brotherhood extends as far as his obligations extend, and no
further.[5]

But is not Abel, whom Cain slays, brother to Cain, descended in
blood from the same Adam through the same Eve? He is not.
There precisely is the tragedy of Abel, and the worse tragedy of
Cain, that the descent which was thought to provide, with a common blood, a common bond, provided no bond at all.[6] So, therefore, the blood—empty ineffectual token—was spilled, and Cain
wanders desolate, without a mask, throughout the world.

15. Power and Justification

The doctrine of Thrasymachus, that might makes right, that justice is nothing but the interest of the stronger party,[7] is so tena-
cious a principle for the reason that it appears in every society to

[5] Compare *Luke* 10:25-37.
[6] Compare *Romans* 9:8: ". . . They which are the children of the flesh,
these are not the children of God: but the children of the promise are
counted for the seed."
[7] Plato, *The Republic*, I, 338.

describe the actual operation of the law. What is the civilization of the laws but force disciplined to transmit itself? Is not all government, which constrains men to lay aside their weapons, itself a weapon by which one part of society makes permanent its advantage against all others, securing its conquest by claiming *de iure* what belongs to it only *de facto?* The laws of society, Thrasymachus held, are but the instruments by means of which a circumstantial preponderance of power is maintained. Cain was after all a poor economist. Had he bethought himself where his own advantage lay, he would have kept Abel alive to minister before the altar, and to make still those offerings acceptable to God, in Cain's behalf. Cain, having the *de facto* power to kill, despoils himself of his advantage in exercising it. For over Abel living he had a real advantage, as his act demonstrated; over Abel dead he has none. Abel's power, though less than his, is nevertheless, when combined with his, a power greater than his own. Why then, if he might add Abel's power to his own, should Abel thus be wasted? Let Abel be armed that he might do Cain's bidding, that he who is vanquishable as an opponent might become indomitable as a tool.

Observe, says Thrasymachus, the actual societies of men. The masters of society are not the hewers of wood, but those whose collusion is firmest, who keep their brothers that the hewers, whom they exclude from brotherhood, may hew for their sake. There will invariably be found in any government of men, so Thrasymachus believed, a discrepance between the professed interest of government and the real interest. The professed interest will in all governments, whatever their real purposes may be, be described as the interest of the governed. That is the indispensable drug of civility anywhere and at all times. If you would have from a people not merely submission, but its belief that the demand for submission is both necessary and justified, then let the real interest be concealed. For men act not according to the truth but according to what they believe to be true. Control therefore their beliefs, and you control their actions. They will die for a falsehood in which they believe more willingly than live for a truth which they repudiate; and if for a belief which they hold true they be denied that vision of alternatives which would enable them to discover it false, they will endure in dumb innocence what would revolt them in clear knowledge.

The real interest served by government is always, Thrasyma-chus held, the interest of a minority, of an oligarchy, an *élite*. The good shepherd tends his flock, risks danger and privation that the flock may prosper. That is only because the shepherd, like the flock, is committed to the role of being used. He too is owned, and his poor hour spent, not that the flock shall eat, but that it shall be eaten. Wiser than either is the collusive interest which has disposed flock to slaughter and shepherd to privation, which eats uneaten. Behind every civil polity is power—power not the less real because it is wielded with the decorum of legal authority. The spirit of a people is in its laws? Alas, only its dispiritedness, its quiescence, vacant and subdued, beneath a conquest which its inherited status perpetuates and its dumb habit forgets.

Why does this doctrine of Thrasymachus continue to command such fierce consequence in all discussion of the law? Because it appears to rest upon the truth, that law presupposes power in order to be effective. Wherever authority *de iure* is divorced from the power *de facto* of getting itself executed, it in that measure appears to lose its reality.[8] The whole sense of the law appears to lie in its claim to bind the *de facto* order. If the divorcement from power becomes permanent, the law appears then to lapse, to oblige no one, to suffer *desuetudo*, disuse, which in effect, if not in claim, cancels it.

Caesar is dead: he is neither feared nor regretted. Hitler and Stalin are dead. Why then should one fear, and act, as if both were still abroad in the world? Because the thing to be feared and countered is in none of these cases the man who has died, but the role which each once enacted in the world and which another may in their place enact again. The role of Caesar, the order of relations *de iure* which were Caesar's, finds no longer, in history's present pulse, the actors to reanimate it. The order of Hitler, Hitlerism, does: it has but changed its lodgement; it actuates its pattern in minorities in most states, and is dominant in some. The order of Stalin, Stalinism, has been, in the harsh discipline of a few, transmitted, and its power propagated, as the effective

[8] Thomas Hobbes, *Leviathan*, II, xvii.

legal order which compels the obedience of half the world. The
principle is in both cases the same: *Gladius custos legis.* Norms
can become effective, historically operative in human society, only
where they are sustained by power.

Yet this circumstance, that the law lapses where it is not sustained by power, does not signify that a norm is identical with the
power that sustains it. The power of a stream is in its waters; the
direction of a stream is in its bed. Deflect the waters: the old bed
lies a dry scar upon the land, the power sweeps elsewhere, insensate, having no direction of its own, flowing first where it is re-
sisted least. Just so, it is the order of *de iure* relations that defines
the partisanship of a human society. The same power, directed
otherwise, had made effective another order, and the orders which
discover themselves athwart the stream, in the condign antago-
nisms of the twentieth century, had become, like the order of
Caesar, dead.

The proper objection to Thrasymachus' philosophy of power is
not that it asserts the coincidence of the *de facto* and the *de iure*
orders. Every system of justice must provide for this coincidence
as the norm which it prescribes and would make actual. The fault
of the philosophy of power is not therefore its assertion, that the
two orders may coincide, but its prohibition, that they should ever
be discrepant. For this prohibition requires assent to the belief,
that whatever is, is right, since by hypothesis whatever is has *ipso
facto* made good its claim to be. There can therefore be no wrong.
In such a consequence, were it ever to be admitted, the master of
society has more to lose than the hewer of wood, since the one
has only his servitude to part with, the other his dominion.

To identify the order of *de iure* relations with the order *de facto*
is to mistake the kind of reality which law has. It confuses the
authority of the law with the effectiveness of the law; it equates
its validity with its actuality. If in warfare one party makes conquest over another, the vanquished is compelled to act according
to the command of the victor. The law of the victor derives its
effectiveness from the strength of the victor; its validity it can
derive only from the respect of the vanquished. The vanquished
who rejects the law of the victor may still, under duress, do the
bidding of the victor. But he submits then only to the sanction

which sustains the law, not to the law which it sustains. The sanction itself is neutral, as a sword is neutral, which will cut equally for anyone who wields it. The same sanction, annexed under a different turn of events to the law of the vanquished, would have rendered *it* effective. The power which is necessary to make law effective is thus in neither case sufficient to establish its validity. The validity of a legal order, what constitutes its claim to be an order *de iure,* is evidently something distinct from the power which sustains it in society. Whence then, if not from power, comes the validity of the law?

16. Consent

It is one of the premises of the Stoic philosophy that no man can be bound except by his own consent. That principle is true. The prisoner of war may be compelled by rifle butt, independently of his consent, to do another's bidding. He will not acknowledge his captor's authority? Then his behavior can be managed by constraint. But there is no force exercised by another which can compel from him a consent to authority which he is unwilling of his own accord to give.[9] From life, from liberty, from property he may be alienated. His consent is inalienably his own, to give or to withhold. He may not indeed withhold it. But that is only to say that no man is made Prometheus by being chained to a rock. The force which constrains the martyr does not make the martyr; neither does the force which constrains the betrayer make the betrayer. Martyr and betrayer make themselves. Each is answerable for his act. Each is what he is by what he consents to be, for except by his consent there exists for him no *de iure* order with which he may be identified, against which, therefore, he can sin and be abased.

This is not an impertinence of moral nicety. It is part of the inanition of contemporary reflection upon the nature of law, that in the effort to describe only what can be sensibly observed reflection has been suspended at the critical juncture at which law assumes its authority, its character as valid obligation. Consent does not suffice to make law moral or benignant, for, as the

[9] Compare Epictetus, *Discourses,* I, i; Marcus Aurelius, *Meditations,* V, 10.

twentieth century has had every occasion to observe, men are capable of consenting to the most abominable orders of justice, orders as insensate as the power upon which they rest. "Know ye not, that to whom ye yield yourselves servants to obey, his servants ye are to whom ye obey . . . ?"[10] The moral question concerning the worthiness of the law, concerning the conditions under which consent deserves to be granted, is distinct from the question of the law's validity. But consent is necessary to the existence of law in society. The law to which consent is given may be that of Caesar or Christ, of the City of Man or the City of God, of capitalist or socialist, of totalitarian or democrat. But without consent there can be no obligation. The question at issue is not whether a given system of law shall in its effects produce good or evil, but what is the indispensable condition under which any system can be law at all.

Machiavelli's Prince may compel the world; only the world can civilize the compulsion. If Princes could make law, then no man could be free. It is because Princes are incompetent to make law that, where men fail to make it, all men are slaves.

Is it sufficient, for the purpose of explaining the political condition of men, that a man's behavior can be compelled? The prisoner's labor is done, the compliance of behavior is exacted, independently of his consent. If then he can be made to comply with or without his consent, is not his consent a superfluity which had been better left to the regret of moralists? The answer, though, alas, only moralists have made it, is, No. For the mere compliance of behavior to a rule externally endured is not what is meant by a political condition. The slave sustains no political relationship to the master, for the very reason that there is, for slave and master, no common rule to which each consents. Each stands, in relation to the other, in a status which is merely *de facto*. A legal relationship holds not between the master and the slave, but between the master and other masters, who bind themselves by mutual consent in a juristic community, so that the slaves of each may be retained by each, and the rights of each preserved, under the civilizing restraint of rule. The slave is not extricated from his servitude by this reflection. He serves no less who serves by con-

[10] *Romans,* 6:16.

straint. The slave may even, as in bitterness he observes the way of the world, despair of a political condition. He may reconcile himself to remaining in his *de facto* status. He may, like the child, expend his hour without reflection or dissent. That is in fact the condition of the majority of mankind, of every child until he reaches the years of reflection, of the majority of men even after, of those who reflect but want the strength of effective protest at all times. In a mute sufferance the failure to dissent may last for an hour, or for a generation, or for an age. But there is in this matter no statute of limitations. The failure to dissent establishes no right, for the sufficient reason that consent is necessary to the establishment of the statute.

By what right is the child, whose consent has been asked neither in its being born nor in its being bound, obligated by the laws? He is bound by no right. It nevertheless occurs that, born naked into its mask, the child is nurtured to the performance of the obligations which the mask requires. The child wants, it indispensably needs, the settled security which a mask provides, not necessarily the security of that mask which it has inherited, but the security of some mask, in which decisions are made for it. Implicitly, in observing the relations prescribed by its role, it acts as if bound by the role, and its habit of obedience to the demands of the role may suffice for its entire life, so that, though the child is not bound by its father's consent, it acts still as its father acted, and as his father before him. It inherits all that it is, the obligations of its father as the substance of its father, his status as his species. Upon this inertia of sheer habit, peeping and unawake, such continuity as human society ever acquires is borne. One generation transmits its masks to the next, undisturbed or unreflectively transformed, as a folksong transforms itself upon the lips of those who sing it, though they sing it with a view only to repeating it. These masks, worn in the fatigue of old habit, are the forms upon which all of the settled expectations of society are grounded. Apart from their implicit residence in the unreflective habit of a people the procedure of the law itself could never operate. Were it ever to chance that all were at once suspended, or even reflected on, society, and the child within it, would be cast completely adrift, disoriented, in the vacancy of an open sea. For the greater portion of all men's lives, the forms by which men live and by which they are bound are passively inherited, uncreatively transmitted. All societies are in this respect, like the child, primitive. The generations within them slumber, regarding only that part of the social pattern as plastic which they chance to work upon, if they work at all; the rest as not less inflexible than the natural laws within whose universal dominion they live and die. Such habit suffices for so long as the man in the child does not reflect. But when the child reflects upon alternatives to the role to which it has been born, it precisely meditates the question, By what authority the law binds it? and to the authority of the law to govern it the giving of its consent is indispensable. That question is the child's precarious emergence from its shell of habit, which requires from it the most fateful of all its decisions: the decision where its allegiance shall be given.

Does not this demand for consent unseat the law and all the settled expectations of men? Not more than they deserve on all occasions to be treated as tentative. Habit is more imperious in human life than reflection. But that is the veritable genius of a civilized society, that it can countenance this reflection. That society is most civilized in which, by systematic intention, not only men but laws as well are put on trial.

chapter V

The Ethical Foundations
of the Market

17. *The Undefended Citadel*

No one can escape the dumb anguish of those lines spoken by a
negro in Lorraine Hansberry's play, *A Raisin in the Sun:*

> . . . There ain't no causes—there ain't nothing but taking in this
> world, and he who takes most is smartest—and it don't make a damn
> bit of difference *how*.[1]

The lines are a modern confession. They convey—not only for
negroes but for all Americans, not only for Americans but for all
men of our century—the modern despair of the moral foundations
of society. All men in all times have experienced that doubt in
some measure. In the twentieth century it has become the desecrated style of the modern consciousness. It touches our own most
intimate awareness of ourselves. It extends itself carelessly, with
indifferent hopelessness, upon all of the institutions of modern
life. But it dwells most relentlessly and with least forgiveness
upon the forms most typical of the society which has called it
forth. In the market it moves unchecked, and our theory of the
economic community has abjectly followed its course. In despair
of civilization we are in peril of rejecting the redresses which only
civilization can afford; in despair of community we are in peril
of rejecting the foundations of community itself.

[1] Lorraine Hansberry, *A Raisin in the Sun* (New York: The New
American Library, 1961), III (118).

Karl Marx supposed that all social institutions are grounded at last in economic institutions, namely, in institutions of production.[2] He conceived all culture—all politics, all forms and manners and observances, all spiritual institutions—to be a superstructure on economic foundations. Every social arrangement is the passive register of an economic distinction, every social transformation a mute obedience to the material conditions under which our lives are passed. The causal relations among social institutions run all in one direction—from economic foundations to spiritual superstructure, from modes of production to politics, from class struggle to poetry.

It is easy to disparage Marx. It is more difficult to answer him. In the present arrest of the modern intellect it must be confessed that we have deceased from the search for an answer. The decline of faith in modern institutions has on the contrary progressed so far that we argue in his terms, extend his conquest, and betray our patrimony.

The only secure path to an answer is to rediscover the moral foundations of society itself, to concern ourselves with the problem which at last concerned him, and to challenge the inversion by which we are committed to our present dumb surrender.

Men must be brought to see that the economic domain is not original but derivative, that it rests itself upon an ethical substructure, and that where that structure of moral covenant is wanting, they have not a society at all but only the illusion of one.

The market is the dominant institution of modern life. It is of all modern institutions the one whose ethical premises are least understood, least spontaneously affirmed, least believed in. The cynical profess to see in the market no ethic at all. The sentimental import into the market an ethic which is not its own, which is drawn from religion or law or cancellable habit.

Where there is no vision, the people perish. We are as a people,

[2] Compare *Critique of Political Economy*, translated by Max Eastman in *Capital, The Communist Manifesto, and Other Writings by Karl Marx* (New York: Random House, 1932), 10-11: "The mode of production of the material subsistence conditions the social, political and spiritual life-process in general. It is not the consciousness of men which determines their existence, but on the contrary it is their social existence which determines their consciousness."

even in our honeyed Canaan, in process of perishing. For we have grown blind to the moral premises of our simplest and most quiet acts.

Therefore I propose to describe the unborrowed ethic which is cognate to the business community itself—the ethic which is found in it, not an ethic which has been imposed upon it. For the task is not to produce an ethic where none is. The task is not to prove that profit is Christian, or that Christianity is profitable. The task is to articulate the implicit covenant which the business community uses but never states.

Let it be confessed that the market is not the City of God. It is nevertheless a city, and unless marketers see it, the city will die.

18. The Economic Community

If by a "market" it be agreed to understand, not the place of the market—the stockyards and depots, the concourses and green-grocers' stalls—but an order of persons making exchanges, of economic actors who, in the phrase of Adam Smith, truck and barter with one another, then I take the market to be the compendious institution to which all economic theory is finally addressed.

For ordinary purposes, among capitalist nations, that decision concerning the use of terms will excite no arrest. It is not, however, in point of consequence, so innocent as it may appear. For I do not intend by the use of the term "market" to restrict attention to any special form of it. In particular I do not intend to restrict attention to that special form of it which economists are accustomed to describe as "the market system," the system regulated by the competition of independent buyers and sellers, in which, without interference from the state, the invisible hand is said unmolestedly to work. The community of exchange is more fundamental than the political agencies which historically have regulated it or have been content to leave it alone. The relation of exchange is the fundamental relation of any economic order, the relation by which economic actors are bound together in their distinctive form of community.

That community is what I shall understand by the "market."

The market will therefore appear wherever the relation of exchange appears; the market system will not.

Wherever economics has achieved the status of a social science, it deals essentially with the economic community, that is, with the community of the market. Its study is the wealth of that community, that is, its marketable wealth. That there are values beyond the values of the market, values which men place beyond all price and forbid themselves to treat as objects of exchange, there can be no question. The wealth of a nation, though men permit themselves to forget it, is invariably wider than the wealth of its economy. If nothing in a nation were conceived to have dignity, then nothing in a nation could be conceived to have price. Yet such values in human society, the goods which men reserve for dignity and withold permanently from exchange, fall beyond the domain of marketable wealth. Within that domain all values are exchange-values, and the market is the structure of their interchange. It is the one institution into which all economic interests are distinctively gathered. It is the one institution in which all members of the economic community distinctively congregate. The parties to that community may never look upon each others' faces; they may never meet bodily in any common place. Yet, as the economist views wealth, against the needs of that community all wealth is measured, in its interest all wealth is produced, for its sake all wealth is distributed, at last to the end of its sustenance all wealth is husbanded or consumed.

Traditionally, theory has treated the economic community as a derivative phenomenon. It has viewed the exchanges of goods in the market as a natural consequence of the division of labor in human productive activity.

In any society whose labors are divided each member must depend upon the efforts of those beyond him for the satisfaction of some of his needs, and the market appears as the simple result of the unequalness of any one man to the supplying of his private wants. The ascetic saint who subsists by his own labors unassisted, limiting his needs to those only which his own labors can supply, will frequent no market. He will draw directly from untenanted nature, without fee of return, its free gratuity—for his meat the body of the locust and for his drink the honey of wild bee. He is party to no exchange, since no need of his solicits an exchange; therefore he is party to no market, which is simply the community of exchangers. The market is the commerce of insufficient saints.

Such in effect is the classical account of the origin of the market. Nor is it without its part of truth. The institution of the market is in fact rooted in the reciprocal needs of men who traffic in the products of their divided labors. That fact is beyond question. Nevertheless, the belief that the division of labor is an adequate accounting for the bond of the economic community is one of the profoundest illusions of social theory.

Economists make after all, as one learns, a very poor priesthood. They would maintain, as a point of method, their own severe detachment from the process which they observe; they have denied themselves the point of view which would enable them to observe it. But here at least is one occasion in which a mistaken positivism imperils their enterprise and ruins their understanding. For they see the market from beyond the market, not as the marketer sees it, who participates in it, but as an external spectator sees it, who views it from without. Therefore, they see only the bare outward show which alone can disclose itself to an unimplicated observer. They see the bare outward behavior and are blind to the norm which animates it and regulates it and confers upon it, for the persons who enact it, its social meaning. They see only the comings and goings of men, their mute trafficking beneath noise of turbine and smoke of anthracite, the bare accident of human neighborhood, of men moving with others of their kind, all poor in the midst of their common plenty, who mend their afflicting poverty without love, without loyalty, without compassion, without rule, in each other's company. The creative resolution of a social problem they do not see, for the civilized achievement is obscured beneath the dumb outward sufferance. Therefore their conclusion has been legislated by their perspective. They contemplate an institution; they describe an inadvertence.

The division of labor does not supply the bond of the economic community; it describes only the condition requiring it. For it does not follow from the circumstance that two men may place a beam more easily than one, that they will join themselves together in placing it. They will join themselves together in placing it only on one condition, that each admits in the other a right to a part in the common shelter. Without that admission their act will not occur. For the bond of their community, the tie which unites them, is not the physical beam which they have together lifted but the unspoken compact into which they have laconically entered. The bond of community among men is never measured by the weight of the beams which they carry. It is measured by the mutuality of their acknowledgements, by the respect for claims which they acknowledge in each other, as parties to a common covenant.

For the market, as one comes at last to see, is a traffic in claims, not in things. Labor is never exchanged for other labor, but always only for a right, either for a right in wages or for a right in the use of another's skill or for a right in a commodity which another's labor has produced.

The bond of the economic community, the covenant under which rights are commonly admitted, may be implicit only; in the terse interchanges of hewers of wood it may be neither spoken nor ever formalized. The majority of mankind are not, thank God, attorneys at law, and it is perhaps foolish to expect men who grunt and sweat under a weary life to solemnize in language the conditions of their fatigue. But these conditions are, in the measure that men act voluntarily, clear enough on the whole. The covenant may go unspoken. It is nevertheless essential and is always, wherever men have willingly contracted an exchange, mutually acknowledged to be binding on them both. For apart from their covenant exchangers have no community; apart from their labors they may have it still. The right, the claim, outlives the act which earns it. That is why the economic community preserves its uninterrupted life even when a city sleeps. Its labors cease, its concourses are emptied, its goading needs are for a little time quiet or unfelt; yet all that potent mass of life slumbers still beneath a common sky of its own making.

19. *Property and Exchange*

Economists are by profession disposed to study the factor of wealth in the economic community. I am concerned with the same community. But I attend to the factor of commonwealth. Where the economist sees in the behavior of the market a creation and a flow of goods, I see in it a transaction, an exchange of goods, in short, a commerce of persons.

We are by long habit accustomed to viewing the relation of goods exchanged. I shall be viewing the relation of the exchangers —not the ratio of exchange of bread and meat, but the conditions essential to the peace of the baker and the butcher.

Therefore, in order to provide the terms which will be found useful for this purpose, let me consider a simple limiting case, a community of two parties only, a community of two who contract an exchange with each other.

Ordinarily, men contract exchanges within an already established legal order which has defined in advance their relations to each other and supplied a constable to oversee their good behavior. We unheroic moderns suffer the illusion of supposing that the constable is essential to our community: we assume that where there is no constable there can be no contract. But that is an illusion of our positivist mentality. A constable may institute a jail; he is powerless to institute a society. He may by force protect a society which others have framed; he cannot by any act of force supply their omission in framing it. Political science, as it is cultivated in our day, celebrates the constable. It forgets the community instituted by consent, which alone can ever justify his act or require it. That is why in our day we have no science of politics. We have only police administration. We live in the dispirited tradition of Thomas Hobbes, who wrote in the *Leviathan:*

> Covenants without the sword are but words, and of no strength to secure a man at all.[3]

Well, even if it were so, it would remain an error to imagine that the sword without a covenant is a civil security. We should be more candid in confessing the limits of what power can accomplish in human affairs: the failure of Othello's union with Desdemona was not after all the failure of a sword; it was the failure of a trust.

Therefore, for the sake of simplicity, let us be rid of the con-

[3] *Leviathan,* XVII.

stable and of all of the adventitious securities of the legal order. When Martin Luther was asked where, if the ban were put upon him, he would go, he replied: "Under the sky." In the moral ambiguity of the twentieth century we shall do well to imitate his example. Consider simply a community under the sky, the community constituted by two parties who have, out of the wilderness of the world, entered into a relation of exchange. Then, for any concrete analysis, certain elements will immediately present themselves as essential to that relation.

The two parties to the exchange I shall describe, borrowing a term from the law of contract, as "persons" (*personae*): persons are the *subjects of exchange*.

These subjects contract their exchange with respect to certain objects: the "things" exchanged (*res*, in the language of the law) will then be technically described as the *objects of exchange*.

Thus, if Tom Sawyer trades with Huck Finn an apple core for a bent nail, Tom and Huck are persons, the subjects of exchange; the apple core and the bent nail are things, the objects of exchange.

For a discussion of the foundations of the American economy this exchange is hardly a translation of goods which shall have any appreciable effect on the destiny of nations or even upon the economy of the Mississippi Valley. Nevertheless, for a philosophical purpose, that simplicity is precisely the thing wanted. It is possible, but it would be very unwise, to begin with an exchange in which the persons implicated were General Motors and the United States Government, and the things exchanged were trucks and tax-dollars. I am interested for the moment less in the identity of the terms than in the structure of their relations to each other. Such dignity as marketers may ever claim will be found at last to depend upon their standing in that simple structure, related as Tom and Huck are related, as subjects of exchange, in the mutuality of a covenant into which they have freely entered.

Economists have been content to focus their interest exclusively on the relation of the things exchanged. The relation of the exchangers, though it is everywhere assumed as the social condition of the economic domain, is nowhere attended to. The ethical premises of the market remain therefore systematically obscure, and men walk ignorant of the institution which has civilized their concert.

The fault is that we refuse to think concretely enough. The economist conceives concreteness of analysis to reside in turnips and hominy grits and sidemeat, and not in the community of exchangers who truck and barter with these things. He wants to make economics a matter of commodities and prices, and for certain limited purposes I grant the extraordinary convenience, and even the genius, of that abstraction. But the economist cannot afford, having made that abstraction, to forget it. If he does, he commits the error which the philosopher Whitehead used to describe as "the fallacy of misplaced concreteness": he is guilty of mistaking an abstracted set of elements for the concrete phenomenon which it is his business to analyze. Thus, it is all very well to attend to exchange-values and prices. But a serious economist will remain aware that the objects of exchange which bear price tags are simply elements in a complex transaction in which subjects of exchange stand also related; that these subjects are as essential as those objects; and that, if we had not both, there could be neither an exchange nor any exchange-value nor any tag to be noted.

Concretely, the topic of economics is a social fact, and we are forbidden to ignore the circumstance that that fact embraces persons as well as things.

That, for an economist, is the experimental evidence of Lidice. All of the villagers of little Lidice are dead in the ashes of their burned church. In a single stroke of Nazi vengeance for the death of Heydrich their village has been reduced to a desert of things. The village still stands. Every market-stall remains still stocked. But there is no market, and neither wealth nor commodity nor price.

Let me return then to Tom and Huck, who were meditating, under the full afflatus of the profit motive, the exchange of an apple core for a bent nail. Tom examines the apple core, Huck the nail. Visibly, the objects have changed hands. An exchange has therefore occurred? No, the exchange waits upon an agreement, which is not yet. For the moment they simply meditate what it would be to make permanent this new distribution of the goods of the earth of which now, provisionally and experimentally, they make trial. The exchange does not consist in this merely external transfer of objects which an unimplicated observer sees. The transfer essential to exchange is a transfer not of things, but of rights. The objects may or may not pass between hands. But unless ownership passes, there has been no exchange.

The exchange, in short, if it occurs, will consist in a transfer of titles, of rights which are held, and are commonly admitted to be held, by the two parties.

That common admission of rights is the curious invisible bond which unites Tom and Huck at this precarious and painful moment of decision in which each weighs the marginal advantage to himself of acquiring what the other owns.

Tom and Huck stand related as persons for the one sufficient reason that each admits the other to be the bearer of a right: each admits in the other the right of governing the disposition of the object which he himself now holds. For that, and never anything short of it, is what we mean by being a person: to be a person is to be a subject of rights. And that, as you will observe, is already a *social* fact. To be a person—to be the subject of a right—is a fact necessarily and essentially involving, besides the person who has the right, another person who accredits it.

John Locke supposed a man's right to a nut picked up from the forest floor to be conferred by the labor expended in the act of picking it up. For, as he thought, in the act of picking it up the gatherer as it were congeals into the nut, which belonged till then to nature's great common, the labor of his own body. That is a delusion. For it must then follow that if another may by force of seizure take from him his nut, the usurper then holds it by the same ground of legitimacy, having mixed his labor with it. On the contrary, no one can have property in anything except as others acknowledge it. My property in a thing is the consequence not of the labor which I have put into it, but of your willingness to accredit it, your willingness to accredit the labor as the ground for a claim. And if you have not that willingness, then though I labor with all my heart and expend my very gut, I have no property.

My right of property in a thing depends not upon my claim to it, but precisely upon your readiness to admit my claim as privileged. Thus, I own a house by right of title. Which is not to say that I physically occupy it. On the contrary, I continue to own it even when I venture out of doors. Owning it does not signify that I use it. Ownership, as the law interprets property, means only that I have the right to exclude others from the use of it. I may have no interest in making that exclusion: having the right, I may have no interest in exercising it. But the house is mine independently of my interest, whether or not I choose to exercise it. For ownership consists not in my act or failure to act, but in your willingness to admit, with respect to that house, the priority of my claim to dispose of it as I choose.

There lies the paradox of all property: my property in anything depends not on my interests or my claims but on the acknowledgements and forbearances of others, just as your property in anything depends not on your interests or your claims but on the acknowledgements and forbearances of others. We here confront the fundamental condition of all peaceable intercourse among men. It is the radical sense in which all property is public. Private property is a public fact, or it is no fact at all. It is public for the reason that it depends quite abjectly on a public concert. It is always a reciprocal engagement, never a unilateral one.

Government, lawcourt, and police may be invoked to preserve property. They are powerless to originate it, and in fact they everywhere presuppose it as the social condition of any political arrangement.

For we have property only because first we consent to have community, and there is no greater mystification of human understanding than the belief that men establish community in order to preserve rights of property which they had apart from it.[4] Apart from it they have no property, and can have none. Outside of the bond of community a man owns nothing. He has only what he holds, and only for so long as he holds it or can by force unassisted prevent another from holding it in his place.

When in America the framers of the Constitution sought to

---

[4] See John Locke's *An Essay Concerning the True Original, Extent and End of Civil Government*, IX, 124: "The great and chief end . . . of men's uniting into commonwealths, and putting themselves under government, is the preservation of their property. . . ."

establish government, their motive was to preserve an order of
consent in which Americans already stood. To ratify the Constitution was to confirm in law what already they had, and acknowledged each other as having, beyond the Constitution in
society. The legal order proceeds from the social order. The Constitution did simply define in explicit article a system of rights
which were already implicitly admitted in social consent. Our
habit of reflection conceals that circumstance, conceals the circumstance that society is itself a relation of men under implicit
covenant. We are all in this matter the children of Hobbes, who
conceived that without politics there could be no society, that all
social relations are at last political relations, that men have no
bond with each other except in the stomach of Leviathan. In such
measure, in the political suspense of our world, have we become
addicted to the opinion that rights issue only from the sword and
fasces. We suppose political community to be the only form of
community, all rights to be legal rights, that is, rights politically
conferred, rights sustained by political sanctions. We are profoundly deceived. The American Revolution is history's clearest
evidence that men do not wait upon Caesar to prepare their
tables, nor upon Caesar's knife to slice their cheese. Their society
subsists in their alliance with each other, not in their allegiance to
him. That is the lesson of every revolution in all the world. The
legal order is temporarily in relapse. Then men discover, in a precarious hour, the effective limits of their society. It extends as far
as their mutuality extends, and can never by any political dispensation be made to extend further.

That is why, whatever else may be said of property, the proposition of Prou'dhon, that property is theft, is sheer nonsense. Every
right implies a correlative duty, and is real only in the measure
that that duty is admitted. Thus, the right which lies in you implies a duty in others not to interfere with your free exercise of
the right, and unless that duty is acknowledged by others as an
obligation, as a restraint upon their act, your right is empty and
delusive. A man's property in the market depends not upon performances which he requires of others, but upon forbearances
which others require of themselves.

Therefore, by reason of the circumstance that rights and duties are correlative, rights can appear only where the demands of moral community have been acknowledged, only where men are content to observe the minimal restraints which are necessary in order that they should form normal expectations of one another. There is never any point in asking whether *A* apart from *B* has any rights. *A* apart from *B* neither has them nor for that matter ever needs them. The only serious question is: Under what conditions will *B* admit rights in *A*? And to that question there is a direct and simple answer: on the one condition that *A* reciprocate by admitting rights in *B*. All rights are grounded in such reciprocity, in the mutuality of persons who, for the sake of rights which run against others, admit duties which run against themselves.

Our sceptic generation has lost sight of its own artifice. In the universal priesthood of all disbelievers we have separated our theory from our act, our science from our moral substance, our belief from our intercourse. It remains still true, in spite of the profound demoralization of all modern belief, that the appearance of rights and duties in any society is an index of its moral community. If you would know the limits of a community, do not attend to what it will think to say of itself. For it will make of itself, in what it says, either more than it is or less than it is. If you would know the limits of a community, look to the rights which it actually confers. For wherever rights are acknowledged, there also there must be persons, and wherever there are persons, men stand under covenant in each other's presence.

20. The Productiveness of Exchange

I confess that I have gotten a little afield from Tom and Huck. I now call attention to two matters of capital importance in the transaction which we left them meditating.

First, a paradox, that if they consent to make an exchange, then though each has treated the other fairly, yet nevertheless each will go forth from the event conceiving himself to have gained.

Such is the genius of their community of exchange, that each is better off in it than either could be apart from it. That, I say, is a paradox, for the sum of goods, the wealth of their community, is precisely the same after their transaction as before, namely, an apple core and a bent nail. The exchange has been fair. The right to the apple core and the right to the nail are commonly admitted by the exchangers to be equal, so that, with respect to the rights involved, Tom and Huck, as they entered the transaction as equals, also leave it as equals. Yet, in spite of that, each conceives himself better off than he was. By the simple act of redistributing the goods of their society of two, an increase of well-being has been achieved: Huck has more satisfaction in the nail than in the apple core, and Tom more satisfaction in the apple core than in the nail. If it were not so, the exchange would not occur.

The belief that exchange is sterile is the strangest of all of the consequences which stem from the fallacy of misplaced concreteness. Quesnay regarded the trade of the market as unproductive, a mere trafficking in wealth which failed, for all the wear and effort, to increase its quantity. The wealth of a society, as he conceived, is never by trade increased, but simply redistributed, equal parts being equal after transfer as before. In that assessment he was mistaken, for he supposed the wealth of society to reside in the poor aggregate of things which changed hands. The wealth of a society is, on the contrary, never measured in things, but in the felt satisfactions which can be drawn forth from them.

The persons who make exchanges in the market never regard the things exchanged as being of equal value. If they did, they should have no motive for trade, since the effect of the trade would be to leave each as he was before, neither richer nor poorer, except for the wisdom gained, that the wages of commerce are an illusion of men's restlessness.

But that is never in fact as the men who make the exchange see their act. As they see their act, the things equal in exchange are rights. The commodities which pass from hand to hand are regarded by each party to the transaction as unequal. That is why the exchange occurs. For though the sum of commodities has remained unaltered, the ready sources of satisfaction have been increased.

Therein, in that margin of improvement, lies the productiveness of exchange. By a simple substitution, though no additional utility has been extracted from the parsimony of the land, and no man not party to the transaction observes any increment of wealth, yet still that community of two, who have made the exchange, is richer than it was, and economically superior to its former estate. For the parties to the exchange have realized a mutuality of interest which binds each to the other, for the duration of their act, as person to person, in a bond which no mere watcher ever sees or can ever perfectly assess. Their society with each other, though they form only a community of two, is a society in which the goods held are more efficiently distributed in relation to actual need than in any society in which, with the same aggregate of goods beforehand, that mutuality has not been found.

21. The Rule of the Market

So much for the first point. The second matter of importance is that Huck's and Tom's exchange has occurred, their community of exchange has been constituted, without benefit of church or state. Priest and constable alike would view their exchange with contempt. Nevertheless, Tom and Huck at this moment compose a rudimentary community under the sky. If either offends against their community, there is no sanction afforded by the rest of mankind which will by force or fear supply remedies of redress for the injured party. Yet they stand in relations of positive peace. Not merely is there no outward offense; there is a positive acknowledgement of rights even in the absence of offense.

It is the habit of social theory in our day to suppose that Tom and Huck behave in so civilized a fashion each out of fear of a black eye. But that at least is not as Tom and Huck see their relationship. They have the essential civility to know that you can sin with an ethic, but you cannot sin without one. Covenants must precede the instruments of justice by which covenants are enforced. For where there is no rule, there can be no offense against rule; and where no offense is possible, the wages of sin are superfluous. A black eye in community is a punishment; beyond community it is as morally inconsequent as a thunder shower.

Property is an institution of the market, not of the state. The institution of property is authorized in the habit and comportment of the market even where there is no legal community to support it, no civil sanction to defend it, no political arm to enforce it. International law, such international law as men have, is for its greater part an *ex post facto* confirmation, by consent of the nations party to it, of an order of rights already acknowledged in practice, already consecrated in custom, before formal consent was given or sanctions were thought to be necessary.

What the state institutes and attempts in the interest of its citizens to maintain is not property, but a normative distribution of it. The institution of property is itself invariably assumed. The state undertakes only to articulate and preserve it, to regularize the procedures under which it is held and alienated—in short, to confirm it by rendering unto each that which is his due. A state may as a political dispensation invoke a principle of distributive justice. In the exercise of sovereignty it may by its power of taxation redistribute the wealth of a nation, searching out a distribution which the operations of the market, undirected, will not afford. But the tax is resorted to only because the institution of property has been already admitted: confiscation has been preempted as a remedy even from the sovereign.

It is therefore a mistake to suppose that the economic community ever perfectly coincides with the political. Political economy is an institution of politics, not of the market, and economic theory has been in all of its seasons misled by the exclusive attention it has lavished on the parish. In the face of other nations a state may profess to institute a political economy, an insularity of its market from the market of its neighbors. But in that enterprise its success is always as delusive as it is temporary, and at last it must always fail. For it works then beyond its competency and beyond its power. The market respects exchangers, not boundary-stones or compatriots. Traders are your true cosmopolitans, citizens of no state but of the world, who treat with a fillip the most heroic defensive measures of every political wall. The economy of the *polis* or of the nation is for them, in their strict capacity as tradesmen, as essentially non-isolable as the economy of the household. The most formidable barrier to trade which a nation institutes, and surrounds with its most condign sanctions, in order to protect the market it professes to own, is all undone by the pettiest smuggler of contraband in shirtsleeves and a rowboat.

Tom's and Huck's community deserves therefore to be attended to. It is grounded neither on force nor on fear. It is grounded on a simple respect for each other's claims, on what (if I dared to say it in the presence of constables, priests, and doctors of political economy) is simple good will. In any proper description of their relation coercion has no place. Each respects in the other a simple dignity, confers upon the other the status of being party to the community which they have realized as their proper new creation out of nature's ignorant solitudes.

Nature is a web of things, of bent nails and apple cores, and it is only constables and priests and doctors who suppose dignity to lie in the things which indiscriminate nature owns. But the community of exchange which embraces Tom and Huck is not nature's dispensation. It is their own, their proper act and commission, the concert of persons which they have instituted by a creative silent artifice on nature's stage. By their unspoken covenant they have secluded their community, they have set themselves apart, from the total residuum of nature which falls beyond covenant. Their community is in nature but not of it. For under their covenant they stand related to each other not as apple core to nail, nor as man to thing, but as person to person. That is the irreducible significance of such community as they have, that in it they stand related as *I* and *thou*. Each respects in the other a person, a bearer of rights, whom he forbids himself to treat merely as a thing, as a mere *it* in nature beyond his society. Price he assigns to things in nature; dignity he reserves to those only who walk equal under his covenant.

Competition is so characteristic a feature of capitalist economy that one is apt to see in the economic community a simple extension of that struggle for survival which occurs in universal nature. Power and collisions of power are as real in society as they are real in nature. The demand for adjustment is inexorably the same in both. There is nevertheless the most radical distinction between competition in nature and competition in the market. Nature is beyond covenant; therefore in nature there can be no offense against covenant. The market is a community under covenant; therefore an act which in nature is possible may be in community forbidden. Thus, men compete in the market; yet, in spite of competition, they deny themselves the unquestionable advantages of theft. For they hold no act permissible which shall suspend the conditions of their permanent intercourse with each other.

Around competition in the market this boundary is ineffaceably drawn, nor shall any man transgress it without losing his status in the community of which he claims to be a part. The market is simply that order of human affairs in which men are content to purchase their satisfactions, in which, in a word, power is exercised according to rule.

I am willing to be told that marketers are very imperfect saints. It is nevertheless a point of unimpeachable merit that they do not behave as the ascetic saint behaves, who seizes without recompense the wealth of the unoffending honey-bee and strikes water from the unrequited rock. They may walk noisy and contentious in a soiled tobacco-cloud, each haggling for the last fierce ounce of private gain. They walk nevertheless in implicit acknowledgement of the covenant which has civilized their oppositions. Each, despite his antagonism to another, forbids himself any act which would suspend the market common to them both.

I will not sentimentalize about this matter. The fault of positivism before any normative structure is not that it will admit only what it sees. Its fault is that it will admit *whatever* it sees, the breach of a covenant as well as the performance of it. It supposes that men stand in relations of community wherever they have a mere neighborhood in nature. The thief knows better, and so also does the marketer. The thief belongs to the neighborhood; he does not belong to the community. The marketer belongs to both.

An authentic account of the market must enable us to mark this distinction. It must enable us to distinguish between the real institution and the dumb show which outwardly resembles it. There may be, and even usually are, thieves in the marketplace, men parasitic to the economic community, men related to it as the parasite is related to the body of the host which harbors it. But a market in which all men are thieves is a contradiction in adjective. For the prime fact of the market, which keeps it populated, is not that men eat of each other, but that they are content, in the interest of satisfying their needs, to make orderly exchanges. Marketers may subsist without sympathy; they cannot subsist without mutuality.

The behavior of marketers is not, in short, mere behavior; it is normative behavior, behavior in obedience to a rule. That rule is the rule of their covenant, the bond of their community with each other. Subscription to it is the condition of their membership in the economic community, and without it they have neither membership nor community at all.

What is this rule of the market which obliges all marketers in a common consent? It is the joint affirmation of two principles.

The rule of the market stipulates, first, that for something given something shall be received; in short, that every exchange shall be a reciprocal exchange.

It stipulates, second, that no transfer of rights shall be regarded as binding into which the parties to the exchange have not voluntarily entered; in short, that without consent there may be no valid bargain.

That two-fold rule states the condition of all peaceable exchanges in the market. It is not a matter of sentiment; it is a matter of covenant. It is not the matter which we wretchedly describe (always with inward moral qualm) as "enlightened self-interest." It is a matter simply of peace, of the form which peace takes in the economic community. It assumes nothing beyond the conditions essential to the peace of the market, and is binding on marketers only for so long as they would stand permanently beneath its shelter. For the market is wherever its rule is observed. Wherever its rule is observed, rights have been conferred, and community established, though there is no statesman to solemnize it, no historian to record it, and no lawcourt anywhere in the land. Thomas Paine wrote: "Government, like dress, is the badge of lost innocence."

22. The Dignity of Marketers

I do not intend, in describing exchange as a relation of persons, to impute to marketers any dignity which they do not in fact acknowledge in each other. They are incorrigibly extrovert by long habit, and are more apt in the conduct of their daily offices to speak of things claimed, of *mine* and *thine,* than of themselves. They speak always only of property, never of the persons in whom property is vested, as if the bonds of their real community were hogs and corn, the space of the earth, blast furnaces and tools of steel. But that is a difference of words, a difference only in their way of describing their circumstance. The parties to a relation of exchange are nevertheless related, despite their anonymity behind machine and desk and counter, in the dignity of persons. Which is only to say that they are related as *I* and *thou*—as subjects, not as objects, of exchange. Apart from the exchange which they contract they may represent any of the conditions of which mankind are capable, as rich or poor, great or humble, simple or wise, illustrious or abased. In all of these respects they may be unequal. Yet with respect to that relation of exchange into which they enter they stand prior to their bargain as equals, each equally empowered to give or to withhold the consent which alone can bind it. Before the loaf of bread on a baker's shelf Dives who will not confiscate the loaf is at last but the equal of Lazarus who will not steal it. The loaf may be had only by way of exchange, and as both in bargaining for exchange are equal to the baker, they are equal to each other. It is another matter that though they are equal, Dives shall have the loaf and Lazarus go hungry away.

The dignity of marketers does not imply that all men shall be fed. It implies only the mutual willingness of all marketers to procure their satisfactions by trade. The baker is as ready to sell his loaf to one buyer as to another. All buyers stand in equal dignity opposite to him. But not all stand in equal preparedness to pay his price. The plight of the poor is not that they have not the dignity of buyers. Their plight is that they have not the means to make their dignity effective. They would buy. They have not the wherewithal to command an exchange. When men accuse the market of inhumanity, they pick the wrong object for their reproaches. The proper object of reproach in an ill-ordered society cannot be the community of exchange which must reappear identically in a well-ordered society. The accusation runs properly not against the market, but against a distribution of power in society which forbids dignity to be exercised by all men. The decision concerning the proper distribution of power in a society will always remain a dispensation of politics, and this circumstance has led men to suppose that power is the source of all dignity, that where no power is no dignity can be allowed. But that is an inversion, the typical illusion of all social theory in our times. The source of power in the market is property, and wherever the capacity for property is admitted, dignity has already been allowed.

But it must be confessed that nowadays, in our manifest community, the latent community recedes from sight. "Things are in the saddle," wrote Emerson,

> Things are in the saddle
> And ride mankind.
>
> There are two laws discrete,
> Not reconciled,
> Law for man, and law for thing;
> The last builds town and fleet,
> But it runs wild,
> And doth the man unking.[5]

Nothing in nature forbids that a man should be treated as a thing. Only men in community can forbid it.

That is why Nigger Jim, who floats down the Mississippi on a raft, is so pathetic a revelation concerning the larger and formally more civilized adult community that lies beyond the community of Tom and Huck. In that adult community Nigger Jim is a man. But he lacks the status of being a person, of being party to that community. He is not a subject of rights; he is an object of rights. He may be bought: he is a chattel, a thing with a price, a piece of capital or land according as you regard him as a producer's tool or as a raw natural resource. He has price, but not dignity. The distinction is of such fundamental importance that I shall let Kant make it:

> In the realm of ends, everything has either a *price* or a *dignity*. Whatever has price can be replaced by something else as its equivalent; . . . whatever is above all price, and therefore admits of no equivalent, has a dignity.[6]

[5] *Ode, Inscribed to W. H. Channing*, 50-57.
[6] Immanuel Kant, *Foundations of the Metaphysics of Morals*, translated by Lewis White Beck (New York: Bobbs-Merrill, 1959), Second Section,

If you would know the value of a thing, ask what it would cost to replace it: its value is equal to the cost of its replacement.

Thus, among the traffickers on riverboat and cotton wharf, Nigger Jim's value is the cost of his replacement. And if he may be replaced by a machine or a mule, his replacement is a matter of indifference so long as an equivalent utility is assured. But the traffickers forbid themselves with respect to each other the license of substitution which they allow with respect to him. A buyer may choose to trade with one seller rather than another. He may even hold that the opportunity of choosing among sellers is essential to a free exchange. Thus sellers are interchangeable in the market. But they are never exchangeable. Their status under the same covenant in which the buyer himself stands confers upon them an intrinsic worth, a kind of value which the machine, the mule, and the nigger are forbidden to share. For whatsoever stands under their covenant has dignity; whatsoever, man or thing, is foreign to their covenant has only price.

A distinction without a difference? No, that is what we have to learn from Tom and Huck. All communities are at last under the sky. And the sky is as wide as we make it—as wide and as narrow as men's sympathies, as benignant or cruel as the restraints we put upon ourselves. The sky may embrace the cotton wharf, it may embrace the raft and the river, it may embrace the ends of the earth. Lofty or low, it extends as far as dignity is diffused. It extends as far as the obligations we acknowledge to one another, and can never by dispensation of God or sanction of government be made to extend further. With things I have no commerce; I make contracts with my brother.

When a businessman sets a value on the good will of his firm, his language is ambiguous, but his thought is innocent. But when a cynic says that there is no man who cannot be bought, he impugns the foundations of our economic community. The language is again ambiguous, but the thought is no longer innocent.

---

53. Contrast Thomas Hobbes, *Leviathan*, in *English Works of Thomas Hobbes* (London: Bohn, 1839), III, 76: "The value, or worth of a man, is as of all other things, his price; that is to say, so much as would be given for the use of his power; and therefore is not absolute; but a thing dependent on the need and judgment of another."

We are meditating the fundamental ambiguity which attaches to the concept of *labor* in economics and to the concept of *human resources* in all contemporary theories of management.

If one man labors for another, he exchanges the labor which he gives for the wages he receives, and the wages are the price of his labor, not of him. Only the labor which he parts with has a price; the laborer who parts with it has a dignity. In contracting his employment he is the subject, not the object, of exchange.

That is why we are able to mark a distinction between employment and servitude, between free laborer and slave, though outwardly the act performed, the neutral modicum of labor, is the same. Employer and employee are parties to one community; master and slave are not. If A employs B, then, however else they stand related, they must nevertheless stand equal with respect to the relation of exchange. For each is free to give or to withhold his consent to entering into that relationship, and each is free at the termination of their contract to detach himself from it. All that A acquires, all that he can ever acquire by purchase, is the direction of B's labor—neither B, nor strictly even B's labor, but only the direction of B's labor. During the interval of his employment B consents for the price measured by his wages to substitute A's direction for his own: he channels his labor according to A's interest. He stands nevertheless before A with his cap on, since exchange has been the condition of his act.

Such is the condition of their free community. The claim of Marxists to have transcended this condition is a delusion. The Marxists have simply substituted the public for the private employer, and in doing so have suspended the right of free entry or detachment for the employee. The concept of wages is an economic, not a political, category, and the profession of communist nations, that by eliminating the wage-system they have afforded economic in the place of political freedom, is one of the frauds of our century. They have shrunk freedom in both kinds, and extinguished it in one. Their narrow accomplishment is the security of the voiceless.

The object of the free labor movement in America has been nothing of the sort. Its proper object is now, and has always been, to secure the conditions of free contract for all men. The proper object of employers in America can never be less than to afford those conditions. In our modern industrial civilization collective bargaining is as essential to the freedom of laborers as corporate employment is essential to the freedom of enterprise. But we Americans are guilty of mud in this matter. If the shutdown is a sin, it does not follow that the strike is a civility. Both are in error; both equally have suspended the covenant of the economic community. The right to bargain for employment is a right to make contracts on equal terms. It is not a right to dictate employment or to abrogate the conditions of employment by contempt.

It is a confusion of thought to suppose that the right to one's labor is a right to one's job. If that were so, there would be no need of bargaining at all, since one party would be already admitted to own both the nail and the apple core. The job with its wages is, on the contrary, in negotiations for a labor contract, the employer's commodity for exchange; and though it remains less than likely in America, it is nevertheless still possible to reduce employers to servitude by denying to them their equal powers of contract.

But it is equally a confusion of thought to suppose that the ownership of land and capital confers upon the owner a right to direct the labors of a society by constraint. Alexander Hamilton's assumption that the interests of property are the bulwark of a stable society is in fact literally true. But it is true only if the labor which journeymen and mechanics own is understood to be itself a part of property. The assumption is false and dangerous as Hamilton's contemporaries understood it, since it supposes that the vast majority of men who labor on the land and in the factories are licentious and have no stake in the stability of society. For, whether the control of the instruments of production be vested in the public or in the private party, no society can be accounted stable in which the only free option afforded to its laborers is either to labor constrained or to die unconstrained.

I refuse to speak as a partisan in this matter; therefore I shall satisfy no partisan. Distributive justice is the great political problem of our century. But the path to a distributive justice in American society must be found through our institutions, not in spite of them, and we do not mark out our clear path by making ourselves party to the confusions which obscure it.

The right to dispose of one's labor in exchange is not equivalent to the right to command an exchange; it is not equivalent to "the right to work." A free society requires indispensably that employer and employee shall bargain as equals; it does not assure that there shall be employment. The two rights—the right to dispose of one's labor and the right to work—are distinct. The first right runs between the laborer and the person who freely chooses to employ him; the second between the laborer and society at large. I have no right to labor in your employ, unless you choose to employ me. But as a member of the political community which falls beyond us both I have every right to expect of society that my labor, such as it is, limited as it always is, shall not by default of society itself go permanently unused. In the long run employers have as profound an interest in guaranteeing to all men in society the right to work as any employee can ever have in claiming it, and the capacity of free government to remedy the market's blind cycles of arrest and unemployment is in fact, in our world, the condition of the market's permanence. That is, however, a matter of our political, not merely of our economic community. There is no single problem of contemporary life for whose solution clarity of thought is so essential a prerequisite.

23. The Bond of the Economic Community

Men live in societies, some in societies which they have actively constituted, the majority in societies into which, passively, they have suffered the adventure of being born.

Within these societies their labors are divided, so that each depends abjectly on the other, and so far keeps the other that he shall himself be kept.

That may be the extent of the accredited bond. The factory worker, who shapes the plow, may nurture no love of the farmer, who grows the food he eats; nor may the farmer nurture any love of him. Each in society may be so separated from the other that the other's individual identity, as he lives or dies, suffers or prospers, never impinges on awareness. Each simply works, works in community, but works lonely without communion in a voiceless solitude.

Are factory worker and farmer, then, by virtue of the interwovenness of their acts, allied to each other? That they keep each other there can be no question. But it must be admitted that under the conditions of modern life, where anonymity is the habit of our intercourse, where men are timid of each other's presence and society but a peopled solitude, their circumstance is on its face ambiguous, and is always obscurely understood.

Community extends only as far as obligation extends. Men and dairy cattle have no community with each other. The dairy cow, though it keeps the man and is kept by him, is forever beyond the man's society. Each is parasitic to the other. Each does simply use the other. The cow is a machine for transforming fodder into milk. If the milk could be had without serving to the cow its fodder, the cow would go unfed. But it is not so with the factory worker and the farmer. Each has a stake not merely in the produce of the other, but in alliance with him. Therefore, the taking of the plow without the giving of the food, the taking of the food without the giving of the plow, is not cunning or economy, but malice, theft, a rupture of their social bond.

Where then, if not from the simple circumstance of interdependence, does the social bond arise? It arises from the circumstance that the members of a society act implicitly out of respect for one another's rights. Each acknowledges rights which the other holds, and in that measure (though it may be only in that measure) acts under a self-imposed restraint for the other's sake.

Each member of society acts also for his own sake, and until the web of society is torn, reflection may carry him no further. Reflection may leave him to suppose that "Hell is other people," that men endure the sight and company of each other only because without each other they cannot live. That limited reflection is the error which tragically colors our conception of our free world and gives to it, in the indecencies of our season, its unrelenting harshness of aspect.

We are in this matter the victims of our own peace. For it is only peace which allows us even for a moment to hold so desperate a conception of the foundations of our common enterprise. Nothing in all our world is so dispiriting, or so perilous to the interests of free men, as our inability to discover a positive sense and value in the commonwealth of the human community. We have permitted ourselves to cultivate, in defending free institutions, the very illusion which Marx cultivated in accusing them—the illusion, namely, that a free society, in the market as elsewhere, is but a raw collision of private interests. The truth of the matter is, if we had only the wit to see it, that mutuality may be wider than the market; it can never be narrower.

The market is not the truce of God; it is not the union of a political or religious or scientific or artistic community. It is nevertheless a union of persons. It is a condition of peace, the distinctive form which peace takes in the economic intercourse of men. To speak of it as amoral, as falling beyond the bounds of morality, is to condemn in it what in those other forms of community we excuse—namely, the claim to autonomy, the claim of any part of human life to unqualified separateness from a total image of man.

We are wrong on both counts, as wrong in degrading the market as in elevating politics or religion, science or art. Morally, no form of human community can be defended which suspends its total concert, which forbids its other forms their proper and liberating place in the harmony of the human effort. For morality is simply our implacable affirmation of our wholeness, our demand for concert, for organization, and for total sense, and the steadfast refusal to substitute for the human well-being the undisciplined autonomy of any fragment of itself.

If man shall not live by bread alone, so neither shall he live by politics alone, or by religion, or by science, or by art alone. Each is a moral community; no one of them is a sufficient community. The fragmenting claims of the domains of civilized life have by our ignorant assent become the literal terror of our world. For they have suspended the conditions of the fundamental human covenant which is beyond them all, the covenant without which at last all dignity in all men shall be cancelled in all roles—the dignity of saints and scientists as well as the dignity of marketers, and the dignity of saints and scientists no less than the dignity of marketers.

chapter VI

Value and Economy

24. *Utility and Value*

The feature of the world which the science of economics isolates
for special analysis is commonly entitled "utility." By the utility
of a thing is understood that property which enables it to supply
some need on the part of an animal organism. The need in question the economist does not attempt to circumscribe. It may be,
indifferently, a brute animal hunger or a religious hunger for
salvation. In the one event as in the other, the bare existence of
the need is a sufficient condition for imputing value to whatever
in fact will serve to satisfy it. The utility of a thing is the ground
of its value, its objective fitness for ministering to a need wherever
and whenever the need is felt.

Thus, water is fit to slake thirst, and retains its fitness, even
when no thirst is felt. That inherent fitness is its utility. It is an
empirically determinable property, a property of water considered in relation to the needs of the living. Needs are capable of
being instituted or extinguished. Utility is always found. The Ten-
nessee flowed harnessable for its million years before ever men
chose to harness it, or knew to see in that careless flow a power
suited to their uses, an inexhaustible resource for man and society, there to be had, capable of use even before the use was discerned or an actual user had appeared.

"Rent," said David Ricardo, "is that portion of the produce of
the earth which is paid to the landlord for the use of the original
and indestructible powers of the soil."[1]

[1] *The Principles of Political Economy and Taxation* (London: Dent,
1911), 33.

126

Those "original and indestructible powers of the soil," considered in relation to their possible uses, are what is intended by the soil's utility. Out of relation to any possible use those powers are without utility. But the putting them to use does not institute their utility, and neither can the valuing them institute their value. The original and indestructible powers of the soil are valuable because they are useful; they are not valuable because they are used or valued. The land was before rent and the progress of rent in the land. It was before the landlord, and before him who would purchase the use of the land. Nor had the original and indestructible powers of the soil to wait upon their coming, though the value put upon those powers can appear and be confirmed only with their coming.

The terms *utility* and *value* are commonly assumed to be equivalent, and there are in fact a number of connections in which they may be used interchangeably without offense. Nothing can have instrumental value which has not utility, so that wherever such value is correctly imputed to things utility may also be imputed to them. There is nevertheless a reason for regarding the terms as distinct, as naming different things. The language of the matter is without interest. But the fact of the matter is of the greatest possible interest. Whatever the conventions of language may be, the terms of our discourse must enable us to make the reflection, that nature as we know it would be still a resource capable of sustaining living things even if, in fact, there were no thing living.

Empty the world of life, expel from its precinct all appetite, all conation, all need, there could be no value. The world's poor monotony would be never felt, its insensateness never regretted, its tedium never known. Nor in all the majestic fabric of creation would the majesticalness of its course and frame, or the riches of its detail, be ever loved or sought after or admired. Order of fathomless indifference, it would be the bare mechanic nature which the physical sciences have represented, with such singular detachment, to the eye of intellect. The elemental utilities of nature, though need were nowhere actual, would remain nevertheless as formerly they were, earth, air, fire, and water all in the pulse of time, all fit to sustain growth even in the fallow world where nothing grew.

To impute utility to a thing is never to pronounce upon the present incidence in the world of any actual need for it; it is to pronounce only upon the fitness of the thing to satisfy such a need, were the need ever to become actual. Water has utility for the support of human beings whether human beings discover themselves in a land of drought, or a land of flood, or a land of benignant sufficiency. That there is too much of it, or too little, or just enough, is a reflection not on its capacity to serve need, but on the fluctuations of the need in the organisms it serves. The satiety which extinguishes need extinguishes value. It does not extinguish the utility of water for allaying the need, were the need again to be felt. Therefore, the value of water cannot be equivalent to its utility, since the one varies while the other remains constant.

There can be no objection to describing utilities as *potential values*. But if the two expressions are treated as equivalent, it must be understood in what measure that convention departs from customary usage. For nothing in the causal order can then be excluded from the domain of value; everything in all the monstrous frame of nature must then be admitted to be a potential value. The notion of utility marks simply a causal relation in nature, any causal relation between the properties of things and the satisfactions of needs to which they directly or indirectly minister; and there is no causal relation in nature which will not, for some conceivable need, satisfy that description.

For the purpose of economics that meaning is too broad for what the economist ordinarily intends by value. When a farmer stores his wheat, reserving it from present consumption for later use, he stores it for the reason that, though in relation to his present needs it is superfluity, in relation to his anticipated future needs it is not. The stored wheat is then said to be valuable, though present need for it is nowhere felt. It is a potential value, held for the sake of its usefulness in relation to those future needs for which it provides. Such actual value as it has, it has only in relation to the present need for providing against future needs; but with respect to those future needs it is potential. So much, but never more than that, the farmer understands by prudence in economy: his future need is admitted to have the same reality, the same right to figure in his reckoning, as the actual one. For the rest he leaves utility to nature and to God, and would shrug his shoulders at the curious proposition, that everything under the sun has value if only you are able to find or hatch a need which requires it. The latter proposition is nevertheless true, and economic theory must be capable of acknowledging that truth, of acknowledging it no less than the farmer's truth, that the real and operative values of mankind are those which minister to the real and operative needs of men.

I propose to employ the term *utility* in the broad sense, in the sense in which it refers to any causal connection, direct or indirect, whereby things are related to the satisfaction of possible need. A utility is not a value. It is a potentiality *for* value, the ground in nature which, wherever need is real, enables an ascription of value to be confirmed. The term *potential value* I shall employ as the farmer employs it,

> And pay no worship to the garish sun.

If that offends against the habit of economics, I make no excuse. The habit is confused, and economic theory cannot afford, as the farmer can well do, to suspend the distinctions upon which the truths of science are grounded.

25. The Natural Conditions of Value

The economist assumes, as the minimal condition for the existence of value, an animal organism placed in the midst of nature. Within this its natural circumstance the organism, as it would survive, is required to sustain itself, and since it exists as a creature of needs, the task of sustaining itself becomes for it an adventure. It is but a fragment of the world which environs it, the hithermost fragment of a universal nature which extends beyond it and includes it as its inescapable context. The environment which encompasses it is both its indispensable resource and its besetting peril. For its life is the risk to which nature has committed it. In its natural condition, sunken in nature, isolated with its needs, it makes demands upon the environment to which the environment itself is sublimely indifferent. For the environment varies according to its own insensate habit, thoughtlessly, without malice, without benignity, without regret, but always at last in independence of the organism's natural needs. The organism's abject dependence on its natural setting remains nevertheless constant. So that, if it would preserve its precarious purchase on life, an active response to nature's changes is required of it. If the demands of its nature remain permanently unsupplied, if its hungers remain unslaked and aborted, it will perish. It may live on one condition only, that by its own act it preserve its equilibrium with nature even in the face of nature's changes. To preserve its equilibrium is to *adapt* itself—to seek out within nature the elements which serve its purposes, to eschew those which thwart and frustrate them. In the one set of elements, those which assist it, it finds positive value; in the other set of elements, those which oppose it, it finds negative value, disvalue, hindrance.

It is only by reason of the purposiveness of the organism's activity that it is said to have needs. The needs of the organism, by relation to which things have potential value for it, are themselves derivative factors. They depend on the organism's immanent tendency; they are subordinate to its directed activity toward some end or goal for the sake of which it acts. The stream seeks the sea, the arrow seeks its target, not because of need. The reason for its movement and for the direction of its movement is not within it, but beyond it. For the target belongs not to the arrow, but to the archer; the sea belongs not to the stream, but to the accidental outlet of the furrows of the land. The goal of arrow and of stream is an accident to each which each blindly endures. Each moves subject to an alien claim, moves without purpose or direction of its own, and so therefore without need of its own. Its movement is not an act but a sufferance.

In any authentically vital activity, on the contrary, a need is the symptom of an inner purposiveness: the animal acts, and its activity can be neither described nor understood except by reference to some end toward which the activity is directed and in which alone it terminates.

A seed possesses its end, namely, the reproduction of itself, as a potentiality within it. It does not suffer its direction passively from without, but realizes it actively from within. Placed too

much in the shade, a plant will stretch itself toward the light; its
hunger unabated, its stalk will fatally lengthen till, grown too thin
to support its load, it topples and dies. The plant needs the light,
it needs the support of its stalk, for the sake of an end distinct
from either. The plant's needs are everywhere dependent, subordinate to the immanent tendency to live and reproduce itself
which presides over its career. Its needs fluctuate; the tendency
persists. For the needs relate only to means; the tendency alone
relates to the end, for the sake of which these needs are felt and
these means are demanded. Strictly, the plant does not *need* its
end. This it already has, and the intelligible continuity of its
growth resides in its having it. It wants only the means of realizing its end which exists already potentially, and may be made to
exist actually, within it.

The value of a utility depends as little on any act of mind as
the need of a plant depends upon any such act, and if the human
concern for values were restricted to matters of utility, it would
be possible to elaborate the entire science of value without any
reference whatever to mind.

In the growth of a plant one may properly speak of the value
of the light, since the light has value by relation to the needs of
the plant. The value of the light may, or may not, be apprehended; it certainly does not depend for its existence on any apprehension of it. It is enough that the need exists, and that the
light has utility in relation to it. The value is incident to the need.
It consists in the objective relation between the need of the plant
and the fitness of the light to serve that need. Robinson Crusoe,
who casts his seed-corn incontinently aside, discovers by accident
in the stand of wheat the unpremeditated instrument of his husbandry. The value of the seed-corn remains exactly the same,
whether or not it be apprehended *as* a value. Robinson may practice his husbandry only on condition that he grasps the relation
of the seed-corn to his need, but the value of the seed-corn resides
not in the grasping which discovers that relation, but in the objective fitness of the seed-corn to stand in that relation. In this
respect the value which the light has for the plant and the value
which the seed-corn has for the man are exactly on a par: we
mean nothing else in describing agronomy as a positive discipline.

The sole difference between plant and man with respect to these values is that in the one case the value is barely used, in the other it is used and reflected on as well. But the reflective act of mind, which apprehends the value for what it is, does not constitute the value. It simply discovers it, finds it. If the value which arises from the relation of utility and need were not available as a fact of nature, no apprehension of it would suffice to implant it there.

The history of human error rests on the mistaken belief that man can by taking thought create utilities. In the making of a machine, in the planting of a garden, he does but combine natural elements and canalize natural forces so as to adjust them to his uses. He commands nature, according to Bacon's hard insight, only by obeying her, and in his act of obedience he is permitted to draw only upon resources which nature has supplied.

If m be causally related to x, and I desire x, then m is a means to x, and has the value of a utility, whether or not I reflect upon it, or having reflected, choose to adopt it.

If penicillin be causally related to the cure of an infection, and I desire the cure of the infection, then penicillin is a means to the cure, and has the value of a utility, whether or not I reflect upon it, or having reflected, choose to adopt it.

The need for m depends upon the desire for x. Therefore, the value of m depends upon the desire for x. But the relation of m to x depends neither upon the desire nor upon the need, and would remain steadfast in nature even in the absence of desire or need.

A causal relation is a fact of nature, not of mind. I do not institute it by desire, and neither shall I cancel it by aversion. My knowledge of it, as my ignorance of it, leaves its operation in nature's silence undisturbed.

Such is the fundamental perception of all scientific economy. It is not the physician, but the sick body, which works a cure: the physician does nothing save supply the natural remedies by which the body is enabled to cure itself. And if, by the sick person who has cured himself, the physician be paid for his part in the event, he is paid not for the cure, but only for pointing the path to it. The taking of the path is sufficient to the cure; the physician's knowledge of the path has not conferred upon it any peculiar dignity or any least part of its effectiveness. The patient who submits to ministrations in his sleep is no less cured that he rises with unassuaged ignorance from his bed.

Therein, in this perception of the limits by which nature hedges our acts, is found the sense of the Stoic paradox, that man can be free only by conformity to nature. As human freedom is commensurate only with human power, the freedom of humanity can never lie entirely in the control of means, which nature owns; it must lie in the election of ends, which man owns, and may also disown. All that man is competent to do, he does by government not of nature, but of his own desires. At last he governs, and can govern, only himself. For he shall move on nature's web only as the web is laid. He is nature's denizen, not its architect, and the submission required of him is as abject as that of any other creature beneath the universal sun. The freedom of man, such freedom as he has, can reside, as the Stoic perceived, only in his unlimited capacity of assent, in his capacity to commit himself to ends and to withhold his commitment from them. He, not nature, is the partisan, the taker of sides, and nature shall appear morally insensate only to him who seeks what nature is not qualified to give. Man's distinctive freedom—what distinguishes him from the rest of the animal creation—belongs to him in his independent role as fashioner of his own ends. These only is he ever competent to legislate, meditating for himself the proper objects of desire. The values which alone he constitutes by an act of taking thought are the ends which he affirms, the same ends which he is free also to deny. Given these ends, his needs are determined, and with them the things which can have the value of utility for him so long as those ends are embraced. If a man seeks ends which are beyond his power, he shall be afflicted; if he seeks ends within his power, he shall gain them. But it is not nature which afflicts him, but he who afflicts himself. He is nature's victim or nature's sovereign according as he chooses. It is only as he fails to choose that he is, or can be, nature's child.

All labor of men is, in the last analysis, extractive, simply a form of mining, which seizes from nature the elemental utilities which nature already holds, but holds buried, in its womb. Economy creates no utility: it does but *produce* it, that is, *draw it forth* and make it accessible, according to the needs of men. What economy effects, all that it can effect, is a redistribution only, a new design in nature's impassive face, which supplies utility where need is felt and utility is wanted.

Yet in that simple redistribution by design, though no new utility has been compelled from the parsimony of the land, an emergent value has been realized for the designer. His own wealth in the face of nature has been enlarged, though the wealth of nature has remained steadfastly the same. For his proper wealth is measured not by what nature holds but by what he holds and can efficiently dispose according to his purposes.

A serious economist must finally address himself to the hard perception, that all that economy ever accomplishes, at last its sole concern, is order, a channeling of utility, a redistribution of the resources which nature harbors in indifferent silence. All economy is a study in design. It is form-producing, never thing-producing. It produces form, and form only; capacity—the original and indestructible powers of nature—it is obliged inevitably to borrow. Yet out of that form, out of that liberating form which has but redistributed the utilities of nature according to need, the act of economy wrests value, as the artist wrests value from the form implanted in the unspeaking clay.

26. The Paradox of Scarcity

There are many things which have the value of utility, which have nevertheless no status as *economic* goods. They command no price since they are so plentiful as to require no allocation. They are what the economist describes as "free goods"—the utilities which nature supplies so prodigally out of her bounty, as natural resource, that they need not be economized. To the farmer who ploughs beneath the sun the harvest is an economic good, since it requires his labor to produce it. The air in his nostril is a free good, since he has it without labor and competes with no one to have it in sufficiency to supply his needs.

To call a good "free" is not to say that it is no good. It is to say only that under the circumstances under which it is free, it will command no value in exchange. Let the same farmer become miner beneath the soil. Beneath the soil, as upon it, the need to breathe persists, but the air which upon the soil was nature's free provender becomes beneath the soil an economic good. The miner must labor to procure it, or pay another to procure it for him; and if the measure of the value of air beneath the soil is the amount of labor required to transport it there, the condition of its being an economic good is not that it can be measured (any free good can be measured), but that it has, besides the property of utility, the property of *scarcity* as well.

Economists have everywhere assumed that the property of scarcity is, like the property of utility, a natural relation, a merely *de facto* circumstance which men who economize do simply encounter in nature. They assume that as the concept of utility refers to a causal relation between resources and satisfactions, so the concept of scarcity refers to a simple relation of quantities in nature whereby the supply of a utility may be said to be equal or unequal to the demand for it.

The supply of nitrates in the soil may or may not be equal to the needs of a seed which germinates there. That equality or inequality is a natural relationship which a spectator external to the relationship may determine. The economist is therefore accustomed to supposing that scarcity, which is a function of this relation of supply and demand, is in all cases a merely *de facto* relation. Given a measurable demand and a measurable supply, the supply must be either more or less than the demand, or equal to it, and that, as the economist conceives his task, is a sufficient condition for marking any distinctions of value which he reflects upon.

Regrettably, in a human economy, that is not the case. The concept of scarcity is never, in any human economy, a purely descriptive category.

A Brahmin will famish before satisfying his thirst at a well contaminated by a pariah's hand. An artist will be content to undergo the cruelest physical deprivations in order to practice an art which no one has the wit to demand. A revolutionary will die for a cause, a scientist for a principle, a saint for a compassion, an ordinary man for a fidelity.

A seed does not arbitrate its needs; a man does. A man's needs

depend upon the ends he affirms, and unless his affirmations are
known, his acts of economy cannot be understood. For his needs
are subordinate to his economy; they do not dictate it. He measures scarcity, as he measures superfluity, according to a commission he has given to himself. Any need which runs against his
fundamental affirmations he will renounce as alien to himself.
That is why to be ignorant of his affirmations is to lose the sense
of his act. The need is felt; it goes unheeded and by any act of
his unsupplied, though the means to supplying it may lie ready
to his hand.

Let any felt want be entitled *demand*; and let any demand
which a person experiencing the demand treats as admissible be
entitled an *affirmed demand*. Then economics, in describing any
distinctively human economy, deals properly not with demand,
but only with affirmed demand.[2]

"A man is rich," says Henry David Thoreau, "in proportion to the
number of things he can afford to let alone." That is a hard saying,
and it is one of the blindnesses of economic theory that economists have never been persuaded to treat it seriously. The degree
of human well-being is always, in point of fact, expressible as a
ratio of power to desire:

$$W = \frac{p}{d}$$

Normally, a man's desires outrun his powers of attainment, so
that his "life-fraction," as Thomas Carlyle calls it, is afflictingly
small. He wants more than he can get, and can get only a poor

2 By "affirmed demand" I do not intend the familiar and everywhere accredited concept of "effective demand." Economically, a demand is effective
only if it is accompanied by the power to purchase its satisfaction. Unac-
companied by the power to purchase its satisfaction, a demand, though felt
and devoutly affirmed, begets no exchange. That is the pathetic estate of
the poor at all times: their need is real, they would supply that need, but
they do not command the resources to make their demand effective in the
market. No seller can be found who will part with what he has for the
nothing which they have. Therefore, since the market is a respecter not of
men, but only of exchangers, men starve while exchangers traffic.

Effective demand is demand which is capable of influencing the market.
Affirmed demand is, on the contrary, a restrictive condition of the market
itself. It lays down the limits beyond which no exchange will be contracted
or even attempted.

fraction of what he wants. His condition may be improved in either of two ways—by a path of conquest or by a path of renunciation. He may, his desires remaining constant, increase his powers of attainment; or, his powers of attainment remaining constant, he may contract the range of his desires. By the one device as by the other his degree of well-being is increased. For unity, his perfect well-being, requires only that his power be equal to his desire, and whether that equality come by a path of conquest or by a path of renunciation is economically a matter of indifference. Economics cannot profess to decide which of the two paths a man should take. Economically, he may take either. He will be found in fact, without offense, to take both.

If one would understand the rationality of a man's act, the essential thing is to attend to the economy which presides over it, to see that economy as he sees it who performs the act, not as another sees it, or fails to see it, who views the act from without. His *de facto* needs which another can observe are a very imperfect evidence of his economy. For not all of his needs are permitted to figure in his demand schedule. Some of them, even some which he is perfectly capable of making effective in the market, he will exclude in austerity from any reckoning of his good as he conceives his good. An external observer who views the fact from without inevitably supposes what the economic actor will not at all allow, that every need has an equal right to figure in account. The external observer supposes that all needs are of equal status, that needs differ only in relative urgency. The person economizing knows better: he is an economist, not nature's mendicant and pensioner. Needs differ in admissibleness. The bare existence of a need is never a sufficient index of its status or authority in his economy. It may, despite its urgency, have neither status nor authority. It is felt; it elicits no act. It goes unfed by omission. He renounces the need; he flatly disowns it. He refuses therefore to admit value in the means to its satisfaction. Who shall compel him to elevate another's trifle? Utility is a dispensation of nature, value a dispensation of his own. In his economy the value which another sees he extinguishes by a resolution.

For the grounds of economic theory that fact is most disturbing. It signifies that the economic actor will be found on occasion to pronounce superfluous the very thing which an external observer pronounces scarce.

The difference in description is not a difference of objectivity; it is a difference of object. We are meditating an inescapable illusion of all positivism, the illusion which positivism cultivates before any normative structure whatever. It is a form of the pathetic fallacy. I have entitled it *the illusion of the unimplicated observer*. An unimplicated observer will discover scarcity where the person implicated, the person practicing economy, admits none. That is why, on positivist grounds, we abscond with our economics, we do not study it.

If scarcity is a function of the relation between demand and supply, then whatever affects the measure of demand must affect the measure of scarcity. If the measure of demand is for any reason zero, then any positive supply is superfluity, and the total absence of supply is sufficiency. For nothing which is not wanted can ever be scarce.

A demand schedule is simply a descriptive account of the conditions under which, given a range of needs and the sources of their satisfaction, an economic actor is willing to purchase his satisfaction. The possibility that any *de facto* desire should be excluded from the schedule, that is to say, on any grounds other than the statutory costs of satisfying it, of rendering it effective, is never by an external observer imagined. That possibility is, however, in any market, always actual, actual not only exceptionally but in the most ordinary acts of ordinary men.

Why is Jonathan Swift's *Modest Proposal* never taken seriously as an economic remedy? If the eating of Irish children be recommended as an effective means of alleviating poverty among Irishmen, assuaging hunger among Englishmen, and eliminating beggars from the streets of both, the reason for rejecting the remedy is not that there is not in this a resource of wealth, and among Irishmen a resource virtually inexhaustible. Were men prepared to harvest their young as they harvest herring from the sea or potatoes from the soil, there can be no question that the utility of the one, its capacity to satisfy felt need, is as indefeasible as the utility of the other. Why then does a people so prolific,

ground down with want and privation so permanent, deny to itself this ready means of Malthusian equilibrium, refusing steadfastly to take advantage and sustenance out of the very cause of
its own property?

That is satire too bitter to the taste? It is indeed. I am so far
from trifling with economics as to despair of a perspective which
forbids it to see the satire as an Irishman sees it, and as even an
Englishman can be made to see it. I am told of a French economist who, when he read Swift's *Proposal*, pronounced it with
acerbity a self-defeating hypothesis. He wrought an invincible
argument to show it. It is given to some to be born again; to
Frenchmen, to die twice.

Swift was himself an Irishman. He wrote, out of a mood no less
bitter but more literal, *A Proposal for the Universal Use of Irish
Manufacture, in Cloaths and Furniture of Houses etc. Utterly Rejecting and Renouncing Every Thing Wearable that Comes from
England*. Against an English misrule which restrained Ireland
from importing any manufactured goods save goods from England carried on English bottoms, he proposed a boycott. A boycott rests upon a very simple principle: permit yourself to desire
that which it is in another's power to give or to withhold, you
are slave to that other; but if you be content to desire only that
which it is in your own power to supply, you are slave to no man:
you achieve your independence by a resolution.

This is the Stoic paradox, that scarcity is not a condition which
we find, but a condition we have legislated for ourselves. The
wealth or penury of nations can be measured only in relation to
the wants which they affirm, only in relation to the wants which,
as they see their total good, they refuse to disallow.

The paradox of scarcity lies at the foundation of all rational
economy. The failure to perceive it is what makes the American
economy so profoundly irrational, and American poverty so irre-
mediable and so permanent. In the indigence of our modern
habit we treat the power of production as the licentious measure
of our wealth. An insubstantial economist said to me: "I can tell
you in one word what all men want: More!" And one shall dignify
that as the issue of economics? It is neither detachment nor science. It is a confusion of thought, a betrayal of the terms of econ-

omy. For if scarcity is systematically without limit, no productivity shall ever mend it.

All power is relative to its commissions. Therefore he who governs the commissions of power governs the measure of its efficiency. As its commission expands, its efficiency diminishes; as its commission contracts, its efficiency takes its increase. But power can be efficient in any measure only as its commissions are defined. Restrict your wants, I shall measure your wealth; leave wants unrestricted, I shall measure only your poverty.

27. Constitutive and Statutory Economy

All things which men value merely as means have this common character, that they are without exception dependent goods, things which have their value not in themselves, but only in relation to something else beyond them, as a tool is valued not for its own sake but for the sake of what it enables us to produce.

Let any such good be entitled an *instrumental*, or *extrinsic*, value. Of any extrinsic good it is therefore possible to ask *why* it is valued, and the reason for which it is valued will always finally depend upon a value beyond it which the having it will enable us to secure.[3] Thus, the scientist values his experiment for the sake of knowledge; the physician his medical science for the sake of health; the artist his craft for the sake of expression; the statesman his laws for the sake of governing a free society of men. But the question "why?", which is relevant to the consid-

---

[3] The question why a thing is valued is in fact ambiguous. The answer may be: it is valued because it is *useful*, because it has the inherent properties which fit it to serve need. But the answer may also be: it is valued because it is *needed*, because it is required as a means to some end which falls beyond it.

The first answer is technical, the second teleological. The significance of the technical question depends upon the significance of the teleological one. It can never be asked where the teleological question is not capable of being asked. For if no end commanded activity, no need would be admitted, and if no need were admitted, the thing, despite its utility, would command no value.

The correctness of the valuation put upon a thing depends indeed upon the thing's utility, upon the inherent properties of the thing which fit it to serve need. But a utility will be valued not at all apart from need. Apart from need it is useful but without use, like the wife of a eunuch.

eration of instrumental goods, is evidently misplaced and meaningless in the moment that one assigns to anything an independent value as an end. For if art be valued for the sake of expression what reason can be either given or required, why expression should be valued? If laws be valued for the sake of creating and conserving a free society, what reason can be either given or required, why a free society should be valued? Those ends for the sake of which all other things are done and sought are not themselves valued for the sake of other things: they must, at least in the first instance, be valued for their own sake, not extrinsically as the means, but intrinsically as the ends, of human pursuit.

Let any such independent good be entitled an *intrinsic value*. Unless there were some things which men valued independently, as they value truth, or commonweal, or health, or expression, there could properly be neither a science of value nor any value at all. Nor is this conclusion altered by the circumstance that the science of physics, in addition to being valued for its truth, as the physicist values it, may be valued also for its uses, as the engineer values it. The usefulness of a science may be the predominant motive which impels a man to pursue it. But that is only to say that men have in the world other purposes besides the purposes of science. The parable of Faust who, to have perfect knowledge and perfect power, sold to the devil his immortal soul describes the moral condition of but one intellectual epoch. The Middle Ages were content, contrariwise but with the same singleness of purpose, to subordinate all values to the exclusive claims of salvation in life eternal. The values in particular which a society elevates, to which it subordinates all others, will be found to vary among historical peoples and periods. But the systematic demand for hierarchy, for subordinating some values to others, remains constant for all men and for all generations.

If therefore one would understand the inner sense and meaning of a society, not as others conceive it but as it conceives itself, it is necessary to look beyond its instrumentalities, beyond its laws and institutions, its arts and sciences, to the ends for the sake of which they have been framed. The institutions of a society are its settled and commonly agreed upon means for producing and conserving a certain conception of humanity, that is, a certain system of affirmations according to which it has conceived its own sufficiency. To know that conception of human excellence—to know what the Greeks described for themselves as *arete*—is not possible except by knowing the institutions; but the sole interest in investigating the institutions of a society can be to discover the ideal of humanity which is implicit in them. The serious study of history or of anthropology is not to supply the curious anecdote and incident of a travelogue; it is to understand the common function which institutions have within human society, as societies define for themselves, in the tragic wager of history, the affirmations they have dared to live by.

Consider the building which you occupy, how its degree of architectural excellence is to be judged. It is, good or bad, a very perspicuous essay in economy. It is a contrived artifact, the product of an act of calculation, in which settled needs of men have been anticipated and a parcel of the environment shaped to suit them. Any piece of architecture is but a large-scale tool, in the rough phase of Le Corbusier a *machine à habiter*. This is to say simply that the indispensable condition of its being architecture at all consists in its being addressed to a specific human function: it is designed to serve determinate needs which men have in the pursuit of ends they have independently set for themselves.

For the architect, as for the anthropologist and historian, the ends which a society embraces, therefore the needs which it will in fact affirm, are simply given. In stipulating a design the architect performs for society one of its most critical acts, but he is the critic not of the ends to which society dedicates itself, but only of the means by which its acts of dedication may be assisted, and their hindrances removed.

If society's act in defining its affirmations is described as *constitutive*, the architect's act must be described as merely *statutory*. The ends being given, his statutory task is sufficiently performed in providing a space in which these ends are efficiently served. The form which the space shall take is required to respect the building's function, as house or theater or railway station, and not a single word can be said concerning the excellence of the building except by reference to its function, to that use or purpose for the sake of which it was contrived. The serviceableness of any tool is measured by its efficiency in enabling men to perform a task. The serviceableness of a precision tool is measured by its efficiency in enabling them to forget the instrument in the performance. So, a building has the distinction of architecture in proportion as it emancipates men from the external conditions which it affords, in proportion as it liberates them to the performance of tasks and the pursuit of ends which are independent of architecture. Perfectly contrived, an architectural work not merely serves, it declares and visibly celebrates, the ends of society. It is the spatial emblem, the distillation in outward token, of a good which society has inwardly affirmed, and would persist in affirming still, though not so well, without it. In its forms, perfectly responsive to society's demands, the historian may read, inwrought into space, the ideals of the society which it served.

Men build differently from age to age and from society to society, not because the notion of architecture in human culture varies. They build differently because their uses and purposes are at odds. Every human culture builds in indelible egotism to suit only itself; and as it conceives its tasks, so it fashions its tools.

Just so, as a nation conceives its tasks, so it frames its economy; the economy of any nation can be judged only by reference to the ends which it proposes to itself.

I shall describe any inquiry into the organization of the ends of human pursuit as an essay in *constitutive economy*. And I shall describe any inquiry into the organization of means as an essay in *statutory economy*.

The economy of a nation which men ordinarily think to criticize is typically a statutory design, the more or less successful attempt to accommodate the uses and purposes which the nation regards as essential to its life.

Given the constitutive ends of a community, there is a statutory distribution of the community's resources such that in the interest of realizing those ends every other distribution is only equal or inferior to it. Statutory economics is a study of that formal distribution. That such a science is possible is one of the sovereign intuitions of our world. That such a science is to be had from any description of men's *de facto* behavior is one of the sovereign delusions of modern belief.

28. Sufficiency

Economists are diffident of the concept of perfect sufficiency, that is, in their terms, of that condition in which the marginal utility of any commodity is either zero or a negative quantity.

It must be confessed that the customary impatience of this concept is grounded upon a misunderstanding. The concept is not without meaning; it is simply, for the purpose of describing any actual condition of mankind, without application. Perfect sufficiency is nevertheless the normative equilibrium to which all economic activity is addressed, and exclusively addressed; and were it not for the mistake of supposing economics a purely descriptive science, no one would have ever thought to question its focal importance.

That perfect sufficiency is nowhere realized is no doubt true. That it is everywhere demanded, in the measure that men economize at all, is also true; and to degrade that concept because it corresponds to no actual condition of men is to degrade the concept of the fundamental motive which belongs to any economic order.

Economics has been so anxious to preserve its status as a positive science that it has suspended the normative condition under which alone any economic activity can be positively described. Circumstantially, men live in an order of predominant scarcity in which goods, efficiently used, must be allocated. The farmer who shakes his fist at God in a land of drought may be in fact more typical than the farmer who shakes his fist at God in a land of flood. The fact is that, as the farmer views his economic estate, the one condition is as baneful as the other. Scarcity is one of the conditions of economic value; so also is superfluity. Each elicits an economic act. Neither would elicit any act unless a normative equilibrium, that condition which we call perfect sufficiency, were sought. Such a normative equilibrium is the condition by reference to which any act can be said to have the status of an economic act. Any act which conduces to that equilibrium is accounted economic; any act which fails to conduce to it is accounted uneconomic, wasteful, or inefficient. If men prosper, sufficiency is the measure of their prosperity; if they suffer want, it is the measure of their deprivation; if they experience surfeit, it is the measure of their satiety and disgust. For if Antony's appetite grows by what it feeds on, the marginal utility of Cleopatra passeth understanding.

Sufficiency is the presiding standard by reference to which any act may be determined, in strictly economic terms, obligatory or forbidden.

Economics has always professed to be absolved of the task of determining what at last human well-being consists in. It cannot be absolved of the task of stipulating what the well-being of an economic actor consists in. For unless the conditions of economic well-being be known, no act can be understood as an economic act. Every act becomes then, in the absence of any norm, merely *de facto* behavior, a brute and insensate disturbance of the physical equilibrium of nature, a disturbance of that order of indifference in which men live or die, feed or famish, loaf or labor, beyond the pale of any economic order.

An economic act is never mere behavior; it is normative behavior, behavior in obedience to a rule which the actor has given to himself and with which his act is intended to comply.

The idea of a perfect sufficiency is purely formal. It will not suffice to moralize an economic community. What a man takes to be sufficiency may not, being had, be found to be an authentic sufficiency at all. He may be appalled at last to discover that he, poor collier, bears only the makings of ashes in his hands, that all his fretful sound and fury signifies, after all is done, nothing. He has labored under a delusion, he has pursued an inanity, like those followers of Ulysses who sought Circe and were turned to swine. Yet that delusion whose emptiness appals when once it is disclosed was essential to the economic significance of his act as he performed it. It was essential that it be thought to signify. Such is the tragic risk of any human economy. Nothing forbids that a man should walk in error, conceiving his sufficiency to lie in what would estrange him from his fellowman, empty his mind, enslave his body, cancel his independence, or damn his soul. Nothing forbids unless he forbids himself. There is no guarantee in the human condition that men shall act wisely in pursuit of what is their proper good. But no man can act economically without some conception of his good.

The idea of sufficiency can be given a determinate content on the one condition that the ends of an economic actor are known. A bee economizes; a squirrel economizes; a man economizes. Given the ends of each, there is an intelligible economy for each. But apart from those ends, there is no determinate economy for any.

The bee and the squirrel inherit their ends as passively as they inherit their species. A human being has no such absolution. The content of sufficiency is the most fateful of all human problems. The goals of men are not given to them by nature: men give goals to themselves. They are obliged, creatively and historically, to perform the task which nature has left undone, to supply nature's omission and oblivion by affirmations of their own.

That is why economics is not, and can never become, a descriptive science in the sense in which historiography and anthropology are descriptive sciences. A historian's or an anthropologist's task is done when the behavior of an economic community has been described. An economist's task is but begun. For it is not enough to have observed the behavior and to have described it accurately. Economically, the behavior itself may be at fault. The behavior described is subject to an implicit norm. Exactly in the measure that it professes to be economic behavior, it is *criticizable* behavior. The matter at issue with respect to it is not its factualness, but precisely its rectitude, its capacity to justify itself in terms of its consequences, given the ends to which the society stands committed.

Economics is a critique of behavior, not a description of it. The economist's task is essentially like the architect's: critical, accusative, addressed to a judgment of efficiency. It brings principle to facts; it does not wait to elicit principle from them. For the thing at stake in economic behavior is not the fact, but the claim made in behalf of it, that it is economic. The behavior is subject to fault. It claims to be principled behavior. Therefore it is amenable to a judgment of principle and open to its verdict.

John Stuart Mill rightly regarded the law of diminishing returns as the fundamental proposition of all political economy, a law as fundamental for economics as the laws of gravitation are fundamental for the physical sciences. The law of diminishing returns is a descriptive statement of the conditions of any productive activity whatever. When economics is described as a positive science, what is to be understood is the undeniable fact that it possesses such laws as this, laws which empower men to make firm predictions concerning the consequences of economic behavior. It is impossible to overstate the interest of such laws. The fact remains that they are to economics only what the principles of engineering are to architecture. If I would vault a space, the principles of mechanics permit me to anticipate and allow for the thrusts and stresses which will be generated among the physical members of the vault. So, in the same way, if I would allocate scarce resources, the law of diminishing returns permits me to predict the consequences of using variable proportions. But as the laws of mechanics do not themselves require that a building should stand, and are steadfastly illustrated even if it falls, so the laws of economics are indifferent to success or failure in economic enterprise.

The law of diminishing returns forbids no man to go broke. It simply states the ineluctable conditions under which that melancholy issue shall be suffered or avoided. The law does not itself profess to discriminate among the conditions it impassively describes. That is why economics, which propounds the law, can never end with it. Economics is an exploration of efficiency. It is precisely concerned with determining, under the conditions which the law describes, the *right* distribution of resources, that prescriptible distribution from which the greatest increase of satisfaction might be drawn. In short, the demand to *maximize utility* is no part of the law of diminishing returns, and in the absence of that demand the law would be economically without interest.

29. *The Composition of Value*

Ghandi fasts: an empire is imperilled. The economist is apt, in this predicament, to look rather to the empire than to Ghandi. For that the economy of an empire should hinge thus fatefully upon the act of a private individual, whether he eats or not, must surely appear, to one who regards it from without, an inexcusable weakness of the system. Ghandi's act of abstinence becomes the spasm of all India. Yet it depends for that significance less upon what Ghandi does than upon the response of others to his act. Therefore, the economist is content to look to those others—to regard India and empire and to forget Ghandi and his empty bowl. That is where, in the formation of his fundamental notions, he mistakes. For there he loses the perception which, had he made it, must have enabled him to understand in greater measure not only Ghandi and India, but America and you and me as well.

Meditate the man and his hunger. Ghandi's bowl is not merely empty, it is emptied: *he* has emptied it, and its emptiness is nothing to him. Owning his hunger, he is impotent; disowning it, he commands a nation from his bed.

The circumstance of importance for the economist is neither the impotence nor the power of command. It is the simple act by which the hunger is either owned or disowned, either affirmed or set aside.

So long as the hunger is owned, the food is an admissible value and solicits Ghandi's act. Let the hunger be disowned, the food is an inadmissible value and solicits only his contempt.

What Ghandi governs is neither the fitness of food to supply his body's needs nor the dart of hunger-pang by which his rebellious body importunes him. He governs only Ghandi, but Ghandi he governs absolutely, governs even to the edge of death, and can govern even over it if need be. The power of the man is in himself, not in what lies beyond him. It is a power which shapes his conduct, by whose sovereign operation the world about him, including his own racked body, expands or diminishes, gains value or loses it, as he chooses. For proper value can lie only in what he exalts, and can lie not at all in what he despises. Even his animal hunger he governs, not whether he shall feel it, but whether, being felt, it shall rule him. By that power he is equal to the fateful decision which makes him free from all that is external to himself. Ghandi will die if he fasts too long? That is true. "Thou art," says Epictetus, "a little soul burdened with a corpse." Ghandi is powerless to legislate for nature. But that is not the interest of his example. The interest is that nature is powerless to legislate for him.

The only scarcity which can ever count in economy is a scarcity which the economizer is disposed to remedy.

Ghandi is so far from being a poor accountant that he requires of himself a definition of the terms of which an accounting shall be taken. The value which Ghandi's physician sees is not a value which he, Ghandi, will allow, since the need which the physician sees is not a need which he, Ghandi, has authorized. Ghandi is as well informed as his physician concerning the value of food for the preservation of his life. He is, as a man of larger purpose, better informed concerning the value of life. The physician conceives life to be an intrinsic value, independent, isolable, the source and condition of every other value. Ghandi conceives it as after all, in the birth of a nation, merely contributory, good as it serves his ends, expendable or indifferent as it fails to serve them. The self which he would preserve, the only self which he counts worthy of preservation or of reverence, he discovers in the role which he has given to himself. Ghandi, the essential and invincible Ghandi, is to be found in that role, not in yonder withered body stretched upon a pallet with which all India commiserates, in fear lest it should die and be placed permanently beyond the power of sight and touch. Do you take *him* to be this wretched remnant of an animal body which he uses so utterly without compassion, nursing it along as a scourge of the world on water drops? You mistake the order of the economy which he has constituted.

Every end has its costs. Therefore the relative value of any end can be determined only by an assessment of its costs. We permit ourselves at times, by old habit, to think otherwise, to suppose that because some goods are intrinsically valuable, valuable in their own right and for their own sakes, as men value health or truth or beauty, or honor or purity or love, the cost of their purchase leaves their value unimpaired. We assume that if a good has been identified as an intrinsic good, then its relative importance in the total economy of human good—what I shall call its *contributory value*—has been thereby determined. It has not. Intrinsic goods compete with each other in the human devotion, and we have no right to assume that they stand to each other in a pre-established harmony, that their concert presents no problem, that the composition of our last goals can be assured otherwise than by decisions of our own. That is the cardinal error of all value theory. Even honor, love, purity of heart have their costs, and men who forget it have diminished their conquest of honor, or of love, or of purity, such as it is. The moral task is to make real in the world a design which the world does not afford without our effort; and if honor and love and purity were to be had without sacrifice of other ends which we also prize intrinsically, they would be never so highly esteemed as in fact invariably they are, even by those who find their cost too high.

To affirm the value of any end is necessarily to affirm the value of the means indispensable to the attainment of it. There, implicitly, is the source of our moral problem. For among the means indispensable to the attainment of an end the sacrifice of other *ends* may fall. That sacrifice is the constitutive cost of that end, and for anyone who would pursue that end, that sacrifice is its price.

To declare a good intrinsically valuable is not to declare it absolute. It is to declare only that, *other things being equal,* it will justify itself. But that condition, that other things are equal, is a critical condition, and we are forbidden ever simply to assume its truth. Intrinsic goods are themselves subject to criticism. They stand related to each other, as parts are related to each other in a common whole, according to an order of proportion. Therefore, in Dewey's phrasing, though individually they are "prized," they require still also to be "appraised."[4] The relative importance of their contribution to the total pattern of good which a man or a nation aspires after has still to be determined.

That is why it is essential to distinguish constitutive from statutory economy. Constitutive costs are measured in terms of intrinsic goods; statutory costs only in terms of instrumental ones.

The ends a man pursues are never isolated; they can never

---

[4] John Dewey, "Theory of Valuation," *International Encyclopedia of Unified Science* (Chicago: University of Chicago Press, 1939), II (4), 5. The first clear conception of the centrality of "contributory value" in moral theory appears in Clarence I. Lewis' *An Analysis of Knowledge and Valuation* (LaSalle, Ill.: Open Court, 1946), XVI, 479-510.

therefore, in the economy of his desires, be treated as independent one of the other. He may regard each of them as intrinsically good, as good for its own sake, good in its own right. Yet, if they compete with each other, if the pursuit of one suspends or compromises the pursuit of another, he is then obliged, as he would preserve the integrity of his act, to make a decision concerning them—to decide in what measure the pursuit of either must be qualified. And nothing in the nature of intrinsic value forbids the decision that one or other of them might have to be suspended in total measure, that its proper measure in the economy of his desires should be zero.

That, perspicuously, is Ghandi's circumstance, who places his life in suspense for a social ideal. Life is the constitutive cost of that ideal. The fasting—the renunciation of the means to life—is statutory. The renunciation has no value in itself; the life does. Such is the rigor of the economy which Ghandi has constituted. He takes to himself the renunciation; the life he lays with quiet regret aside.

Ghandi is obliged to decide upon the *composition* of his good; not where the intrinsic values lie, but how, in the ordering of a career, they may be brought together in a single order which can, in a last accounting, command his allegiance. That order, and it alone in all his world, is beyond all price, since it alone in all his world commands all costs, exacts all tolls, and requires of him, beyond every inducement of pleasure or deterrent of pain, his last sacrifice.

If in the human career good competed only with evil, the destiny of mankind would set for men no problem which fell beyond the ready comprehension of a little child. But it is not so. The profound difficulty of constitutive economy arises from the bitter truth that in the human condition good must compete with good. That is why, in a human economy, all ends appear with price tags on them. Their intrinsic value is not equivalent to their contributory value, and their contributory value is, morally, our ultimate and sole concern.

The ends men give to themselves are clear; the economy among them—their relative place in the concert of human desires—is not.

That economy must be constituted, and the decision which constitutes it is, for any man, a decision concerning his last partisanships.

With respect to the problems of statutory economy we have, formally at least, a superior assurance. The question concerning the proper distribution of the resources of an economic actor is capable of being given an answer of scientific rigor on the one condition that the ends to which the actor stands committed are known. Wherever those ends may be understood as fixed, needs also may be understood as fixed, and there will be an ideal distribution of the actor's resources in relation to those needs such that any other distribution would be only equal or inferior to it in the measure of satisfaction which it produced. That normative distribution will be the distribution in which the satisfactions drawn forth from those resources will be at a maximum, and the actor, so far as he economizes, will find no reason to introduce any further change, to distribute any resource to a use other than the use to which it is presently committed. For the normative distribution will be that in which the marginal utility of any least part of his resources is in all commitments equal.

The power of that conception is incontestable. It is one of the extraordinary conquests of the modern intellect, and anyone who fails to appreciate the positive burden of it must condemn his own competency as its critic.

The conception of an ideal statutory distribution of resources is nevertheless grounded on an assumption which economists have been content to leave systematically unstated. The assumption is, that the ends of human pursuit—those very ends which the economist presumes, in static analysis, to treat as fixed—are independent of each other; that the pursuit of one does not affect the pursuit of another; that, in short, all ends are mutually compatible.

That assumption is demonstrably false. And economics is forbidden, on the pretense that questions concerning ends are not the proper subject of economics, to make an affectation of its truth. That is the very interest of Ghandi's example. It is because Ghandi's example requires that assumption to be stated that his example appears both so heroic and inimitable and always so perfectly anomalous.

Suppose m and x to be causally related in nature in such wise that unless m occurs, x will not occur. Then, under this circumstance, m will be said to be an indispensable condition of x.

And suppose the negation of m, namely, *not-m*, to be causally related in nature to y, in such wise that unless *not-m* occurs, y will not occur. Then, under this circumstance, *not-m* will be said to be an indispensable condition of y.

Upon these two assumptions I may then describe x and y as being, for any rational economy, *incompatible objects of desire*. No rational economy can permit them to figure as joint objects of pursuit, since to have the one is necessarily to relinquish the other.

That structure is a very familiar one in the human story. We would have uninterrupted peace among nations; we would also have the unfettered sovereignty of nations. Alas, it cannot be so, and nothing which we do can ever make it so. For the circumstance which forbids it depends not at all upon our doing, but upon the conditions of peace and the conditions of sovereignty. If the restraints of law are necessary to peace, and the total absence of those restraints is necessary to sovereignty (*potestas legibus soluta*), then the sovereignty of nations is incompatible with peace among them. Each cancels the other, and men who pursue both pursue a delusion. The two goals are inconsistent; they are mutually exclusive. We must relinquish the one or relinquish the other, either forego peace or disown sovereignty, since both together cannot, by any expenditure of resources, be had.

We are, however, free, if not to realize this unqualified conjunction of ends, at all events to seek after a civilizing adjustment. We are free to reconstitute our ends so as to render them compatible. The unrestricted independence of nations is in fact incompatible with the peace of nations. But liberty is not incompatible with law. Peace is as little an absolute good as independence is an absolute good. Each has its costs, and if we would preserve both, we must limit both. For where each is laid as limit upon the other, they are together possible. A union of nations under law is such a reconciling economy, a constitutive economy of adjustment, of check and balance, in which rival ends have been brought together, and composed in one order of good, each in its fair measure, for the sake of human community.

Materially, that is a problem of politics. Formally, it is a problem of constitutive economy. For, formally, the same problem recurs even where the ends requiring to be adjusted to each other have nothing to do with politics, as when, for the advancement of knowledge, a Galileo is willing to risk the condemnation of an Inquisitor, or a Fermi the leucemia of his blood.

Economics may, in the interest of describing itself as a positive science, permit the opinion that the criticism of human ends is no part of its undertaking. It may affect to believe that the only values which are amenable to rational criticism are instrumental goods. That belief is the fraud of intellect in our season. It could be true only if the independence of human ends, in men's *de facto* behavior, were in all instances guaranteed, so that the question of the consistency of human ends, of their mutual compatibility with each other, could never arise. But that condition is contrary to fact. Ethics and economics are indivorcible. Their relation is such that unless the problems of constitutive economy can be resolved, the terms of accounting in any statutory economy are systematically indeterminate.

A great economist once wrote: "Questions of ultimate ends are not amenable to direct proof. Whatever can be proved to be good must be so by being shown to be a means to something admitted to be good without proof."[5]

It is just so. But men have drawn from that truth the conclusion that the ends of human pursuit, being subject to no proof, are therefore amenable to no criticism. No single misconception in the theory of value has been so perfectly annihilating to the rationality of men's acts as this belief, that criticism must cease at the threshold at which it becomes most fateful and most necessary. For it is exactly at this threshold that all of the most fundamental problems of the theory of value begin. Upon this threshold every concrete issue of international relations, every unreconciled collision of ideologies, every formative act of law or economy

[5] John Stuart Mill, *Utilitarianism* (1863), I.

flings down its challenge to our rationality. Nor shall our rationality be defended by retreating from it. The retreat from it is exactly the option which we do *not* have.

The ethical problem has never been to prove that that for whose sake all else is sought is good. That proposition requires no proof. It requires only to be given a content. The establishment of that content is the problem of constitutive economy. It is not its business to prescribe ends to mankind. Its business is to compose them, to show how the ends of the human community are to be accommodated into one consistent and harmonious whole, such that every end which men critically affirm has its proper place, and no end which men refuse in any commission to renounce is without a place, in the human endeavor. That composition is precisely what is meant by "that for whose sake all else is sought." It is not itself an end; it is an economy which states the conditions of human sufficiency. Such at last, for men and nations, is the sense of the poet's phrase: "There never was a war which was not inward."

chapter VII

Science and the
Covenant of Inquiry

30. *Belief and Evidence*

Of any belief which a man may hold it may be asked, With what *right* he holds it? It is the most fundamental demand of rational inquiry that this question, whenever asked, shall require an answer. The question may be postponed, it may remain for a time uncomprehended, it can be permanently evaded only at cost of disqualifying the inquiry from its title to rationality. Wherever that title is claimed, the question, *With what right?* may be significantly asked, for in the claim to rationality a right has been asserted, and in knowledge as in law this right must be established.

No less in matters of belief than in matters of conduct, rights and claims may fail to coincide: a man may hold beliefs to which he has no right, he may have a right to beliefs which he does not hold. The right to hold a belief is not established by the circumstance that the belief is held, nor does the failure to hold it imply that the right is not available. How then, if not from the simple holding, does the right to hold a belief arise? It arises from what is commonly described as *proof.* Those beliefs are accounted rational which are capable of being proved. Question a man's right to hold a belief, he will seek to justify the right by citing reasons which support the belief. The reasons, if they suffice, will constitute a proof; the proof confers the right. Where no proof is possible, there can be no question of right at all.

A belief unsupported by reasons is commonly said to be held on faith, that is, without right, *sine iure*. The description is not, at least it is by no means necessarily, invidious. That men hold some beliefs without claiming rationality for them is as neutral a circumstance as that they have a capacity for appetite as well as reason. Among the affirmations of which men are capable there are even some for which no reasons, in the ordinary acceptation of the term, are either necessary or possible. No philosophy ever succeeds in escaping the final contingency of its own foundations. That is why any philosophical argument which attempts to justify these foundations will inevitably appear circular. For in the end a philosophy seeks only to understand that which it already believes.[1] The corrosions of a universal doubt which cancelled all belief would have cancelled at the same time the sole motive of philosophy. Belief is the occasion of philosophy, not its achievement. Therefore, the tradition of philosophy which has made an affectation of rigor in pronouncing *dubito, ergo sum* is not likely to perceive that its most redoubtable champion, David Hume, is nearer to Anselm of Canterbury than to Descartes.

Let it be asked, With what right the sciences of nature seek to predict nature? The answer is, it must be admitted, By no right whatever. For of that future which is predicted we do in fact know nothing, unless it be assumed that the past of the world, of which we have had experience, supplies a clue to the future, of which we have none. Experience of nature will enable us to predict nature only on the assumption that nature behaves uniformly on all occasions, so that the part of its career which has been observed may serve as evidence for the part of its career which has not. Yet for this belief in the uniformity of nature, which underlies the simplest generalization from experience, there neither is nor can be proof in any ordinary sense. Reason will not prove it, for there is nothing contradictory in supposing it false. Nor can experience supply to it any confirmation which will not

---

[1] Compare S. Anselmi, *Proslogion*, cap. i, in *Opera Omnia*, edited by F. Schmitt (Edinburgh: Thomas Nelson, 1946), I, 100: "Non tento, domine, penetrare altitudinem tuam, quia nullatenus comparo illi intellectum meum; sed desidero aliquatenus intelligere veritatem tuam, quam credit et amat cor meum. Neque enim quaero intelligere ut credam, sed credo ut intelligam. Nam et hoc credo: quia 'nisi credidero, non intelligam'."

itself have presupposed the uniformity of nature and therefore have begged the question. That was Hume's momentous bequest to philosophy, the annihilating perception that the fundamental principle of empirical knowledge is amenable to no proof, that it is therefore affirmable by no right.

Of such principles it is sufficient to say only that they are not part of the set of beliefs which men rationally affirm. With respect to the beliefs for which men claim rationality the question, *With what right they claim it?* is admitted in all cases to be relevant, and the admission of this question is equivalent to the assertion, that the notion of legality, of obedience to rule, in some sense presides over the rational enterprise.

There must exist, in any rational inquiry, a ground for making the distinction between beliefs which are held *de iure* and beliefs which are held merely *de facto*. For the rationality of an inquiry consists in an exclusion, in laying down the condition that no belief shall be accepted without title. A belief can be justified, can acquire its title, only from the reasons which support it. In short, in order to be accounted a rational belief, it must be amenable to proof. But what shall be allowed to constitute a proof? It is possible to marshal the reasons which support a belief only on the condition that there is a rule, understood or tacitly assumed, which determines with precision what shall be accounted a proper reason. The will to believe can never be accounted a proper ground of belief, since on this ground any belief will appear to have the same claim to legitimacy as any other, provided only someone chooses to affirm it. The will to believe will justify no belief for the simple reason that it will justify every belief equally. Unless a rule be stipulated which defines the propriety of inquiry, which admits some reasons and excludes others, the normative distinction between faith and reason must disappear. For, in matters of belief as in matters of action, if everything be proper, then there is no propriety.

My child draws. From the tip of her crayon flow forth brave images of a faerie world which she summons, in purest detachment from her nest in nature, out of sovereign fantasy. Asked why she has thought to introduce into her drawing yonder blob of color, she will answer, succinct and imperturbable, without cessation of her work, "Just because." Let it be confessed that the question, as asked, is illicit. It is certain that the answer, as given, is unsatisfactory. The proper answer was to have answered not at all, for if the answer cannot be found in the brave new world where the blob was found, there is no answer. But the answer "Just because," which she finds invariably effective in quieting an intruder, has never yet succeeded in satisfying one. She is asked to give a reason, but the reason which she gives will not suffice to distinguish a legitimate blob from an illegitimate one. It will justify any blob, or none, and she is content to leave her tedious questioner suspended thus astride his query, uncertain in conscience whether he has been answered or mocked.

In the procedure of a court of law, a set of rules enables the court to decide what evidence shall be admitted into its proceedings. The function of the court is to render a decision upon a question of law. But the question of law (*quid iuris*) can be decided only after the question of fact (*quid facti*) has been determined; for until it be known what actually are the circumstances in the case that is being judged, no judgment concerning the application of the law can be rendered. To determine the question of fact it is indispensable to marshal evidence, and since the litigants, who are to produce the evidence for the matter in dispute, cannot be presumed to be disinterested, the disinterestedness of the inquiry is governed therefore by rules.

These rules, *the rules of evidence,* do not assuage the dispute itself; they succeed only in civilizing its conduct. They supply purely formal criteria; they do not depend upon the kind of case which is being heard, nor do they vary with it. They nevertheless lay down, in advance of all testimony, the conditions under which testimony will be heard. They declare, in effect, the conditions of relevance for that inquiry: any evidence is admissible which they do not exclude, but no evidence which they do exclude can, for that inquiry, figure as evidence at all. Judge and counsel alike are bound by them: the pleading which offends against them is overruled; the judgment which abridges them may be appealed. Such disinterestedness as a legal inquiry into fact may have is entirely dependent upon them.

The rules of evidence, like the principles of the common law itself, have evolved out of the experience of the judicial process. Their wisdom in detail is by no means beyond criticism; it is their function alone which is never questioned. Jeremy Bentham was of the opinion that, as the rules of evidence do actually operate, they in some instances preclude the very evidence which would enable the facts to be elicited, so that on occasion, where justice is at stake, of all participants in the legal process, the court is methodically the least informed. The objection is not, however, an objection to the need for rules, but an exception taken to the utility of particular rules which prohibit the consideration of evidence clearly relevant but proscribed. The issue is technical. But that it should arise, that the rules of evidence should be capable of being criticized, is philosophically a matter of the greatest possible interest. For it in effect declares that the rules which govern inquiry, which decide what by definition shall be permitted to function as evidence, exist by artifice, by implicit covenant. They oblige only those whom they govern, but these they oblige absolutely, so that what these the governed conceive and do, they conceive and do within a normative order which the rules have constituted and circumscribed.

The *man* who judges, what shall he believe? He is, like Bentham and like you and me, free to believe what he wishes to believe. But the *juryman* who judges, what of him? He is free to believe only what the rules permit him to believe, and nothing else. The discipline of the rules is the discipline of a mask: it sees light where light is admitted to be seen; to other light, systematically and methodically, it is blind. The *Fiat lux* which God decrees may make light where none was; but, inevitably, the *Fiat lux* which the law decrees must forbid light, even where light is. But suppose the rules be changed, that this light which was concealed may now be freely entertained? We have but exchanged masks; we do not dispense with one,

> And take upon's the mystery of things,
> As if we were God's spies.[2]

The significant choice is never whether we shall wear a mask, or wear none. It is invariably, Which mask shall be worn? and

[2] *King Lear*, V, iii, 16-17.

with respect to this question the evidence, which as yet is undefined, is silent.

31. Transformations of Method

Every science whatever is in similar circumstance. It matters not
at what epoch it is sought, in what place it is found, by what
stamp of mentality it is embraced—a rule of evidence presides
over its enterprise. For science, whatever the historical predicament in which it is generated, is on all occasions a form of rationality, and of rationality there can be none where there is no
rule of evidence which men are content to regard as binding upon
them.

Rationality is, in short, a form of covenant. Rational inquiry is
not merely behavior, but normative behavior, a behavior in obedience to rule, which is at least implicitly acknowledged as governing its procedure.

The rule tacitly acknowledged, which is implicit in the procedure, may be made explicit, so that it is by the agent consciously
respected. But that is as little necessary as that I should, in enacting my duties as citizen in society, be ready to discourse on
the status of the law in which my duties are prescribed. I on the
contrary act dutifully, and only afterwards reflect, if I reflect at
all, upon the bond which is immanent in my act and gives my act
its character.[3] So, in the procedure of a rational inquiry, I search
out reasons that will sustain my beliefs. That rational disposition
which demands reasons is nevertheless normative, though I never
turn critically back upon it, or attempt to formulate the rule or
principle, which is immanent in its demand.

Yet, in the moment that I attempt to formulate it, I find it no
less instructive for what it affirms than for what it excludes. What
might be supposed of it, that since it is a rule of evidence, it is
therefore neutral in what it prescribes, is precisely what is *not*
true of it. On the contrary, it is a mask, a mask which both

[3] Compare *Romans* 2:14-15: "For when the Gentiles, which have not
the law, do by nature the things contained in the law, these, having not the
law, are a law unto themselves: Which shew the work of the law written in
their hearts, their conscience also bearing witness, and their thoughts the
meanwhile accusing or else excusing one another."

disciplines and blinds, which must inevitably blind because it
disciplines the vision that complies with it. *It* is not neutral; it
neutralizes only those who act in common obedience to it, and
acknowledge it as obligatory upon themselves. But with respect
to others, who do not acknowledge its authority, its partisanship
is absolute: it is the very rule of partisan policy, which admits
what they exclude, and excludes what they admit. The rule which
guarantees the disinterestedness of inquiry is not itself neutral
with respect to the matter of disinterestedness. A society which
would secure for its members an openness of mind must, with respect to the closing of the mind, forbid itself a tolerance which
in all other connections it prescribes. Just so, the neutrality of a
scientific judgment is its compliance with the common rule which
binds all scientists. But this neutrality is the property of the judgment which obeys, not of the rule to which obedience is given;
for until the rule declares what is the meaning of neutrality, there
can be no distinction made between what is neutral and what is
not.

It is this predicament which is disclosed at large in the history
of philosophy. Why otherwise should philosophy be found to have
a history, save that in every historical epoch it reconstitutes its
task according to rules which it has legislated for itself anew?
The transformations of the history of philosophy are, technically,
transformations of *method*. All of the radical collisions of philosophic temper, which fatefully divide men into sect and party and
nation, and history itself into peoples and epochs, have their
origin in the circumstance, that what men choose to regard as
rules binding upon them, in the pursuit of truth no less than in
the pursuit of justice, has varied in the human career. The decisive method of any science is its rule of evidence. Where no
rule is, there also no science can be. For truth has no meaning
whatever except in relation to evidence, and will vary as evidence
is variously defined.

The grand divisions of philosophy—divisions which separate
whole epochs of reflection, the Greek from the medieval mentality, and the modern mentality from each of these; divisions within
an epoch, which estrange an Anselm from an Abelard; divisions
out of epoch, of Realist from Idealist, of Rationalist from Em-

piricist, of Naturalist from Transcendentalist; divisions so radical and profound that all philosophy as we know it does but walk within their precinct—what shall one make of these divisions which offer themselves as commentary on the self-same world, or on the grounds of knowledge within it? These are the pregnant historical acts wherein the principles of the rational enterprise are drawn forth with an explicitness which, except at intervals of insight, when the human vision is relentlessly self-critical and self-aware, men do not countenance. They are what make of all philosophy an ultimate confession, "that maketh men to be of one mind in an house."[4] The sciences of nature, which represent the modern genius, do not pass beyond these divisions. They do not reach them. They work within them, taking sides, but (since, circumstantially, all take the same side) taking sides without awareness of it, taking sides unconfessed, as men in society do everywhere ally themselves in enacting their duties, and act honorably and well, without asking for the principle which makes their duties what they are. The philosophers, at whose hands the divisions have been drawn, are all alike rationalists committed— Bacon as well as Descartes, Hume no less than Spinoza. Which is only to say, that each enacts the philosophic function, though each enacts it in a different way: each would have a reason to justify his belief, but by each the rule which admits reasons is differently defined.

Properly, a science has no revolutions: it has only a statutory development. It either evolves or dies. It may progress, it may revise its assumptions, it may expand its purview so as to penetrate into domains where formerly it had no place. But in its total career of expansion it preserves its essential identity unaltered. The norm of method which presides over its expansion is fixed; it is only the execution of the norm that is permitted to vary, as the prowess of its executants is sharpened, or the direction of their interests focalized. It is the same science, and those who execute its tasks belong to the same community of inquirers, because all members of the community respect a common rule. The science evolves so long as this rule is respected; it deceases when this rule is abridged. For the rule of method is the condition of legality in

[4] *Psalter,* 68:6.

any science. By it alone does the science have its character as a juristic order, into which only those beliefs may be admitted whose legitimacy has been established on proper grounds. The unity of a science is, in short, a *juristic* unity. The continuity of its development is a *juristic* continuity. Juristic unity or continuity is exactly what philosophy's history fails to exhibit. The history of philosophy betrays no common rule, no method commonly agreed upon, which will suffice to link the parts of its story into the unity of a single development. That is why, to those men of science who labor in quiet obedience to a settled rule, the story of philosophy must appear so anarchic an affair. It is all unregenerate protest, all reformation, all revolution: the grit of the barricades is indelible upon it. The act which generates an order of law is not itself lawful. So, the act which civilizes inquiry is not itself civilized. The history of philosophy is not the annal of man's obedience to a rule, not even the annal of his disobedience to one. On the contrary, it is the story of the making of those rules by which obedience and disobedience first become possible. Philosophy's role is to civilize, not to be civilized. Civilization is its task, not its datum, for it must decide at last the question, By what rule shall the making of rules be judged?

32. *Knowledge and Partisanship*

To argue and to agree would appear to be very contrary attitudes of mind, for it would seem that where men argue they have no agreement, and where men agree they have no argument. That is why Abelard's observation concerning the structure of argument must inevitably appear as a paradox—the paradox, namely, that no one can argue except on a ground of agreement (*Nemo quippe argui nisi ex concessis potest*). If men dispute, and dispute significantly, concerning any matter, they tacitly concede that there exists some ground beyond dispute upon which they are commonly agreed. Unless this were so, unless there were a common ground to which their mutual consent was given, though they might continue to dispute, they could not dispute significantly. For every significant dispute assumes that the basis for resolving disagreement is independent of either of the disputants: it consists in the admission of a common measure by which each party to the dispute acknowledges himself to be bound.

The waging of a war, if it eliminate one of the disputants, may terminate a dispute; it cannot resolve it. It cannot resolve it even if it eliminates both disputants. The matter disputed remains as it ever was; the dispute wants only disputants that it may be resumed.

Resolutions of argument are like treaties of peace; if they are to last, they can be gained only by consent. A resolution constrained without consent is no peace at all, but only an armed truce, a temporary cessation of hostilities which a more favorable occasion will again unleash. Thus, when it is said that there is no disputing about tastes, the meaning (whether just or not we need not here decide) is that since, in matters of taste, there is no commonly acknowledged standard to which the disputants may refer, the argument is empty. The argument is logically irresoluble, since a resolution precisely requires the common ground which is not allowed.

Just so, when philosophers dispute, so far as they dispute significantly, they assume provisionally the obligatoriness of a rule which binds them both. This rule affords to them the common ground which renders the resolution of their argument independent of either of the disputants. The rationality of the dispute depends upon a covenant which is common to them both. It can be assured by no other means. For though they be divided upon the matter under dispute, the division is not permitted to extend to the ground, or rule of evidence, which alone, by their common adherence to it, can enable their difference to be objectively resolved.

This rule, which they commonly admit and place beyond dispute, is logically of a higher order than any matter about which the dispute is conducted.

I ask you now to consider the kind of problem which typically occurs in any radical collision of philosophies. And I deliberately select for consideration the most critical of all problems, the problem of knowledge, of all problems the least resolved, though it has commanded the attention and exercised the ingenuity of the subtlest and most powerful intellects of the modern world.

Let the matter under dispute be, What rule of evidence shall govern the admission of evidence into inquiry? Then, if the discussion is to be rational, the rule of evidence which is discussed is distinct from the rule of evidence which presides over the discussion. The common consent of the disputants to the latter rule is necessary in order to permit their dispute concerning the former rule to be significantly resolved. About the rule which regulates the discussion the disputants must be agreed, in order that, about the rule which is discussed, they might significantly disagree.

Let the rule which presides over any discussion, and to which a common consent is required in order that the significance of the discussion might be assured, be called the *constitutive rule,* or the *rule of the first order.* And let any rule which is itself discussed, which figures as part of the matter of discussion, be called a *statutory rule,* or a *rule of the second order.* Then it will follow, that in any significant discussion, in any discussion which is capable of an objective resolution, a rule of the first order can never be the matter discussed.

This distinction is of the last consequence, for by reference to it one may decide, with respect to those disputes in which men's ultimate philosophic suasions are at stake, in what measure men significantly disagree, and in what measure they do but legislate. For, unless there be some rule of the first order which necessarily obliges all men, then any rule of the second order must be legislative.

When Descartes writes, and men read, the *Rules for the Direction of the Mind,* the rules in question, about which the argument is conducted, are rules of the second order. The rule of the first order, to which Descartes and his reader do commonly consent, consent to which is indispensable if the argument is to be significantly made or understood, is not the matter which is argued, but a condition of the argument, without which there could be no argument.

And when Hume writes, and men read, the *Enquiry Concerning Human Understanding,* the rule in question, about which the argument is conducted, is a rule of the second order. The rule of the first order, to which Hume and his reader do commonly consent, consent to which is indispensable if the argument is to be significantly made or understood, is not the matter which is argued, but a condition of the argument, without which there could be no argument.

Descartes writes in the *Rules for the Direction of the Mind:*

> By *intuition* I understand, not the fluctuating testimony of the senses . . . , but the conception which an unclouded and attentive mind gives us so readily and distinctly that we are wholly freed from doubt about that which we understand. . . . Intuition . . . springs from the light of reason alone.

> . . . By *deduction* . . . we understand all necessary inference from other facts that are known with certainty. . . . Many things are known with certainty, though not by themselves evident, but only deduced from true and known principles by the continuous and uninterrupted action of a mind that has a clear vision of each step in the process.

> . . . The first principles themselves are given by intuition alone, while on the contrary, the remote conclusions are furnished only by deduction.

> These two methods are the most certain routes to knowledge, and the mind should admit no others.[5]

That is the radical pronouncement of the Rationalist philosophy, its statement of its program. The pronouncement, which bears to Empiricism the same relation, is enunciated by Hume. Hume writes in the *Enquiry:*

> . . . Our thought . . . is really confined within very narrow limits. . . . All this creative power of the mind amounts to no more than the faculty of compounding, transposing, augmenting, or diminishing the materials afforded us by the senses and experience. . . .

> Or, to express myself in philosophical language, all our ideas . . . are copies of our impressions. . . .

> When we entertain, therefore, any suspicion that a philosophical term is employed without any meaning or idea (as is but too frequent), we need but enquire, *from what impression is that supposed idea derived?* And if it be impossible to assign any, this will serve to confirm our suspicion.[6]

[5] *Philosophical Works of Descartes,* translated by E. S. Haldane and G. R. T. Ross (New York: Dover, 1955), I, 7-8 ("Rule III").

[6] David Hume, *Enquiries Concerning Human Understanding and Concerning the Principles of Morals,* edited by L. A. Selby-Bigge (Oxford: Oxford University Press, 1927), 19-22.

Let now Hume read Descartes, and Descartes Hume, the question is, What is the significance of their division one from the other? That they are divided, divided concerning a fundamental rule of method which shall bear consequences, make differences, in a total tradition of philosophy, there can be no question: their division is one of the most radical divisions which philosophy is given to contemplate.

If Hume rejects Descartes' rule, or Descartes Hume's, the rejection is not occasioned on either side by a failure of the one to understand the other. On the contrary, each understands the other but too well. By a sympathetic projection, by a provisional assent —by what in another connection has been described as "the willing suspension of disbelief"—each does that of which he is perfectly capable, adopts tentatively the rule of the other, divests himself of his own rule. The argument is heard, it is understood. Its compulsiveness may even be acknowledged as absolute. But its absoluteness rests upon a provision, and ceases in the moment the provision is suspended, as presently, in each case, it is. The rule which is in each case provisionally accepted, the acceptance of which enables Hume to understand the argument of Descartes, and Descartes the argument of Hume, is a rule of the first order, and for so long as this rule is commonly respected as obligatory on them both, they may significantly argue. But in the moment that this mutuality, which alone will enable argument to be significantly conducted, lapses, so that neither observes the condition of argument of the other (the condition which alone will permit argument to have an objective resolution), Descartes and Hume do no longer argue significantly at all. Each simply legislates, legislates fatefully indeed those rules, rules of the second order, which shall thenceforth bind him absolutely, and shall bind equally all men who consent to be bound by them.

By what rule shall Faust gain knowledge? Upon so radical a question nature herself is silent. That is the tragedy of Faust. Impassive, indifferent, brute circumstance, nature issues no command, and Faust, who has sold his soul to possess her, discovers stricken that there is no obedience save as he shall require it of himself.

33. The Relations of Covenant in the Scientific Enterprise

I may therefore now speak—I would hope, without too seriously being misunderstood—of the relations of covenant in the scientific enterprise. By the covenant of a science I understand nothing besides its adherence to a common method, that is, to a constitutive rule of evidence. The scientific community no less than the political community observes the obligations of a *de iure* order. It is a community *sub lege, non sub homine*, and that is the indispensable condition of any moral community among men, whether in science or elsewhere.

That terrible question of Pontius Pilate, *What is truth?* is rightly regarded as a sign not of his rational, but of his moral, inanition. The substance of Pilate's doubt, that there is no rule that supplies the condition of knowledge or of certitude, no rule of evidence which is not at once man's caprice, is not the civilized suspense of judgment which waits upon evidence: it is an annihilation of the standard which permits evidence to be assembled. Men are nevertheless capable of that doubt, capable as Pilate was capable of it, capable as all men are in peril of it, who perceive the contingency, but do not allow the morality, of the scientific enterprise.

It is man, not nature, who decides what are the juristic conditions under which nature can be known.

By the method of a science of nature I understand something more fundamental than the statutory rules which are implicit in its techniques of discovery. Its fundamental method is, on the contrary, its constitutive rule of evidence, its covenant, which places ultimate authority, in determining the truth of beliefs about nature, in *experience*. That rule establishing the final authority of experience is indispensably required before the task of discovery can be undertaken, since it stipulates the condition under which any discovery could be acknowledged.

A hypothesis can be verified, statutory rules governing the inductive procedure can be elaborated, for the reason that the conditions of verification are presumed already to be understood.

What constitutes an inductive proof—the rule which enables inquiry to proceed—this is not the topic of induction, but its condition, without which there could be no induction, nor any special rules of technique, whether those of John Stuart Mill or another.

Yet now, if one asks what is the status of this rule, which accredits experience as the source of evidence for the truth of beliefs about nature, the natural contingency of the rule is at once declared. No method, no rule of evidence, can justify itself on natural grounds for the reason that apart from evidence we are forbidden to claim knowledge of those grounds. If nature keeps secrets, it keeps no lock, and the method which we use is not a key to nature but the simple index of our moral community with each other. We seek by civilizing our community of inquiry to establish an objective order beyond the caprice of opinion of any individual inquirer. Therefore we respect a common rule of covenant which shall govern us: we constitute a universe of inquiry in which every opinion shall be corrigible according to a standard of evidence commonly agreed upon.

In short, experience affords evidence because that is what, *juristically*, men have chosen to mean by proof. The important consideration is not whether all men have concurred (as in fact they have not) in meaning this, but, supposing this concurrence, what constitutes the *obligation* that the rule imposes? It is simply this, that men consent to be bound by it. Their consent to it, not their agreement with each other, confers upon it such obligatoriness as it has. Their agreement with each other is a consequence of their common commitment to the rule, not the reason or justification for their commitment, and if fewer than all consented, these still who consented would be bound by the rule as indefeasibly as, if none consented to it, it would oblige no man. Sense-experience is not an impregnable obligation: it stipulates no obligation whatever; it is we who oblige ourselves.

If, then, in its own part, sense-experience supplies no impregnable obligation, what shall be said of the relations discovered in logical analysis? Let it be asked, What constitutes a *deductive proof?* A proposition is said to be proved if it can be shown to be analytically involved in premises the truth of which is assumed. Where such an implicative relation exists, the proof consists simply in exhibiting the proposition as a consequence of these premises: it is simply explicative of them, an unfolding of their meaning, and has therefore exactly the measure of truth which they have, so that to deny it is to deny them also. To deny it without denying them is to derange the total economy of one's beliefs, since the existence of that economy radically depends on preserving a consistency among the beliefs which compose it. If it is true that, while temperature remains constant, the pressure of a gas varies inversely as the volume, and oxygen is a gas, then necessarily the pressure of oxygen must, under a constant temperature, vary inversely as the volume. Suppose the consequence to be false, then at least one of the premises must be false: either it is false that oxygen is a gas, or it is false that under a constant temperature the pressure of a gas varies inversely as the volume. The proof is found to hold, the inference is valid, because unless it were so, the consistency which is the indispensable condition of knowledge would be aborted. The condition of proof is thus determined by a normative demand, by a demand for self-consistency, which defines the juristic equilibrium of the logical domain.

The fundamental demand of the logical domain is the juristic demand for consistency. That demand is necessary? Shall one find in it an impregnable obligation fixed by nature? One shall not. That we do mutually consent to it is, in the silence of mere nature, as contingent a circumstance as that we do breathe a common air, and just as, if I would live, so I must breathe, so also, if I would reason, I must observe the conditions of rational discourse. But it is not life which impels me to affirm the value of life, nor is it reason which impels me to affirm the value of the logical domain. The demand for logical consistency is not a logical demand. It is a moral demand, a juristic condition of all inquiry. If in describing it as moral I broaden the meaning of morality beyond what philosophy has been accustomed to regard as its purview, it is not logic, but only a philosophical impoverishment, which is diminished. *Illum oportet crescere, me diminui.*

What shall count as evidence in inquiry is established by covenant, and the covenant which establishes it is not amenable to the evidence which it establishes. Must one then regard any covenant as the equal of any other? Shall animism be accounted a legitimate competitor with our empirical sciences of nature? Are decisions of method, like decisions of style in art, matters about which, as it is said, there can be no significant dispute? The answer is, No. But it is an impoverished defense of the sciences of nature which supposes them to be defended scientifically. The question concerning the distinction between science and superstition is not a question of science. It is a question of morals, of ultimate civilization—the matter of electing whether we shall have a universe or multiverse of inquiry. The issue is not cognitive, but juristic, and it is one of the persistent deceptions of our theoretical concern with method which has permitted us to see it otherwise. What is in question is not a matter of truth but of legitimacy. For the justification of a method can never be equivalent to proof, at least never in the sense of proof according to which one speaks of a theorem of geometry or a proposition of biology as being proved. It will consist of a mode of argument strictly analogous to the mode employed in jurisprudence, where a law for a political society is exhibited as justified by being shown to conduce to the ends to which that society is dedicated. Other justification, in politics, there is not. Neither, in science, can there be.

The order of precedence as between the moral and the cognitive is exactly the opposite of the order which philosophy has been accustomed to draw. Morality has been suspect because it has been thought necessary, in order to sustain its claim upon belief and conduct, to demonstrate its truth. But truth itself is, on the contrary, rooted ultimately in it, and indivorcible from it. The ultimate question of philosophy is not Pilate's query, *What is truth?* but Jesus' query, which Pilate silenced, *What is eligible for human choice?*

chapter VIII

The Covenants of Art[1]

34. Normative Equilibrium

When I was a child, there used to be hung above the dining room table in the Christmas season, as the festive token that its celebrations were in progress, an ingenious device which would nowadays be described as a mobile. It was to me then, and shall always seem, the strangest and most curious of fabrics, made of thread, of a few tenuous wire rods, and of pieces of colored glass and ceramic angels, all delicately strung together in a sequence of suspensions, which floated the rods in space and produced, by deviations from the horizontal, a splendid series of apparent imbalances, angels soaring and sinking as rods rose and fell. Collapsed in the box in which it was stored, it was an insensate tangle of débris. Suspended aloft, lighted, touched, it was a little universe in miniature, which would move with an eerie, majestical precariousness for an hour long before regaining its static equilibrium again. Its motion had the intellectuality of music, a music of pure silence, whose tones were shapes, whose melody was change, whose intricate harmony was enough to addict a childish heart, if it had known Pythagoras, to affirm devoutly the harmony of the spheres of heaven.

The hanging of the mobile aloft was annually performed with a

[1] This chapter first appeared under the title, "The Foundations of Artistic Community," in *The Review of Metaphysics*, XIII, 2 (December, 1959), 235-258. It is reprinted by permission. For a more compendious treatment see John F. A. Taylor, *Design and Expression in the Visual Arts* (New York: Dover, 1964).

solemnity and care suited to so important a matter. For each year, as it was resurrected from its storage place, it hung foolishly askew, demoralized by vicissitude, like a drunkard's hat crushed out of shape. Not that it had not still an equilibrium, a static balance, which it would assume and, if disturbed, would assume again, as if to declare idiocy alone immortal. It did not wait, in order to have an equilibrium, for an artful hand to give it one. Such equilibrium as it had, from the accidental concert of its parts, it had with the indifferent equanimity of all things merely physical. Beauty was its accident, as idiocy also was its accident. It was as innocent of virtue as it was innocent of sin: it knew no propriety, therefore deserted none. I admired in it only what I demanded of it, a virtue of which it knew nothing. Yet, for my part, I permitted myself no such egotist reflection. I regarded it all as the contrivance of the hand which adjusted it. In my child's world, that was the secret of my mother's hand, which no other sought to compete with, much less to penetrate. She knew, at least her hand knew, that of all of the possible equilibria which were available equally for choice, there was one special equilibrium needed, only one which was alive, resonant, essential to the production of that effect to which it intricately ministered. That equilibrium was indispensable to the music which the mobile gave forth, its beginning and its end, the poise from which its movement issued, the cadence in which it came with perfect finality to rest.

The indispensableness of that equilibrium I learned when at last, the usual hand grown quiet, I tried to hang the mobile unassisted. There it was, the same mobile, the same in all its elements. No element was wanting. The effect only was wanting. It was an offense to the eye, crippled, disproportioned, grotesque, the dead corpse of what it was capable of, and I took it down. Who was demoted, it or I? I, surely, for the partisanship, the predilection, was, like the disappointment, in me, not in it. The demand which conferred rightness on it, like the incapacity which could not set it right, was mine. Therefore I was desolate, not because of what it was, but because of what it failed to be, because of what I wanted of it and had not the craft to produce in it.

In such simple incident lies the image of all art. Let that equilibrium which was needed in order that the mobile should work its desired effect be described as the *normative equilibrium*. That equilibrium will be the rightness of that structure, that which is sought after whenever any adjustment is made of it. By reference to the normative equilibrium of the structure one may then mark a distinction between a right adjustment of it and a wrong adjustment of it, between a valid essay and an invalid one.

The normative equilibrium may never in fact be struck, as I was never able to strike it, so that, unstruck, it is never available in perception for experience. It is therefore nothing? On the contrary, I who have failed to strike it know, in my dumb despair, that I have failed to strike it, just as, if by accident I had struck it, I should know that too. The sensitivity which finds the normative equilibrium of the structure nowhere realized is nevertheless regulated by the idea of it: I am aware of its absence when it is unrealized, I am able to acknowledge its presence if it were to be realized, I remain dissatisfied until it is realized. Its positive function in experience is confirmed not by the circumstance that it is on any occasion actual, but by the circumstance that it is on all occasions demanded. As with any object in which the human soul finds its own sufficiency, the constancy of its hold upon us remains unabated, even when the possession of it is denied. A normative equilibrium is that which every artistic imagination is committed to producing; that which, once produced, it is committed to preserving; that which, being lost, it is committed to restoring.

Such a normative equilibrium will be found to be assumed in all artistic activity whatever. It is assumed in any productive activity in which art is created. It is assumed in any receptive activity in which art is critically interpreted. The undeflected vision of every artist, the contemplative imagination of every interpreter, is addressed to it. It is what actually all men mean by the artistic vision, by that vision of rightness which presides prescriptively over the acts of persons who in any way participate in art. Out of respect for it, solely out of respect for it, are the activities of artist and critic ever commonly obliged, or their imaginations joined, in a communion of sympathy. Were its operation ever for a moment to be suspended, then neither artist nor critic could perform his proper work. For the work of either presupposes that a distinction may be drawn between what is done and what is necessary to be done, between a merely *de facto* performance and a performance *de iure*.

On occasion, as Horace irritably affirms,[2] even Homer nods. If that is true, how is it possible that another should ever know that truth? If men may judge of Homer's art only from what Homer has done, how then shall any man judge of what artistically he has left undone? When Homer nods, he leaves not art, but a defect of art. The defect alone is actual, there to be observed. It is a defect not because of what it is, but because of what it fails to be. To acknowledge the flaw, to know it *as* a flaw, is implicitly to discern the rule of rightness against which it offends, to mark the discrepancy between what it is and what it ought to be, between what it makes real and the normative equilibrium which it is committed to making real. To be aware of any matter of art is to be aware of the rule implicit in it: in default of this awareness of rule one apprehends a matter not of art but only of fact.

35. The Consistency of Forms

The experience of art is never simply an experience of forms. It is an experience of claims, of claims made in behalf of forms, regarding their propriety, their fitness, in the function to which they have been committed. That propriety which is claimed for them may or may not be sustainable, but the forms, apart from that claim, have no artistic status whatever. They have the status of artistic forms precisely in the measure that the order which they have is perceived as the order which they are committed to having. Their order is obligatory, necessary, never merely factual. Suspend the perception of their obligatoriness, you have suspended the condition under which alone those forms can be perceived as deficient, or as superfluous, or as poised, just, inevitable.

That is why no merely descriptive account of the forms exhibited by works of art ever suffices to grasp the art of those works. For their art consists not in the circumstance that they have those forms, but in the circumstance that the forms they have are the forms required, and unless the necessity of those

[2] *Ars Poetica*, 359: "Indignor quandoque bonus dormitat Homerus."

forms is seen, their art is not seen. For their art resides in their necessity, and in nothing else.

Upon the ceiling of the Sistine Chapel Michelangelo painted, among the scenes of the Creation and the Fall of Man, the *Creation of Adam*. God stretches forth his hand to animate this splendid dust which his hand has shaped. Adam's hand, not yet touched, as yet unarmed with the will which shall presently condemn it, waits, waits languid, moveless, strength divorced from will, power from desire, accepting the fateful gift of life as no rich guerdon eagerly to be grasped, as Eve will grasp it. Elsewhere it may be seen again, that hand, or at least the consonant echo of it, in Jeremiah, melancholy prophet in the image of Michelangelo himself, clad even in his sculptor's smock, the same vacancy and immobility, the same paralysis of power unreleased, unreleasable, sunken in a profound and tragic lassitude which divorces it from will.

The hand of Adam is, as I believe, one of the most eloquent motives in all pictorial art. Consider only that hand. Detach it from any literary or psychological associations which it may have or which it may be thought to convey. Consider it only as the formal complement of the figure of Adam. That figure conforms to no convention save the convention which itself makes real. But that convention, which it at once declares and establishes, is so imperious in its essential motive that it requires, visually and formally, the extension which it has, the extension which this hand gives it. Not every hand will fit it. The animated hand of God, for example, will not fit it, fit it as the necessary visual extension of it, implicit already in the formal convention which it makes visible. That kind of implication, that kind of necessity, which is here ascribed to visual forms, is not the implication or the necessity to which philosophy is used. The worse for philosophy. That kind of implication and necessity is nevertheless the essential fact to which an artistic sensitivity is invariably addressed, and exclusively addressed.

Physically, nothing forbids that Adam's hand and God's should be transposed; artistically, everything forbids it. The two hands are in distinct formal idioms, and the idioms are dissonant, mutually exclusive. The prohibition against transposing them involves, for any eye sensitized to formal art, no mystery at all. It will appear mystery only to him who looks to find in physical shapes a prohibition which shapes merely physical are impotent to declare. The inconsistency which forms evince is never in themselves. It is in the function to which they have been committed, and apart from that function there neither is nor can be a prohibition felt to any combination of them.

There is nevertheless a stamp of mentality which will profess to find no prohibition. It will allow only what it sees, and in that positivist resolution I find no fault with it. Its fault is, that it will allow *whatever* it sees. That is the dissoluteness which disqualifies it before any normative circumstance, even before its own. It perceives before it, in the *Creation of Adam,* only these *de facto* forms. Considered simply as *de facto* forms, they are as neutral in their declaration as the scaffolding on which Michelangelo once stood, or the curved surface of the plaster which he stained. The art of these forms is not in what they are, but in what they make actual. They are physical forms because they are sensuously perceivable; they are artistic forms because, in addition to being physical, they are the sensuous embodiment of a formal decision. They make objective, make sensuously available in this raw physical stuff of stucco and pigment, a visual covenant. The stuff is in nature, and in a manner of speaking the work of art also is in nature. Undeniably it is physical, as the cracks in its vehicle prove. Yet what makes it art is precisely the responsiveness of its vehicle to the artistic prescription which requires its forms to be as they are. The work of art is not, and is never perceived to be, these merely *de facto* forms. The *de facto* forms perceived, even those forms wrought by Michelangelo, have no residence in art except as their title *de iure* is also perceived. No eye which sees only their actuality will see their art at all. For the measure of their art is nothing less than the measure of the normative equilibrium which they make real.

It is with this as with the vision of moral perfection. Had there been no Gethsemane, the moral purity of Jesus had remained permanently unperceived. For, except for the agony in the garden, the holiness of Jesus obscures his moral grandeur, leaves totally unbetrayed the annihilating possibility which is the anguish of every repentant conscience. Between what Jesus does and what morally he is obliged to do there is, except in this one instance, no discrepancy. The performance done is unerringly the performance necessary to be done, and this apparent inevitableness leads one to place his example beyond the precinct of our moral world. The purity which can suffer no pollution is not human purity. The purity which can, but does not, is human enough, but it is to the outward eye indiscriminable from that purity beyond morality which is reserved to beasts and gods. Its perfection blinds us from perceiving the steadfastness which is in fact its moral achievement. Let it fail but once, it need not fail again: that coincidence of outward act and inward demand, which formerly, because it seemed inevitable, could not be seen as moral, is now at last discerned.

It is just so with art. Its proper achievement is least seen when its achievement is most perfect and most complete. For when the equilibrium which is wanted is at the same time had, when there is no discrepancy between the forms actually presented and the forms necessary to be presented, when, in short, the equilibrium is visible, its normativeness appears to be inevitable, and its achievement merely natural. Let, however, the sufficiency of that achievement be in any measure diminished, the same objective structure, the same in all respects save as that diminution has affected it, will be felt as deficient, as in that measure wanting, in need of redress. That perfection which, being actual, was once presumed inevitable is perceived to be inevitable not at all, but on the contrary a conquest over the intransigent stuff in which, precarious and alterable, it appeared.[3]

[3] It is for this reason that one discovers, from the contemplation of a fragment, what was grasped imperfectly from the contemplation of a whole. When Michelangelo attempts to restore the hand of the *Laokoon*, what condition limits the solutions which are available to him? It is possible, given three angle columns and their entablature, to reconstruct the entire elevation of a Greek temple upon its ground plan: in the simple fragment is contained the principle upon which the whole edifice is reared. A Gothic jamb-figure, estranged to the promiscuous isolation of a museum, declares its own incompleteness as an excerpt: it demands a context which its setting does not supply, and rejects the context in which accident has placed it.

36. *Freedom and Rule in Art*

Artists generally, it must be confessed, misunderstand the task of philosophy, as they misunderstand the task of criticism, in connection with their art: it is the task of neither to make rules for artists. The making of rules is, on the contrary, the artist's task. He is his own legislator. The rule which obliges him he has given to himself, and except as he gives it to himself the role of artist is denied to him.

"When precedents fail to spirit us," wrote Tom Paine, "we must . . . think, as if we were the first men that thought." It is so. No artist, not even the most original, ever wants the material of precedent if he chooses to make use of it. Here, as in every other connection of importance in the human economy, the dead are always with us, always there to be embraced, but it is only the living who can embrace the dead, or who can reject them, in a living act. The dead speak nothing and command nothing except to those who choose to hear or to be commanded. Therefore, to each generation of men it is given to think as if it were the first generation ever to think. To each generation it is given to make that decision by which men determine what work of the dead shall have the status of precedent among the living.

In this lies the freedom of every artist in every generation of men. The artist can find authority in precedent only because he treats precedent as authoritative. He can find authority in nature only because he has constituted it there. He may place authority in neither. He is in his role as artist free to legislate as he chooses, to make whatever rules of art he chooses. Only one thing is forbidden to him, which circumscribes his freedom, because it is the condition of his freedom: he is not free *not* to choose. He is not free to work without a rule. That is the paradox of the artist's freedom: there is no rule which governs all art; yet there is no art without rule, and can be none.

Once, when I had still the innocence of a child, I flew aloft a kite and watched it soar like a snared gull in its wild element against the sky. Proud, untamed thing, pulsing in glorious insecurity in the wind at its dizzy altitudes, it struggled against the bond which denied to it its freedom. Out of love of it, to set it free, to give it freedom, I loosed its string. It fell tragically dead upon the soil. Broken, torn, irreparable, it would not fly again, and I, too suddenly grown wiser, wept above it. The restraint which held it to the earth was the condition of its mounting to the sky. Its freedom was in its bond, not beyond it. Without its bond it had no freedom, but only brokenness and cessation.

Just so, though every artist is free to choose his rule, there is no art without rule, and can be done. The freedom of the artist is in the rule which his activity respects. Lawless freedom, freedom beyond rule, he neither has nor ever in fact wants. For the only authentic freedom which men do ever seek, in art or elsewhere, is a freedom under law, whose sanctity lies in the fact that they have sanctified it, that the law is theirs because they have constituted it theirs, and stand committed to preserving it, and themselves in it.

Art no less than politics involves a kind of *legality*. It is the worst result of the sentimental positivism which we passively inherit that it can make nothing of human freedom in any connection. Everywhere it equates freedom with caprice. Therefore, history, which is the scene of human freedom, everywhere confounds it, and confounds it most abysmally in those areas of human activity in which it refuses to admit law because it sees no legislature sitting.

The freedom of the artist cannot be understood apart from the sense of rightness by which his activity, as *he* sees his activity, is governed. No rightness, no art. He will speak as simply as that, and if you cannot see the rightness of his work, neither will you have seen the art of his work. For that rightness is the measure of his art, and for him at least who makes art, as for those who know its virtue wherever it is made, its caprice is not is freedom, but its fault. Rightness is imputable to art only where caprice has been excluded from it. Properly, the arts are free not because they have no rule, but because the rule which they have is a rule which men have given to themselves.

Things so perfect in their art as Keats' *Ode to Autumn* abash the critical faculty by their simple presence. They enchant and disarm. They seem to exist by unsolicited simple gift, like sculptured rocks carved by erosion. Their effortlessness is their premeditated quality, yet lets them appear as a species of natural growth innocent of design, the simple issue of earth's thoughtless abundance, exhibited by no one's act, by no one's calculation, in undesigned felicity. These are things of law? Shall one speak here of rules? One shall and must, for all that one means, in speaking of a rule, is the condition indispensable for any cognition of that kind of rightness which these things are admitted to possess. If there were no rule, there could be no art, nor could this art be thus admired. For wherever rightness is, there also a rule must be. Even in these cases in which art is so effortless as not to betray itself, the mind which is capable of admiring that quality in it knows, knows decisively, that its artlessness is a part of its fiction, that its naturalness is an artifice which nature can never own.

There are works of art in which craft operates less consciously than this, works whose art is as complete, but unpremeditated. Such art is seen in those houses made for meetings of Quakers, whose austere beauty attaches to them even in the absence of any conscious design that they should wear it. It is seen in factories and bridges and aqueducts, in railway terminals and plans of cities, works of engineers, who, thinking only to satisfy a need of utility, have wrought eloquently as artists despite themselves and have celebrated what they touched. It is heard in ballads repeated in the anonymity of the human voice, through which a folk speaks, and the individual only as a member of the folk, in its immemorial accent.

These too are things of rule? They are. Nor would anyone suppose otherwise except for a misconception almost universally shared, that only that part of activity is lawful in which principle is consciously reflected on. My child's ear is attuned, just as mine is attuned, to hear a solecism of speech when it occurs. The difference between my child and me is that I can state the rule of propriety which my child uses but cannot state. That she uses the rule is evident from the circumstance that she hears the offense against it. The rule's presence is betrayed by the act in which the offense is identified. She knows no rule. She knows not even that there is a rule. She simply obeys a rule, senses propriety in obedience to one. *"Je me l'imagine parce que je le sens. Voyez la belle raison!"* The same rule is implicit for us both; it is explicit only for one. Which is simply to say, that the explicit awareness of it is not essential to its operation, and it will continue to operate, and to operate with equal imperiousness and nuance, though its operation remain permanently undisclosed. Grammar knows nothing, and can prescribe nothing, which is not in this instance already at work in the disciplined tact of speech that goes before it, and could go still without it, in a little child.

So the law which is implicit in the artist's act of making and in our act of apprehending has been articulated neither by the artist nor by us. It simply informs the act that employs it and complies with it.

But suppose in his act the artist nods, strikes still the chisel to the stone, but strikes it vacantly. What guarantee do I have, if the formal covenant is but partially realized in the work of art, that that physical object which is beyond me has necessarily implicit in it this covenant which is within me? The covenant by which I apprehend its imperfection is not actual in it, but only imperative in me. The covenant is simply ideal, my idea of an equilibrium which it falls short of realizing, which nevertheless I regard it as committed to realizing. By what right do I impute this ideal covenant to that object, and regard it as necessarily implicit in that object?

By what right has the artist imputed it, and treated it as necessary, to yonder half-formed lump of stone which he still works at?

Simply by this right, that unless that object be grasped under the idea of a formal covenant, it cannot be construed as art at all. Its status as art is what we confer upon it in regarding it as the embodiment of a claim. It is not merely the sediment of an artist's act, it is the sediment of a lawful act. It is not merely another form which experience meets; it is a form demanded, a form for which indispensableness is claimed. It is criticizable, either by the artist or by us, for that reason only, that the claim which it embodies requires to be assessed. Strictly, its art *is* its lawfulness, and nothing else. Its art is its compliance with a normative demand. The artist implants that demand; we read it forth. If the demand were not independent of the performance, the question of the validity of the performance could never significantly arise. That at last is what men *mean* in distinguishing an object of art from an object merely of nature: an object acquires its status as an artistic object by its amenableness to that kind of legality under which alone it can be regarded as art at all.

The sculptor creates no form; he does simply, as Michelangelo knew,[4] liberate it from its bed of stone. In that emancipative act his work is concluded. All that human craft has done, or can ever do, is to canalize in nature effects which remain still nature's. The sculptor elicits from nature a possibility which nature already includes, but which nature includes indifferently along with that total range of possibilities whereby stone is marred as well as made. The artist discovers form, he does not make it, but it is he, not nature, who constitutes the rule by which his discovery can be acknowledged. What he thus sets free is what art has required of stone, what stone, which is silent, is without capacity to require of itself.

37. The Artist as Legislator

A rule is a condition for the meeting of minds. It does not follow that minds will meet upon it. They may not, and when they do not, that which is authentic art for one will not be art for the other.

When in the formation of civil community men frame constitutions to themselves, they confer legality upon a form of society which they already commonly want and in part already share. They work out of community. Being met, they announce in a constitution the rule which is a condition of their permanent association. Law in general presupposes such a preliminary concert. The law implicit in art does not. The artist works invariably out of the solitude of himself. That self may be in fact so perfectly socialized, so perfectly attuned to the shared inward spirit of a society, that its voice is a voice which society will spontaneously adopt and acclaim as its own, as if in the poet's words all of its dumb

----

[4] *Non ha l'ottimo artista:* Michelangelo's sonnet has been translated by J. A. Symonds in *Renaissance in Italy* (New York: The Modern Library, 1935), I, 827.

aspirations had been spoken, and the babel of many tongues stilled, in a common idiom. But that reception is a piece of fortune which the poet has himself been powerless to arbitrate. He arbitrates only his own act; he is powerless by his simple act to govern the concurrence of society beyond him.

The poet, despite his residence in society, is committed to a solitude which society does not of itself afford. He works solitary out of his "soul's invincible surmise."[5] He works still solitary even when his soul's surmise is one which society will embrace as its own unspoken dream. His act, whatever others shall make of it, is for him, in its initial occasion, simple soliloquy, and is, as soliloquy alone can ever be, the same whether it is heard, or overheard, or unheard. It is soliloquy because it depends upon no hearing. It is an artist's soliloquy because the soliloquist legislates the condition of its being heard.

In the ancient world the sculptor Polykleitos formed a masterwork, a work of bronze, which came to be known from its motive as the *Doryphoros,* the *Spearbearer.* He regarded it, and his contemporaries joined him in regarding it, as the canon of his art. A canon of art is a rule of art. The work was, as Polykleitos intended it to be, the sheer distillation and pure concentrate of his proper idiom, a visual declaration of his artistic principles.

The *Doryphoros* has, like most bronzes of the ancient world, long since been reduced to the metal implements of war, cattle-trough, and kitchen. The work is nevertheless, despite that adventure of its vehicle, preserved, translated into stone, in a number of copies. The finest of them, from Pompeii, is to be seen, bearing still its ancient title and presumably even still some of its former distinction, in the Museo Nazionale in Naples.[6] The thing preserved is not of course the vehicle, but the canon, the rule of proportions, in which, for the representation of the human nude, an ideal covenant is fixed upon, prescribing, for anyone who would grasp the Polykleitean type, the kind of relationships that are to be sought after. The copy is luminous rather for the covenant it embodies than for the material vehicle which embodies it.

---

[5] George Santayana, *O World, Thou Choosest Not the Better Part,* 7.

[6] A. Ruesch, *Guida illustrata del Museo Nazionale di Napoli* (Naples, n. d.), No. 146 (6011).

A form conceived in bronze now impregnates stone. Yet such value as it has attaches in the copy, as once it attached in the original, to the covenant which has presided over its physical estate.[7]

When in the Renaissance in Italy men rediscovered in the silence of such stones the implicit vision of a way of life, it was the rule, the spirit of this presiding covenant, which actually they appropriated. The stones had not themselves to be rediscovered. They had lain there to be seen, the human litter of a landscape, for more than a millennium. Men saw in them obstacles to plows, benches for shepherds, or marble which a kiln could reduce to good lime; or if they saw relics, broken artifacts, they saw in them only the image of a dead pantheon which they rejected. What then, in the Renaissance, for Ghiberti, for Brunelleschi, for Donatello, was to be found which had not all along been seen? A rule simply. The Renaissance unearthed canons, not stones; rules of men, not images of Hermes and nude Aphrodite. It was the pantheon that was dead, not the rule by which men had once celebrated their vision of it; and one may in some part still share that astonished vision which found, in the idealized form of Apollo impaled nude upon a cross, a way of humanizing the mystery of an incarnate God. Strange mixture this, of oil and water, of snow and fire? That remained still to be seen. It remains still to see. For

---

[7] The sense of the canon is at last singular. It is conceptually informulable exactly in the measure that the work is individual and unique.

The proportions of the *Doryphoros* which one succeeds in stating will exhibit ratios. For example, the head being assumed as a module, the height of the human figure is expressible in the ratio 7:1. But such ratios, even geometrically stated ratios, define in fact the style of Polykleitos' work in general, not the style of the *Doryphoros* in particular. The singularity of the convention eludes description. It is not otherwise available than in a translation which visibly duplicates it.

Language has been designed to appropriate only those aspects of the sculpture which omit its singularity: for the singularity of the *Doryphoros* it provides, and can provide, only a proper name. Beyond this it refers to the convention only by relating it to what falls beyond itself—to the bronze which Polykleitos cast, to the marble in which Rome sought to capture it. The intrinsic singularity of the convention is literally ineffable. For ordinary purposes that singularity falls beyond the propriety of interest. For artistic purposes it is, on the contrary, the intuited convention to which all sensitivity is addressed.

the moment, only this was seen, that in these ancient stones was embodied a principle of vision, a rule and canon, which an eye capable of acknowledging it could appropriate.

Every artist projects thus a canon of art, and aspires to realize a canon, in every masterwork which he produces. Every appropriation of his canon is a renaissance, a rebirth of the spirit which animated him. The artist will not always, with the self-awareness of the ancient sculptor, so describe his work, describe it as a canon of art; nor will men who apprehend his work always so describe it. Yet that is what we mean in speaking of the art of Shakespeare or of Bach or of Michelangelo or of Rembrandt. Soliloquists, they legislate, and those who hear or overhear, or who see or oversee, see or hear by complying with the rule which they have laid down.

The artist is a legislator. His is a very peculiar act of legislation. It binds no man but him. But the binding of others is nothing essential to his act. It is sufficient that he be bound by it. His act is legislative because it commits himself. He constitutes a type of order, he establishes a formal covenant of equilibrium, which for his own part he treats as obligatory. His work, the thing in nature which he shapes by craft, is a physical exhibition of that covenant, and he will judge critically the measure of its rightness in terms of that covenant. That covenant is the ground of any disinterested contemplation of his work, whether he himself or another contemplates it.

That is why the satisfaction taken in a work of art is never a sufficient index of its proper value. A work of art, unless it produces satisfaction, can have no value. But satisfaction can be acknowledged as a criterion of art only if it be known already what kind of satisfaction is admissible as evidence. A work of art may elicit satisfaction as a historical document, as an instrument of propaganda, as an economic commodity, as a legal chattel, as a sexual excitation. In all of these cases the satisfaction is indefeasible; in none of them is it relevant, relevant in the sense of providing a criterion of art. The only relevant satisfaction is the satisfaction which accompanies a *disinterested* contemplation, and while that satisfaction will be a serviceable index of art wherever it occurs, it can be known to occur only where the conditions of disinterestedness are known. It is these conditions which the artist, in his act of legislation, has laid down.

38. Style

Technically, what the artist legislates is a style. That, however, is a concentration of idiom which, in the present degradation of the term, will not communicate the meaning intended by it. Style is of all elements cognate to art the one whose function is least understood. To be a work of art is essentially to have style. More than that may be necessary. But that at least is necessary, and any theory of art which cannot account for its stylistic feature is as empty as it is useless. The almost complete irrelevance of aesthetic theory to the positive investigation of the arts is owing precisely to this defect. For the style of a work of art is not a cosmetic ornament which an artist adds to it, having completed it, as a girl adds a ribbon to her hair or rouge to her cheek. Neither is it an adventitious resemblance which a work is found by comparison to share with other works. A work has style, whether or not it be compared to works beyond it, whose style it shares. Style is the obligatoriness of the formal covenant which presides over it, the gut of law within it by which it is understood to reflect, in an objective presentment, the formal decision of him who made it. For the historian, as for anyone who considers art concretely, this feature is the central pivot about which all his investigations hinge.

In comparative analysis the historian meditates the phenomenon of style under a deliberate restriction. Provisionally, for the purpose of ordering his subject matter, the function of style in art is subordinated to its external feature, and style becomes then simply a ground of formal classification. It refers to that characteristic property of a work of art which it shares with other works by the same artist, or with other works in the same cultural epoch or milieu.

One may thus speak of the style of Rembrandt, intending by that description to indicate the objective feature of his work which remains constant throughout the course of his development

and the range of his subjects. The subjects vary, the times of execution vary, the manner remains one. By the identity of the manner of Rembrandt all of the works by his hand are allied to each
other, as, by a difference of manner, any work by his hand is
distinguishable from a work by the hand of another. Rembrandt's
style is his distinctive idiom, the individual stamp by which his
handiwork may be identified as his, by which it is set decisively
apart from the handiwork of Hals or Vermeer, who share with him
only a national idiom, or from the handiwork of Poussin or Velas-
quez or Rubens, who share with him only the idiom of the
Baroque.

There are styles not merely of men, but of the seasons of their
individual development. So, one may mark a distinction between
the early and late styles of Rembrandt.

There are styles not merely of men, but of nations and of
epochs. So, Rembrandt and Vermeer, despite their obvious differences, are more intimately related to each other than either is
related to Raphael; and even when Rembrandt composes his own
portrait in imitation of Raphael's *Baldassare Castiglione*,[8] the
more intimate affinity persists: it is a Dutchman who paints,
though Rembrandt, as little as Raphael, affected to paint as a
Dutchman.

Under this restriction of its meaning, style is the common de-
nominator discovered in works of art by comparative analysis of
their objective formal features. It is simply form, form of a higher
order of generality, but form considered in abstraction from the
function which required it. So by this means, in literature no less
than in painting, in architecture and sculpture as well as in music,
all of those affinities and distinctions have been noted by which
the arts have been ordered according to men and epochs, and
schools and nations.

The historian for reasons of convenience orders works of art
according to styles as the biologist, for the same reasons, orders
living things according to genera and species. He simplifies the
domain of art by classification as the biologist simplifies the do-

---

[8] Raphael, *Baldassare Castiglione*, c. 1515, Louvre, Paris; Rembrandt, *Self-
Portrait*, 1640, National Gallery, London. The more direct allusion is to be
found in Rembrandt's etching, *Self-Portrait*, 1639 (B. 21; H. 168; Münz, 24).

main of living things; and both alike choose, as the basis of their classification, intrinsic structure, structure cognate to the things to be classified.

But there ends the similarity of their tasks, and if the historian, forgetting the restriction which he has placed on the meaning of style, were to persist in thinking the biologist's act and his identical, he would desert his proper function.

Of the forms which the biologist discovers, a hypothesis of natural selection will be regarded as a sufficient explanation. A fish has its form because nature has not prohibited its form: nature has not chosen it; it has simply failed to extirpate it. But such a mode of accounting, with respect to the forms of art, leaves all that matters, all that matters positively and historically, unexplained. It fails to explain why, when nature permits either of two alternatives, one exhibits itself and the other does not.

A people obliged to build in stone will not fling poetically into space those cantilevers which require the tensile strength of steel. They will not because they cannot: stone will so quickly fracture, under a stress of tension, as to mend their error and mar their art. So men's acts, in art as well as life, are limited by the conditions which nature sets.

But still, within the limits of these conditions, a people which builds in stone may build either with posts and lintels or with arches and vaults. Why, given the means, the materials and the knowledge, to build with either, does it build with one rather than the other? The answer lies in the decisions which men make within the limits which nature indifferently allows. Those decisions are not negative conditions; they are positive conditions, positive acts of men in the face of nature.

Style is such a decision. Divorce it from the demands of men, treat it merely as form abstracted from the function which required it, let it, like Hamlet's sicklied resolution, lose the name of action, you naturalize it indeed, but you take from it the significance which led the historian to interest himself in it and to classify those objects that exhibit it.

If style had no significance apart from classification, it would have none by it, and it is an empty erudition which knows the stylistic affiliation of a thousand works of art but knows the intrinsic virtue of style in no single one. For style is a cognate feature of art. It belongs properly to the making of history, not to the writing of it. A work of art, concretely apprehended, *has* style; it is never merely *in* one. In its primary sense style signifies the responsiveness of a work of art to the formal decision which produced it, and has no connection whatever with the circumstance that that formal decision which produced it produced also other works comparable to it. The latter is a historical contingency which may or may not be realized. The responsiveness of a work of art to some formal decision on the part of the person who fashioned it is, on the contrary, essential to its being considered art at all. It is what makes of art, in Longinus' phrase, the echo of a soul. Style belongs in the first instance to the dispositions of men; it belongs only derivatively to things, as these dispositions have generated them.

Emile Zola has described the work of the novelist as "nature seen through a temperament."[9] In that phrase the function of style in all art has been caught. Style is the covenant by which a parcel of nature has been transformed. In this transformation the permanent interest attaches not to the nature which is transformed, but to the manner of the transformation, for in that manner the vision which subjectivizes nature has objectified itself.

Greek and Early Christian confront the same order of natural happenings; they confront it with the same physical organs of vision. Why then should their arts so differ, differ so fatefully and so irreconcilably that men discover in them the signature of a change of worlds, the broadest which in Western history men do ever contemplate? Nature has not changed its habit, they have changed theirs; and by these changes they body forth alternatives of the human condition. Greek and Early Christian confront the same nature; they differ only in their way of confronting it. They differ in the way in which, by their own act, they have related themselves to it. They differ, in short, according to the rules which they affirm; and as the rule of one differs from the rule of the other, so shall their arts differ. We therefore speak, and speak properly, of the Greek temperament and of the Early Christian temperament, of Romanesque and Byzantine and Gothic, of Ren-

[9] *Le Roman Expérimentale,* 5e éd. (Paris, 1881), 111.

aissance and Baroque and Rococo. By such descriptions we mean to indicate a partisanship which belongs to those who exercise themselves within the covenant of one attitude of mind or the other. Philosophically, this partisanship of the artistic temperament is a matter of the most extreme importance. For it precisely requires that we in reflection address ourselves not to those theoretically vacant classifications by which works of art are catalogued, but to the concrete activities of producing art and of interpreting it, in which, in differences of idiom, we discover the purest embodiments anywhere to be found of the freedom that belongs to all that is human.

39. Partisanship and Innocence

Art is partisanship. Artistic perception is a partisan act. That is why the disinterestedness which is said to belong to the aesthetic attitude is everywhere so ambiguously misleading. For the beauty of art is never neutral. There is no such thing as neutral art. There are only men neutralized by their common adherence to a rule of art. That rule is the condition of their disinterestedness, and apart from that rule they can have no disinterestedness.

No art is so little understood as the art of those Impressionist painters and Imagist poets whom theory represents as reinstating the innocence of vision. An artist's vision is never innocent; it is simply never jaded. As a child sees the world with unjaded vision, so the artist sees it, and enables us to see it. But he is, despite that, no child, nor are we. He sees with predilection, and if his predilection seizes the transient image of nature, he values that transient image because he sees in it what is permanent in himself.

What is permanent in himself? The manner of the seeing. That only, the manner of the seeing, not the image seen. The image may change; the style of mind, the attitude that informs it, remains fixed. Such is his independence of the image, that he will not be governed by it, but governs it, that so it might become the mirror of his affirmation as a man.

When Christ speaks of himself as *the Way*, he speaks as moral artist and as partisan, and you understand him as both. Not the act, but the principle of the act, which the act does but make overt, that alone is permanent and prescriptible. The act varies according to the circumstances of the actor; the principle does not.

In the most merciless series of portraits which the world has ever known, Rembrandt turned an unrelenting vision, relentlessly detached, upon himself. It is, I suppose, the longest sustained, as surely it is one of the richest, of all soliloquies.

> I, painting from myself and to myself,
> Know what I do, am unmoved by men's blame
> Or their praise either.[10]

He worked before a mirror; he grew old before it. The mirror, itself vacant, passive, reflected its indifferent silly lights from first to last. The features of him who stood before it changed; his body aged and declined; the style ripens. That is the pregnant revelation of the series: as the one diminishes, the other takes its increase. The manner of seeing enlarges, gains breadth and depth and amplitude, discards its own accidents, purifies itself, as if, out of the nakedness that shrouds us all, in the solemnity of those features which years since had lost their capacity to surprise or to transfix, was distilled the whole destiny of mankind, its grandeur and its independence, its pathos and its finitude.

That is the work of innocence? No, only the mirror is innocent, the bare conduit of that play of lights which it indifferently transmitted. The mirror affirms nothing; it has nothing to affirm. Its innocence is perfect: its innocence is its vacancy. Had Rembrandt's canvases reflected only its silly lights as it reflected his, the series would have been no revelation of a man. The canvases too must have appeared, like the mirror, things among things. The art of Rembrandt is in the rule which he constitutes, not in the image which he reflects. He impregnates the image. The image embodies a convention which he has imparted to it, which requires of it what it does not require of itself. That is why, as the sense of the requirement becomes more clearly divined, and its embodiment more assured, the status of the image lapses, and only its sufficiency, its pure equilibrium, remains. The most profound of Rembrandt's portraits are those in which the raw image

[10] Robert Browning, *Andrea del Sarto*, 90-92.

counts least, and at last counts not at all, except as the mute occasion for exhibiting a covenant, a world ideally ordered, visible but transparent, in which out of dust a spirit breathes. In those last emancipated works purified of the dross of things, in which his sovereignty is made perfect, what does it matter that Rembrandt was the sitter? Shall you not have had his presence sovereign and unmistakable, and with the same economy, in any other subject? The equilibrium is all, and nothing of thinghood remains, in those last acts of his journey's end. For such is the revelation of Rembrandt's art, and of all art wherever it has become in this measure complete, that the proper image of a man is nowhere in nature, but in the allegiances which he has given to himself.

40. The Moral Dimension of Art

The artistic function is a role which actors may perform, and which they will perform alike on condition that they observe a common covenant in performing it.

As a role may remain unacted, so an artistic function may remain unperformed. As a role may be ill acted, so an artistic function may be ill performed. The philosophical question with respect to the artistic roles which men have given to themselves is never whether there are living actors, or faultless actors, who move within those roles. The only question is, What are the conditions which must be observed by any actor who *would* move within them?

A work of art is a permanent possibility of enactment, a ground for participation, for membership, in an artistic community. Men, living men, either belong to that community, or they do not. If they do not, there is a covenant unused, the fossil of a vanished act, which men could, but do not, resuscitate in themselves. But if they do, they gain their character from the covenant they perform as certainly as it gains its life from their performance of it.

What are the conditions of a living covenant? Tolstoy supposed that without a universal communion there could be no art. But art does not depend for its validity upon the number of its communicants. Essentially, it is as little concerned with the extent of its acceptance among men as Christianity is, and as Christianity would remain a distinctive attitude of mind if there were but one man who professed it, and even if none professed it, so the alternatives of artistic community remain still defined even though no one chooses to animate the roles which they provide. One still may ask what it is to be a Christian, though a Christian is nowhere to be found. One still may ask what it is to be a Wordsworth, though the man Wordsworth is dead and lies buried beneath the English landscape he wrote of.

There are as many artistic communities as there are styles of art. Each style commands, for those who participate in its covenant, a good which is proper to it; each proscribes goods which are not proper to it.

In that covenant a human being discerns a role, a human alternative, a possibility of participation. It is but one of the possibilities. Its educative and civilizing virtue is that it exhibits this possibility, that it enlarges the range of human alternatives by one.

It educates, it disciplines, it may not please. Taste is never pleased save where it is followed. To fashion taste is not to follow it; it is, on the contrary, to oblige it, to require of it that it be led. Before Rembrandt or Michelangelo, before the *Book of Job* or the *Oedipus at Colonus*, before *Hagia Sophia* or *Chartres*, before *Lear* or *Faust*, what matters least of all is what by accident I like. For what always I shall like by accident is what ministers to my egotism unconfessed. But these are embodied alternatives of confession. They were not fashioned with a view to predicting my sensibility, nor does their value lie in having anticipated it, as some in fact have done. I may reject a confession, I may accept it; I must acknowledge it to do either. To acknowledge it is to discern the role which it has laid down.

Aesthetic satisfaction is the problem, not the incorrigible datum, of the philosophy of art. The matter at stake is not what pleases men, but where satisfaction is to be sought.

That is why, though art is not itself moral, it sets for men a moral problem. Our commerce with art is inevitably, in Matthew Arnold's phrase, a "criticism of life." The twentieth century practices a concealment in this matter. It has diminished its relation to art as it has extended its knowledge of it. It discovers in art no vision of the roles of men, but only goads to feeling, cozened passion. Therefore, in the contemplation of "aesthetic objects," it is not likely to experience the contrition of Jerome, who suspected in anguish that he loved Cicero as well as Christ. It is not likely to say with Erasmus: "St. Socrates, pray for me!" To the Renaissance the Gothic was barbarous as to the Middle Ages the Classic was profane. The covenants of men were opposed. They were opposed in art no less than in philosophy. "Dead things with inbreath'd sense able to pierce," they pierce contrarily; and as we who regenerate these alternatives of the human in ourselves are not immune to their challenges, so neither can we be immune to their oppositions. Our historicism is a cultivated delusion that the dead, if they were wakened, would be at peace. They would not, nor, alas, shall we, who in inheriting them inherit all that they in dying left unreconciled. I count nothing human as alien to me. Yet in this is no moral absolution, but a moral problem, the very form which the moral problem takes, in art as elsewhere, in the twentieth century: to find and preserve the limits between tolerance and dissoluteness, and between intolerance and fanaticism. The question will always arise, for us as for those before us, What it is to be human, and what to be alien? That question is precisely the question which the artist, among other legislators for mankind, puts and answers as a partisan, renouncing a promiscuous inheritance in order to labor at a pure bequest. Humanity is what no man can passively inherit. We are human according to the covenants we keep. Whether a man shall keep a covenant, or shall keep none, is not given him to decide. The only question is, What covenant? What is the covenant in which human sufficiency shall be found? The necessity of putting that question is what preserves us in the human estate. It is what preserves art in the moral economy and soliloquists in its parliament.

III

The Reconstruction of the Human Covenant

chapter IX

The Crisis of the Law
in Modern Economy

41. *Freedom of Enterprise and the Moral Commonwealth*

Nothing so commends itself to the American mind and character as belief in the virtue of the free market. The popularity of the notion is very easily understood. It is the perfect automation of morals. It justifies the private vice as the public benefit. It works righteousness in ratios of exchange.

A commissar will seek in vain to accomplish by premeditation what the free market accomplishes in the simple absence of anyone's design. Its astonishing achievement is to determine the ratio at which any one good in the market will exchange for any other —for example, the number of eggs required to purchase a lamb chop, or a cement block, or an oil derrick, or a surgical operation. These ratios are declared, in the sleep of all commissars, in what we describe as *prices*. They are declared in the rents of land, in the wages of labor, in the interest which is paid for the use of capital, in the profits of risk-bearing.

Prices are the object of a most exquisite solicitude in every market. The peculiarity of a purely competitive market is that no one governs them. A buyer governs what he bids, a seller governs what he asks, and there can be no exchange until they freely consent to trade. Yet though each has governed his own act and the exchange is their joint institution, the price to which they consent has in the long run been determined by neither of them. For in a free market every buyer has been obliged to compete with other buyers, and every seller with other sellers, and no one of them is permitted to escape the neutralizing implications of that circumstance. The unconstrained neutrality of prices is the distinctive index of the free market system. Every marketer is controlled by prices; no marketer is equal to controlling them.

When men say of a commodity that it has a "market price," the meaning is not that all marketers have in fact bought or sold it at that price. On the contrary, in every market there are those who do better and those who do worse. But in a free market these cases all occur in the short run. In the long run only those buyers and sellers will contract bargains who meet at the market price, since sellers will have learned to carry their wares, and buyers their trade, where it is to their greatest advantage. The price generated from this concert of private interests has therefore been chosen by no one of the interested parties: it is simply the going price, the exchange ratio at which in the long run, given the motives of marketers, exchanges will in fact be made. Such is the cunning of the market as a social institution, that it produces this ratio, produces it anonymously, mechanically, inexorably, not by anyone's deliberation or design but out of the unintended concert of our interchanges.

Ideally, in a purely competitive market, the buyers and sellers are so numerous that the act or omission of any one of them makes no difference in the equilibrium to which the market will gravitate. In the American scene there are still some branches of agriculture which illustrate this condition. Even the largest producer of raw cotton could withdraw his entire contribution from the supply on the market without affecting the price at which the remaining supply would sell. For the total supply is so large, and the part offered by any single producer is by comparison to the total supply so small, that the market remains impassive whether he tote his crop to auction or burn it at home. Therefore, since the grower cannot influence the price at which his product will sell, he does what he can to accommodate the price. He adapts his output. In the next growing season he varies the measure of his contribution to the total supply, increasing it or decreasing it as the price in the current market suggests his advantage. Since every other producer acts from the same motive and in the same way, the next year's price will respond to the glut or scarcity which they have jointly produced. That price is the unwilled consequence of the behavior of independently competing actors. Each seeks his private advantage: the scene prospers in spite of his egotism and becomes depressed in spite of his good will.

A free market is surely the strangest and most democratic of all parliaments—the most democratic because its resolutions proceed always from a universal ballot universally exercised; the strangest because its members, though they sit in one assembly, permit themselves to converse only in pairs.

The impersonality of the market was, as Adam Smith perceived, its great utility as a device of social order. For if a perfect competition were permitted to operate without external interference, it would automatically secure a social result of more goods at lower prices than any known alternative. The prices of a competitive market are as reckless of sentiment as a baby-scale. They nevertheless afford in the life of nations a kind of justice, perhaps not a sufficient justice but at all events an objective and exacting one, which systematically distributes the goods of society so as to reward the most resourceful, the most inventive, and the most enterprising of its members.

No dispassionate assessment of man's social condition can afford to despise that result. The weight of an infant is no measure of its proper destiny. Its weight is nevertheless, as every physician knows, one of the conditions of its having a destiny. A vacant spirituality may conceive the well-being of society in contempt of the fact that men are sheltered by brick and mortar, warmed by fuel, and fed out of the procreant earth. But the obdurate material fact remains. Men do not elevate themselves by penury, neither are they exalted by want; and if other things were equal, that system would be by all men preferred which sheltered and warmed and fed them best. In this at least socialist and capitalist are at all times allied. Both equally affirm, and affirm rightly, that a social system which affects to confer freedom by denying its material conditions is a fraud. The quality of civilized life is measured at last by the uses of our freedom, not by its conditions. But from this it does not follow that the spirit of civilization is better served by poets who shiver unfed. The material conditions of civilization were the undismissible concern of the classical economists who saw in the operations of a free market the vision of a social good.

Yet, for a disinterested observer, concerning the sufficiency of this justice of the free market, there were real grounds for reservation. For the impersonality of the market allowed men in the heat of competition to forget that society is first and last, whatever else it may become, a moral commonwealth, a community of persons. Prices may rise or fall, business may advance or recede, it still remains essential to our community with one another that the dignity of men not be thought to fluctuate with the business cycle. Nothing forbids that issue in a society which confuses its fact with its covenant. The presiding peril of the system of free enterprise is the common peril of all free institutions, namely, the forgetfulness of men, the forgetfulness of men who treat the mechanics of the social process as their release from social obligation.

Saint Augustine's *Dilige et quod vis fac,* "Love and do whatsoever thou wilt," is so terse a commentary on the human condition that it has shocked the ear of every generation since his day. That redoubtable old saint is the stoutest free enterpriser of us all. His dictum is not a counsel of anarchy. The meaning is: "So long as you preserve your concern for one another, you may do as you please: no other restraint may ever legitimately be put upon your act." The dictum is an explicit avowal of the covenant of a free society. It affirms the moral condition which underlies all voluntary association. It announces the imperative which men are forbidden to abrogate as they would institute or preserve their community with one another. Whether we humans would have community or would be without it, we are at liberty to choose. But if we choose to have it, we are by that choice committed to observing the condition under which alone it is possible. A respect for persons is the absolute condition of any community whatever. That is why the central problem of the free market is how to reconcile liberty with fraternity, freedom of enterprise with a community of interest, or (if I may state the problem in a form suited to my present purposes) private freedom with public responsibility.

In a competitive market the problem of adjusting freedom with fraternity is most immediately visible as the market affects labor. For the inflexible efficiency which supplies to society the greatest quantity of cotton at the lowest cost operates also, and operates with indiscriminate rigor, to supply the greatest quantity of labor at the lowest cost. The price which will in the long run attach to any parcel of labor in a free market is as perfectly independent of the employer who buys it as of the laborer who sells it. It nevertheless remains that the buyer and the seller stand very unequally related to the contract into which they enter. For the one it is at least in the short run an option; for the other it is in any run a necessity of life. A piece of land untilled, a mine unworked, a machine unused retains still its residual utility unimpaired; a laborer's stock of energy unemployed does not. For the labor which he cannot sell is, like the power of a stream which flows unused to the sea, permanently lost both to society and to him. Therefore, since any return upon it is better than none, he will before wasting it endure the condemnation of parting with it for what it brings. The merciless severity of that consequence in a purely competitive market has received its classical expression from Ricardo. Under the conditions of a perfect competition the tendency of wages will be to fall to the lowest level at which the labor force is barely able to subsist and beget its replacement.[1] This is the proposition which Ferdinand Lassalle characterized as the Iron Law of Wages. Considered from the point of view of the nation, the Iron Law represents the nation's pure gain; considered from the point of view of the members of the nation, it represents the nation's pure peril. For the very motives which, left alone, have produced this allocation of the nation's resources will also, if left alone, presently destroy it. They will destroy it not because its efficiency is less than ideal, but because men refuse to substitute the wealth of the nation for the commonwealth of their society.

[1] David Ricardo, *The Principles of Political Economy and Taxation* (London: Dent, 1911), 52: "The natural price of labor is that price which is necessary to enable the laborers, one with another, to subsist and perpetuate their race, without either increase or diminution." Compare Anne-Robert-Jacques Turgot, *Réflexions*, 6: "En tout genre de travail il doit arriver et il arrive en effet que le salaire de l'ouvrier se borne à ce qui lui est nécessaire pour lui procurer sa subsistance."

They refuse to allow the very proposition which the classical framers of the theory of free enterprise have always assumed without argument, that the nation is the only subject of economy, and its wealth the only object.

It has become customary among economists to dismiss Ricardo's law of wages. They rightly hold that the tendency described in the law is after all ideal. The law states the ideal limit of a tendency which is never cleanly realized in historical fact. It would be true of the market only under the conditions of a perfect competition, and those conditions, only in part actual in Ricardo's day, are no longer even approximated in our own. Ricardo mistook the transient accident of the market in his generation for the permanent feature of the market in all generations. He reflected in the raw pathetic season of the birth of an industrial new world, when circumstantially the population was too numerous and jobs were too few, when Luddites had been tamed and Factory Acts were still unwritten, when labor combinations were prohibited as a restraint of trade and the memory of Peterloo hung bitter, virulent, and admonitory in the coalsmoke above every mill town in the English land.

And all of this is true. But we have drawn from it a wrong conclusion. Because the conditions of the truth of the law are incompletely actual, we have concluded that its truth is therefore irrelevant. That conclusion is mistaken. The tendency described in Ricardo's law of wages will show itself overtly, relentlessly, cruelly, in any season in which no contrary tendencies hold it in check. But the tendency itself is, like the poor, always with us; and the opposing tendencies which in our day, by the grace of imperfect competition, temper and soften its effects are witness rather to the countermoves of free men than to any inherent benignity of the market itself. The evolution of the American economy has shown, beyond all ritual of belief, that if men are denied the security of a social estate in the unregulated drift of the market, they will seek it in spite of the market in their covenanted community with each other. In the absence of public controls they will institute private combinations—unions, cooperatives, and alliances which afford to them as groups the tolerable expectations which the market has failed to afford to them as individuals. The alliances which men

institute defensively, in order to forestall the bare mechanical out-
come of the market, are a betrayal of the principle of pure competition; they are nevertheless in all seasons the clearest outward
measure of our positive society. A perfect competition would require a perfect independence of all competitors, in effect that
every marketer move stranger to every other, alien, unanointed,
cut off, naked, and alone. It is the one perfection which no one
wants, and except where society has failed it is never found. In a
word, the market does not by any inherent virtue beget its own
correction. It never has. It is we who have corrected ourselves in
relation to it, procuring out of our coalitions such immunities as
only the mutually allied may ever find from its blind effects.

The harmony of the private and the public good is the problem,
not the datum, of a free industrial economy. That harmony is not
pre-established in the stars; it is not written in the operation of
economic laws. It is like all other achievements of authentic civilization a matter of contrived balance, of instituted community, in
which the public and the private interests have been reconciled,
and made complementary to each other, in one order of design.

42. The Compromise of the Public Standard

Why is it no longer possible to assume, as the classical economists
assumed without hesitation or misgiving, that the public interest
lies in the unhindered operation of the market?

Very simply for the reason that the impersonal justice of the
market has been compromised. Whatever the limits or deficiencies
of that justice may be, its claim upon men's minds has always
been that it supplies an objective norm of the public interest, a
norm independent of the acts or omissions of any of the actors
who in their private estate are party to it. In the transformed conditions of modern industrial society the independence of this
measure of the public interest has been suspended.

The conventional defense has always been to impute the loss of
the market's freedom to a political intercession: the innocence of
men's free exchanges has been despoiled by the external interferences of the state. In one word, the fault is government. But this
diagnosis mistakes the symptom for the cause of the malady. The

market has not been compromised by any external factor: it has been compromised from within.

The tendency of all capitalist economy is to concentrate power, to draw together the diffused powers of many competing agencies into a few large concentrations, each so compact and considerable that the behavior of any one of them is capable of influencing the behavior of all others. Wherever such concentrations occur, the behavior of the market no longer functions as an objective, impersonal norm, the measure dispassionate and impartial against which anonymous buyers and sellers discover the value of their labor and enterprise. On the contrary, where powers are thus concentrated and the concentrations have become by merger and alliance large enough to influence the market, and few enough to control it, the neutrality of the standard can no longer be accredited. The parties to the economy are obliged to measure themselves not against a standard set competitively by those who people the market, but against a standard set collusively by those who dominate it.

If a wage-earner can sell his day's labor for $10 with one employer and for $11 with another, then $10 is the measure of his power to command an exchange with either, $1 the measure of his opportunity with the second employer.[2] That opportunity-value depends upon the competition of the employers with each other. But suppose the employers who stand in need of labor to be so powerful that they exhaust the market, and so few that they can see the advantages of combination. Then since competition among themselves does not affect the supply of labor but only its price, and they have no option except to share the labor which is on any occasion available, share it they will and on such terms that the opportunity-value will be eliminated.

An opportunity-value does not depend on the circumstance that labor is the commodity in question. Control of the demand for any exchangeable commodity will produce the same consequence of eliminating the opportunity-value from the seller's price.

That, however, is but one side of the story. Control of the supply of any commodity will do the same. The organization of labor

[2] Compare John R. Commons, *Legal Foundations of Capitalism* (New York: Macmillan, 1924), chapter II.

is the precise and inevitable response on the part of wage-earners to the same set of conditions. If laborers bargain collectively, they do so always with the motive of eliminating the opportunity-value from the buyer's price for any part of labor which they control. Nor is it proper to obscure the circumstance that the $1 which measures the opportunity of gain for the wage-earner measures also the opportunity of saving for the employer. In any bargaining for a labor-contract, opportunity-value is in fact the sole subject of deliberation: the negotiations will continue for exactly as long as either party believes an opportunity-value can be gained by dividing the precariously allied counsels of his opposite. Where labor and management bargain, and each bargains without competitor, the contract which issues from their bargaining stipulates a price in which opportunity-value has played no part. An opportunity-value can appear only where there are, for buyer or for seller, freely available alternatives. The opportunity of either depends always on the possible competition of others for the commodity he would acquire or part with. If I were to represent what is intended by the transformation of the free market under the conditions of modern economy, it would consist in this, that opportunity-value is in process of being eliminated from the marketplace.

The transformation has nothing to do with the interferences of government; it has to do only with the immanent forces and incentives which are loosed in the market itself. The loci of effective decision have been transferred from the private individual to the private alliance, and the alliances stand opposite to each other, bloc confronting bloc, in uneasy, precarious, and temporary truce.

The fashionable opinion that this result was intended is unquestionably false. Men saw in the union of their separated powers a resource of competition, not a suspension of it, and if nowadays we see in the exaggerated combinations of power in our society a threat to the continuance of the free market, we do not see as they saw at whose hands the combinations were once wrought. In any competition the opposing power which I cannot cancel I take pains to accommodate. I do not consent to it. I simply allow for it and contrive my place as best I can beneath its shadow. It is so here. Powers imperfectly equal are met in competition. The larger parties avail themselves of the advantages which their concentrated power confers upon them. The effect is to compel those whose independence has become their peril into alliances which are capable of competing on equal terms. So that at last the contestants who remain upon the field stand opposite to each other sharing it, each so powerful as to command respect, none so weak as to be driven from the scene, together capable (if they should think to civilize their oppositions) of excluding any Lancelot who, coming late, dares to challenge their occupation.

It is customary to describe this tendency of capitalist economy as "monopolist." Such a description is not untrue, but it is invariably misleading. For though it correctly describes the tendency, it mistakes the issue. The issue of the tendency is never in the long run a strict private monopoly. A monopoly can be strict only on condition that it at last ceases to be private. In a capitalist economy the art of monopoly consists, like any other art, in knowing where to draw the line. Of all of the conditions of capitalist economy a private monopoly is the most unstable. It is always and necessarily a phenomenon of the short run only. The fault of a private monopoly is not that it is uneconomic; its fault is that it is impolitic. A single telephone system is a more efficient allocation of society's resources than any competition could guarantee. But in the absence of competition a public rate commission inevitably presides. For in capitalist as in any other society the only power which can in the long run remain perfectly unopposed is the public power. That is a principle of politics, not a sentiment of the Sherman Act or the sermon of a socialist. The only permanent monopoly is a public one. Therefore, the natural issue of the monopolist tendency which belongs to every capitalist society is everywhere privately postponed, held permanently in abeyance, not out of any moderation of sentiment or egotism, not out of any excess of the social consciousness, but precisely out of a rational interest in preserving the privacy of enterprise itself.

The actual issue of capitalist economy is the phenomenon which has been described as an industrial "concentrate," not a monopoly at all but, in that inexcusably ugly phrase of the economists, an oligopoly, a division of the industrial market among a few powerful interests, typically corporations, who in tacit concert divide among themselves an exclusive power which they hold but dare not confess or fully use.[3]

The giant corporation and the labor federation are the representative institutions of modern industrial society. They have transformed the character of industrial relationships in all capitalist countries, creating in the place of individual free enterprise what already at the beginning of our century men characterized with premonitory accuracy as a "new feudalism."[4] The feudalism of the Middle Ages was in fact the product of a reverse tendency. It was the result of a dissolution of the public power, not of a concentration of private powers. But the effect was the same, an equilibrium of dispersed but mutually limited centers of power, each committed to the pursuit of a private interest, each aware that the right to privacy must be cancelled in the moment that all power had been arrogated to itself.

Let all power in any connection be concentrated in one agency, that total concentration carries with it a public responsibility. Such was in fact the decease of the feudalism of the Middle Ages: the perfect concentration of political power among a people was the modern nation. So for the same reason, in the modern world, the perfect concentration of industrial power is not the triumph of privacy, but the obliteration of it, the total abrogation of its proper conditions, namely, socialist economy.

Total privacy implies total responsibility. Only the state can afford that absolute risk. What private enterprise signifies in America is always enterprise of relative risk.

43. The Private Corporation and Public Accountability

The private corporation is the most fateful birth of modern industrial society. It is by law empowered with all of the resources of competent agency. It has the legal status of a person, capable of rights, capable of duties, capable of act and policy, "one body corporate and politic, in deed, action, and name," as the old phrase has it. A corporation can sue or be sued, it can acquire

[3] Adolf A. Berle, *The 20th Century Capitalist Revolution* (New York: Harcourt, Brace and World, 1954), 26.

[4] W. J. Ghent, in *The Independent*, LIV, 2783 (April 3, 1902), 781-788.

property or alienate it, it can make contracts, execute trusts, marry for money, produce and market goods, pay taxes, quarrel with government, prosper, or go broke. It commands resources, resources of intelligence as well as capital, with a precision and efficiency of ordering which in another day would have spread terror among the sovereign nations of the earth.

A corporation has, like the university or the nation, a continuity of life which transcends the generations of men. Men come and go within it, live, exercise their talents, and die within the system of roles which it provides. So that the time shall come when none of its original members, nor even their heirs in blood, walk any longer quick within its precinct. The organization, the system of roles, survives, animated still by others who labor in mute oblivion as men before them have labored, neither speaking nor spoken to nor memorialized, beneath its shelter.

I am speaking of private corporations, not of the public corporation which in political community men call "the State." The public corporation is no novelty. It is as old as the peoples of the earth, as old as the relations of tribes and families, as old as the conception of a common good; for it is found wherever one is charged to speak, with the authority of a group, its corporate decision, acting, as we say, in its person, joining together in one voice and commission the syllables of the public consent. In a society at peace with itself the public corporation has always the character of singularity. It alone can lawfully exercise the powers of government; it alone is vested with the right of eminent domain. Let its singularity be challenged, the society is in revolution and is torn by the divisions of civil war. For the public corporation is a jealous god and will tolerate no other gods. Its singularity is essential to its sovereignty, and its sovereignty is the confession of its public character.

But the private corporation makes no such confession, and therein effect lies its radical novelty as a social invention. The modern private corporation is a political, not merely an economic fact. It has all of the advantages of a public concentration of power; it has neither the risks nor the responsibilities which normally attach to the conduct of the public interest. It exhibits, in the external habit of its behavior, the outward similitude of a state. But it is less exposed to outward peril. The state is compelled to protect itself from any lawless assault which may come from beyond it. That is the price of sovereignty which the state pays. The private corporation is not required to pay it. The private corporation experiences therefore an advantage which no sovereign entity can ever share, the capacity to act within a scheme of normal expectations which another will protect, and will if threatened guarantee, under the beneficent operation of a civil law.

The artificiality of the corporation confers upon it an obdurate and passionless identity which no ordinary individual can ever share before the law. The law of France admits the circumstance with a most disarming honesty. Its phrase for the private corporation is *société anonyme*. The corporation is an anonymous society. The distributive sense of the term imports an irony which is as profound as it is unpremeditated. The corporation itself is not without a name; it is we who are anonymous, the nameless ones who discover in corporations the characteristic estrangements of all modern life. In the twentieth century it is the salesman who dies; two centuries ago it was Willy Loman.

The device of incorporation arose out of an attempt to limit the legal liabilities of partnership. As a legal relation a partnership has had always this serious fault, that each partner stands under an unlimited liability for the acts of the other. The advantages of combining capital are therefore always attended in partnership by a risk which can, and at times does, involve one partner in common ruin with another. The limited partnership which the English use was never specially favored in America, mainly for the reason that the corporation was discovered to be, in operations of any magnitude, a more convenient instrument. The act of incorporation enabled thousands of investors to pool their resources, each assuming only that part of the total risk which was measured by the shares he owned. Risk was proportioned to ownership, and ownership could be diffused as broadly as the opportunity of a private profit could command investment. The corporation was of all forms of combination the one best suited to the taming of the continent. Shall men capable of thinking in continental magnitudes, mining the earth, felling the forests and linking the oceans with rails of steel, hesitate before the social consequence, or even pause to meditate it? The consequence deserved nevertheless to be meditated. The consequence was to transfer the powers of decision concerning the use of capital from owners to managers. Ownership was in process of becoming a passive function, and the law which protected property—the law in whose eye, as old John Marshall said, a peppercorn is of sufficient value to found a contract—the law grounded on property relations was baffled to discover that use and possession were more decisive of the public weal than property ever was. The ownership of a corporation's shares constituted a simple equity in the corporation's holdings, and the owner, exempted from the management of his own capital, relied upon employed executives to realize, and to give or withhold at their discretion, the profits to which the right of ownership abjectly admitted him. The liability, which it had been the initial motive to distribute, was now so broadly diffused that neither law nor legislator nor judge in court knew quite well how to localize it. The corporation, as Lord Chancellor Thurlow once lamented, had no easily discoverable backside to kick.

If I rent land from another, I purchase the use of the land, not its title. For rent paid I acquire a right of occupancy which the law describes as *possession.* The right of *ownership* remains still vested in the lessor. Were the owner to choose to work the land directly himself, or to leave it unused, ownership and possession would then lie coincidently in the same person. But that coincidence is inessential, and the law allows for the possibility of their separation.

In the corporation the two rights have been separated. They have been separated not *de iure* by purchase but *de facto* by delegation. Ownership is divided among the shareholders; possession has been delegated to a group of employees, the actual directors of the corporation, who, though they may have no part or at best a very minor part in the ownership, nevertheless exercise the right of possession in the corporation's name.

In Jefferson's America, the decisive actor in the business firm was the owner. Farmer, shopkeeper, or small manufacturer, he typically bore the risk of his own undertaking and managed it as well. If he employed another to assist him in his labors or even to manage in his place, he reserved still to himself the basic powers of decision which conferred control and implied liability. In particular, he hired and fired, and there was never any question as between his employees and himself that the acts of the firm proceeded from his initiative, that it was he and not they who entered into the primary legal relations with his customers and creditors. An employee might enter or leave the firm: the identity of the firm was not affected by his coming or his going. For the identity of the firm, its legal continuity in time, was everywhere presumed to reside in the person of the employer, in the person of the owner whose legal responsibility required his permanence.

In the twentieth-century corporation the relative importance of the two estates—the estate of owner and the estate of employee—has been inverted. The owner comes and goes in the firm, the employee remains and governs. The shareholder is transient, the manager permanent. Such continuity as the corporation has depends not on the identity of its owners, but on a board of directors who manage without claiming to own, who risk without standing to lose, who maintain an apostolic succession without benefit of doctrine, advice of saints, interference of government, or kiss of the Holy Spirit.

The "divorce of ownership from control" has very justly become the subject of commentary by a long succession of distinguished social critics. Without exception they regard it as the most momentous transformation of twentieth-century society. Thorstein Veblen saw in "absentee ownership" the last dissolution of the capitalist institution of private property. Joseph Schumpeter discovered in it one of the primary evidences that capitalism nurtures within itself the causes which must inevitably destroy it. The degree of concentration of private power in the American industrial scene was the revelation of a book written some thirty years ago by Adolf A. Berle and Gardiner C. Means, *The Modern Corporation and Private Property*.[5] Concerning the fact of the matter there is no room for dispute. Concerning the construction which is to be put upon the fact the authorities are sharply divided. The critics of capitalist economy see in it the last decline

---

[5] New York: Commerce Clearing House, 1932. See also Berle's article, "Corporation," in *Encyclopaedia of the Social Sciences* (New York: Macmillan, 1937).

of an expiring social order. Adolf Berle sees in it, on the contrary, "the 20th-century capitalist revolution," a new order of social relations which, rightly used, will enable free men of good will to enter at last into the City of God.

I confess that I see in it neither of these things—neither capitalist apocalypse nor socialist jubilee. I see in it only the profound estrangement of life and law, an inability of the law to discipline the agencies which it has itself authorized. The divorce of ownership from control is, in the political experience of mankind, a perfectly familiar phenomenon. It lies at the basis of all representative government, of all government where the collective interest is placed by a society in the discretion of some of its members, who are then charged with exercising authority in its behalf. Why then, if this structure of relations is so familiar at law, should the law find itself arrested before the fact of the corporation which is its creature? The reason is that the modern corporation has eluded the law which created it.

44. Legal Theory and Moral Fact

The control of the means of production has always been understood as the typical aspiration of a socialist economy. The control of the means of production is the typical achievement of corporate management in capitalist society. Our exclusive attention to merely legal relationships conceals the political fiction in both systems. We mark only the trivial distinction between the public and the private ownership. We obscure the social reality in which ownership has become passive in both, use alone decisive in either. In both societies the fact of law has ceased to correspond with the fact of agency. The law which is manifest fails to discipline the fact which is furtive. Estranged from the realities of our social life, the law reflects not the action of society, but its passion only, the society's dumb spectatorship of a power of decision which has eluded its controls, compelled its act, and cancelled its democracy.

Corporation directors are pained to be told that the relation of management to shareholders in the modern corporation is the same as the relation of the Communist Party to workers in the Soviet economy. In Russia the ownership of the means of production lies, or at least is said to lie, with the workers; the control is lodged decisively with the governing hierarchy. In the American corporation the ownership lies with the shareholders, the control with management. The divorce of the power of decision from the right of ownership is for all effective purposes the same, and if a distinction is to be made between the two systems, it shall not be made on that ground with respect to which they are in fact indistinguishable. The public versus the private ownership of the means of production is in fact external to their opposition, for ownership either is, or is in process of becoming, a passive attribute, an attribute without social consequence, in both forms of society. American law no longer securely answers to the actual terms upon which the affairs of American society are conducted. For the fact to be attended to in modern industrial society is not the location of ownership but the location of responsibility.

The demand of the law in a well-ordered society is that responsibility shall lie where the power of decision lies. Where that demand is met, men have a legal order; where it is not, they have only the illusion of one.

Politically, a society can live with the divorce of ownership from control. But no society can live with the divorce of control from responsibility. Wherever in any society, all fictions apart, the responsibility for the exercise of power is no longer unambiguously imputable to those who determine its employment, the power has become arbitrary and the law of society has been emptied of its moral significance. The rights and duties which the law defines no longer coincide with actual conduct, and the law becomes phantasmal, impolitic and inconsequent, dead to the actual movement of the society which it fails in fact to regulate.

This reflection has led some to represent the corporation as a fiduciary, as a private agency charged with the exercise of a trust in the public's behalf. But it must be confessed that this legal device has in the present connection only the specious utility of a cosmetic. It conceals with a dust the blemish which it has failed to recognize or remedy.

Suppose a corporation were, out of accumulated earnings equal to its assets, to recall all of its own stock, so that in effect it owned itself. Its character and justification as a trust, as "the people's capitalism," as "shareholders' democracy," at once would disappear. It would continue, under the solemn fiction of legal personality, to do business, employing men, making contracts, taking risks, marketing goods and services. But it could no longer be thought to execute a trust, for it would then no longer affect to act in the interest of others, but only in its own. It would move powerful but untouchable in society, society's unjailable civilian, legally armed with a soulless, immortal privacy which no mere mortal could ever equal, with an unpopular independence which no mere state would ever risk.

I do not consider this a very likely ghost. But its likelihood is not at all in question. Its interest is not that it is likely to occur, but that nothing in the law of corporations forbids it to occur. The law treats the corporation as a fiduciary. We are observing that its fiduciary character is in fact an accident of its evolution, which is by no means essential to its idea. A translation of ownership from shareholders to corporation would occasion no single readjustment of internal relations. All of the basic functions within the corporation would remain perfectly undisturbed, and the corporation would pursue with unruffled tranquillity its former goals. Employed directors would continue to set the same policies, employed executives to command the same efficiencies, employed laborers to work the same routines. But while, internally, the translation of ownership to the corporation itself has made no difference, externally it is a shaking of the foundations of our legal community. It lays bare a still unreconciled conflict between American pluralism and American society. For it has exposed a power in society which society is neither prepared to regard as a sovereign nor yet equipped to govern as a subject.

The code of equity law prescribes for every wrong a remedy. If A injures B, B may seek redress at law for the injury done to him, and the court will restore the justice of A's and B's society by requiring of A, under the peril of its sanctions, a reparation. In the simple interchanges of ordinary men that relationship is clear enough: the responsibility for the offense lies unambiguously with the offender. Intermediate agents may on occasion complicate this relationship, but the principle will remain the same. If A through the agency of C injures B (so that, though C performs the act, A is its admitted author), the primary responsibility will still lie with A who is the principal of the act, only an accessory responsibility with C who is the agent. The life of the law in any society will depend on this condition, that the responsibility for any offense against its order shall be thus determinately localizable and distributable.

The legal right of B to be protected in his property runs against the world at large; that is, in the language of the law, it is a right *in rem*. Such is the peculiarity of all of the basic rights which men claim in a legal community: they are rights *in rem*, rights which oblige all men generally; they imply in all others a duty not to interfere with the holder of the right so long as he acts within his privilege. But just for the reason that a right *in rem* obliges all men generally, it obliges no one peculiarly. That is why a right *in rem* can never directly beget a legal action. Directly, it begets only another right. It begets a right of particular incidence, which enables an injured party to press a claim against his injurer. If A invades B's property, B's antecedent right, the right *in rem*, which ran against the world at large, is converted into a right *in personam*, a remedial right, which runs against A in particular. If it were not so, all of our basic rights in society would float permanently in ineffectual generality, unenforceable for the reason that the law's sanctions could never be brought determinately to bear on any definite person. When it is said that the court interprets law, that is what is meant. The law's incidence is general; a judgment's incidence is always in the first instance particular. The court always deliberates directly over a right *in personam certam*. The effect of the rise of the giant private corporations of our day is to make that concept radically equivocal.

As the giant private corporation has evolved, the idea of collective agency has become a danger to the interpretation of the law itself. All acts of commission originate in the ambiguous and obscure shelter of the corporate entity. Who shall be held answerable for the corporation's acts of commission? The law says that the collective person itself, the artificial entity acting through the agency of its officers, is answerable. To these officers, since they are presumed to act only under a delegated authority, the law is prepared to impute only an accessory responsibility. The initiative responsibility lies with the corporation. But since the corporation, which is the legal principal, can act only through the agency of its officers and apart from their agency can act not at all, such authority as they have has been delegated by themselves. In spite of all theory to the contrary, they are in fact responsible only to themselves; which is to say, that they are irresponsible and their power is arbitrary.

They are irresponsible and their power is arbitrary quite independently of the motives which guide them in their performances. Nothing is gained by supposing the modern captain of industry wicked or malevolent. Unread in the arts of Machiavelli, he could school philosophers and princes in the real conditions of power. Yet there can be no doubt that he experiences the same consternation before the rulelessness, the *anomia,* of his circumstance as do we. Any power is arbitrary, however benevolently it is used, if its uses fall beyond the controls of law. Any actor is licentious, however benignant his intentions, if being accountable to no higher authority he is judge in his own cause.

Grover Cleveland once said: "It is a condition which confronts us, not a theory." Basically the condition is that the directors of the modern corporation are clothed with a most exorbitant power. Therefore, whosoever controls the directors controls the corporation. That is what is meant when behind closed doors the business world speaks of the "silent control" of a corporation, that is, of that individual or group which is able to elect, and therefore also to recall and replace, corporate management. The control is silent not because it refuses to speak. It speaks very effectually. It is silent because it speaks, makes decisions, produces effects, without liability proportioned to its power.

45. The Pluralism of the American Economic Community

The great genius of the American pattern of society has always been its pluralism—its capacity to accommodate, in the peace of one society, the manifold private motives and energies which are generated by the social life. The society is one; the centers of initiative for its acts are many. Such a distributive pattern of power is inherently precarious, for it depends upon the preservation of a balance between the claims of the society and the claims of the centers of initiative which appear within it. In the past, the main threat to the balance of the social pattern has always been the tendency of the public interest to increase itself at the expense of the private, reserving all initiative to itself and extinguishing all pluralism in its members. In order to prevent that issue, the American society has instituted checks and balances in government itself, limiting the powers of government by opposing them one to another according to a rule laid down in the Constitution. The principle of privacy in American society was thus fortified and defended against the public assault. No one apprehended that an equal danger to the American balance might one day threaten from the private sphere. No one apprehended it because in the private sphere liability always ran with initiative, and no one imagined a private initiative which fell in systematic immunity beyond the reach of the law. That precisely is the problem set by the rise of the giant private corporations of modern industrial society. The systematic immunity of the collective agency is the profound political problem of all capitalist nations in our century. It is a problem which public ownership has exaggerated rather than remedied in the communist nations of our century. Aristotle once said that the individual who is capable of living beyond all law must be either a beast or a god. Modern corporations are neither beasts nor gods. In theory, they are creatures of the law; in practice, they are beyond it. It remains for our day to bring them under it.

Has the corporation, in fact if not in law, lost its private status? Has it in fact become a part of the public machinery which our society employs in producing and distributing its wealth?

We are by long habit accustomed to supposing that whatever subserves the public interest belongs by implication to government. But that way of thinking obscures the singularity of the function which the corporation performs in American society. The corporation is no part of government; it has nevertheless a public character. It is a trustee of the public interest. But the public whose interest it is charged with conducting is society at large, not the segment of society which claims its profits but the moral community which requires its services.

It is regrettable that those who describe the giant modern cor-

poration as a "quasi-public institution" everywhere fail to draw
the inference which they have prepared, the inference, namely,
that the kind of privacy of which such an institution is capable
can never be more than a quasi-privacy. Our actual path in this
connection is very similar to the path we take in education. American education is a public function the direction of which we in-
sist upon reserving to local authorities, so that though the society
is one, its patterns of education are many. In the same way, modern industrial production and distribution in America are public
functions. They are public functions which our society persists in
principle (the same principle which causes us to separate the
powers of government) in reserving from the direct controls of
any single public authority. Our economy is, like our educational
fabric, a systematically decentralized federation of corporate
powers. Such is the originality, at least as I conceive it, of the
actual solution toward which our economic community is tending.
That solution is not yet reflected in the law. That is why a too
assiduous attention to the merely legal relations of ownership fails
to isolate the real alternatives of our society. The significant option in America is not between a public ownership of the means
of production and a private ownership. The significant option is
between a singular and a plural initiative.

With respect to that option the American community is now,
and has always been, perfectly decisive. Pluralism is the affirmation of American society in all of its branches and in all of its seasons.

Under the conditions of modern economy it is no longer possible to maintain the old sharp division which an agrarian society
could draw between the public and the private enterprise. When
in the last century the railroads had been flung across the land,
the heroic accomplishment was imputed to the vigor of private
enterprise. But even then there was no question whatever that the
transportation system which was left in private hands was a matter of profound public concern, and government did not hesitate,
in order that the undertaking might be encouraged and hastened,
to make grants of land to the railroads which exceeded in value
the total costs of construction. Never before had the success of a
private enterprise been so despotically assured or a failure so

despotically forbidden. The individual enterpriser might faint in the desert or the mountain passes or the counting house; his place was taken by another and the enterprise went always on. Who then built the railroads, the public or the private enterpriser? The question is empty. For it omits the prime fact, the fact which must preside over any understanding of the actual movement of our society, the fact that the essential character of our form of economic community is guaranteed not by the privacy of our enterprises but by the pluralism of our initiatives. The Sherman Antitrust Act of 1890 is a slap on the invisible hand. That law is inconsistent with the theory of private enterprise as the nineteenth-century economists understood that theory. It is nevertheless profoundly loyal to the American temper. It is the direct consequence of the radical pluralism on which our society is founded.

Americans have always experienced a difficulty in reconciling the theory of their society with its practice. We exalt our rancid acquisitiveness; we leave unexalted our vision of a free society. But it is this vision which prescribes the permanent feature of our society, its openness to novelty, its respect for diversity, the search for an order of law which is capable of preserving its multiple centers of free choice. A pluralist society is obliged to proceed always on a principle of counterpoise: it discovers its equilibrium not by eliminating oppositions but by using them, by making them party to a larger design which exhibits the public dimension of every private act. In the normative pattern of American society there can be no power, public or private, which is not checked by other power. This check is not an assault of government on privacy; it is the cost of our freedom in the shelter of society.

We do not solve the problem of governing the modern corporation by extinguishing its independence; we solve the problem by defining the limits within which its independence is admissible and beyond which its independence is an encroachment on the public interest. When society has defined the duties of corporations to itself as securely as it has defined their duties to their shareholders, the public character of the corporation will have been acknowledged in the law.

chapter X

The Commonwealth of the University

46. *The Idea of a University*

In defining the idea of a university, I do not intend to state an ideal. I profess only to describe what is implicit in the simplest act of the academic community. It is surely a real and very serious question to reflect what is indispensably required in order that a community should enact the role of an academic community, and that precisely is the question posed when one sets out to define the idea of a university. "The ideal is the spirit of the actual." That is why men, who pass their lives in the crush of actualities, have once and again to reflect, lest, being crushed, they lose sight of the spirit of their simplest acts. There is a bond implicit in the touch of a child's hand, and as anyone who has loved a child knows, the strength of the bond is not measured by the strength of ligatures and digits. So, there is a bond implicit in the community of the university, and if it is not customary to reflect upon it, or to honor it by protestation, that is not because it is not real or worthy, but because we honor it, as we honor all things best, in the quietness of our acts of every day.

I am aware that I shall be thought, for what I have just described as actuality, irreparably soft-headed. I speak of circuses when I should speak of bread. Let it be confessed that I earn my living in the academic community, that I eat out of it, that, even,

I should be destitute without it. That is one of the reasons why, to me, philosophy is a consolation. It is nevertheless true that, consoled or unconsoled, I eat out of our community's pocket. Nor should the brute actuality of the case be less than fully stated. If my residence in the academic community had no motive except the earning of a living, no other incitement except to labor and be paid, no one should ever be the wiser and I might live out my life with my belly full. No student should go untaught, no administrator unsatisfied, no publisher unglutted. But I should have committed nevertheless a fraud. What is worse, the fraud would run not only against the community whose function I had betrayed, but against myself, the member of the community, whose part I had deserted. For the simple fact is, that the community of the university is not a community of bellies, although I am persuaded, and the university should never forget, that each member of the community has one. That motive which belongs to every vocation is the distinctive motive of none, and if you make the idea of a university to consist in money-getting, you forbid yourself your problem, which is to distinguish between one form of money-getting and another. That is the Marxist deception wherever it occurs, that it professes to analyze what it leaves untouched. The economic livelihood which each gets from his labors is no doubt one of the motives for the performance of his labors, and to suspend that motive, to treat it as unreal or capricious or ignoble, is to imperil the academic community and to divorce it from its proper act. That act can be performed only when the material conditions of its performance have been supplied. Cancel those conditions, you cancel the act by forbidding it. Supply those conditions, you render the act possible by permitting it. But in no case, by these conditions alone, is the act ensured. Fishers of men, you shall not have your object by purchase. You are still left with the problem of the idea of a university, of the obligations of the academic community, even when the conditions of its existence have been supplied. That is why presidents and deans are, in the end, so vanquishable a lot. They are like women. They supply the conditions of generation, but can't do it alone.

So I am compelled again, even at peril of being thought softheaded, to address the idea of a university and the bond of allegiance which unites men—men and presidents, and even deans—within it.

47. "The Delegated Intellect"

A society has a continuity of life which transcends the lives of men. Men come and go. The society anticipates their coming hither and survives their going hence. It supplies the forms whereby the germ of originality which is in them is either stirred or extinguished. If its forms are foolish, men are wise only in spite of it; if its forms are generous, it makes possible an honesty in men which they could not have without it.

The university is such a society, the sieve of generations through which we, proud dust, are strained. The society of scholars isolates itself, in the broad world, as a special group. Its bond of community is so peculiar that men are not accustomed to reflecting on it. It is a voluntary association. No one has inherited his status in it, as men inherit passively, by the simple adventure of being born, their status in a species, in a race, or in a nation. Its membership is distributed not according to what men suffer, but according to what men do. Each belongs to it only by what he freely affirms, and there is no belonging to it except by affirmation.

What is this bond which unites man to man and overleaps the boundaries that divide generations and nations? Among scientists it is a rule of method, the common rule of evidence which presides over the conduct of their inquiries. The society of scientists, as we have seen, is bound together by common commitment to a rule of evidence in precisely the same way that the citizens of a political community are bound together by common commitment to the principle of a legal order. The peculiarity of the society of scientists is that, unlike the nation-state, its members have no single geographic locus. It is an international community whose members never congregate, surely the most tightly-knit, as it is the least centralized, community on earth. Its executive and judicial functions are distributed universally among its members. The community is where they are, and they are dispersed wherever their rule is respected, without regard for the boundaries and moral separations which in other ways, for other purposes, divide men and communities from one another. Its members are scattered athwart time and the world. Men who have never seen each other's faces find themselves nevertheless to participate in a common task and common dedication. The universal priesthood of believers finds nowhere else its so perfect realization, not in sect of Protestant, neither at Walden Pond. Protestantism is soliloquy, Walden is egotism: science is neither. Of the tolling of a bell when one of his parishioners died, John Donne wrote:

> No man is an Iland, intire of itself; every man is a peece of the Continent, a part of the maine; if a Clod be washed away by the Sea, Europe is the lesse, as well as if a Promontorie were, as well as if a Mannor of thy friends or of thine owne were; any mans death diminishes me, because I am involved in Mankinde. . . .

He who regards the university as an island, he who lets it become one, is treasonable to it. He provincializes its community, and diminishes himself. He gains a province and loses the world. He may even gain the world, but he shall have denied its soul.

Therefore, proud dust, if you would make a university, conceive it to be no less than it is, for it is inevitably more than you are, singly or in aggregate. It is your responsibility, not your presence, which is in question. Let no administrator presume himself to direct a world, who directs only a colony; let no scholar profess to have the truth, who has only his limited vision of it; let no teacher claim to form a man, who is capable only of forming an idiom. Academics are of all breeds of men, I suspect, the worst sentimentalists; and sentimentality is in framing the idea of a university, as in all things that matter greatly, the cardinal sin of all, cardinal because it is sheepish, sheepish because it leaves the object of sentiment everywhere exposed. In this the professors of the sciences are, according to my observation, the worst offenders. For they describe science as if it were their precinct, the scientific method as if it were exhibited in themselves, so that to applaud the one or the other were to applaud them. I do not fail to applaud them. But what I honor by applause is the role which they enact, and themselves only so far as they enact it. I revere the obligation which they observe and the demands of the community which they nurture. In the performance of so austere a role the egotist has no place. He wears priests' robes, but has not the humility of priests, who regard the robe only as the token of the office, and the office as a set of claims upon them, which every man should aspire to honor, but to which no man can without arrogance claim to be equal.

48. The External Obligations of the University

Out of his tragic sensitivity Pascal used to meditate the spectacle of the man who hunts the hare. Why does the hunter search out the hare and pursue it, heedless of the absurd disproportion between his effort and his prize? Does he so value the hare? Not at all. If you offer him the hare ready-caught, he will regard it with proper contempt. The virtue of the hare is not in the having of it, but in the pursuit of it. For, so long as the hunter looks abroad for the hare, he is absolved of the really insupportable task of looking inward upon himself. That is his special peril as a man, which the pursuit of the hare enables him to escape, or at least for a season to postpone, the sere reflection that, except by what he affirms, except by the obligations he imposes on himself, he the pursuer is, like the hare pursued, a poor nothing, the proper object of contempt.

So, in the university, the university acquires its character from its affirmations. In part its ends are given to it, given to it by the society which is beyond the university. It is but society's instrument and tool for the pursuit of ends which not it, but society, has chosen. Yet the society which creates the university in its midst, and sustains the university by its support, is not competent, except in the broadest terms, to define its program. It may, since the university is its creature, place a veto on any of its acts, or suspend its acts entirely. But in this it is prepared to govern the university only negatively. What positively the university shall do, what its positive acts shall be, society leaves undefined, leaves undefined because it is not itself competent to define those acts and has created the university to act for it to that purpose.

Emerson regarded the scholar as "the delegated intellect," as "Man Thinking." I so regard the university.

The university is the gathering of society's powers of reflection in order to liberate all of its other powers.

Such is the plenitude of the university's task in a free society. That is why the simple existence of a university is socially so extraordinary a phenomenon. The society which creates a university creates its own critic. The Lord God who made Adam out of the dust of the ground may be presumed in foreknowledge absolute to have known that in the will of this creature which had the capacity for obedience there was implanted the capacity for disobedience as well. The society which has dared to create the university has not the assurance which foreknowledge can give. It has no assurance that it will not be disobeyed, and except through us no way of discovering the disobedience when it occurs. This is *its* civilized and civilizing risk. But it is also the reason for regarding the work of the university as a civilized and civilizing trust. The university community is under no effective law save as it gives laws to itself. Its freedom is its responsibility. It is the single instrumentality of society for which society has devised, and can devise, no effective control. It has only the knowledge—not sufficient to bind it unless it chooses to be bound—that as it builds society, it builds itself, that as it tears society's vitals, it tears its own. Nevertheless, the university's service to society is, and will ever be, as it interprets its responsibility to society. Make no mistake. The treason of the universities which Hitler captured was not Hitler's treason; it was the treason of the academic community. Hitler succeeded; it was they—men like you and me—who failed, who failed because they deserted the role which society in its dumb trust, with the innocence of a child, had consigned to their care. I am by no means sure that we should have acted our part better. But that is not the point. There is always a Hitler. Society is always, with respect to some matters, a little child. There is therefore always, so long as there is a university, the part to be acted. Of that part Hitler knows nothing, and society knows little. The part can be played only by those who know what are the demands of the part and what is at stake in the acting of it. Unless the academic community acts it, the part shall go unacted, and the idea of a university shall become, like Othello's occupation, a thing gone, heroism without hero.

In its relation to society the university's function is, in the first instance, to provide the means to ends which society has chosen for itself. But it is a lame architect who houses an activity without civilizing it. You do not sensitively house the life of a man by providing only for the movement of his bowels, and if in seeking to serve his needs you search out only the known needs which he declares and will think to define, that he needs a kitchen and a place to lay his head, you will serve him very ill indeed. He buys the services of an architect; you give him the services of a privy-carpenter. You leave him where he was, still vexed by desolations which he feels but cannot state. "The foxes have holes, and the birds of the air have nests; but the Son of man doth not know where to lay his head." What really he wants is not a space in which he can be sheltered, but one in which, in addition to being sheltered, he can be made perfect, in which he can realize such goodness as he finds real but undeveloped within him. Just so, then, as obedient critic, the university has a function beyond the satisfaction of any needs which society now knows. In the ripeness of its performance it has the function of illuminating ends which society is not now equipped even to discern. No person, least of all the university, has the right of prescribing ends to mankind. But there is a duty which falls, if not only to the university, yet still to it no less than to other communities of men, and certainly to it more than to some, the duty of discovering the ends implicit in mankind's perfect and unhindered development, ends not now chosen because they remain in society and in us unimagined or incompletely affirmed, ends nevertheless real because, given the alternatives of free choice, mankind would embrace them as its own.

I despair of making mathematics moral. Even should I succeed, there would still be the mathematicians, and with respect to them everybody is agreed that such an aspiration were madness. But that is not what is required. I have not set out to define the idea of a mathematician, or the idea of mathematics, but the idea of a university, and though it is true that mathematics is amoral, and mathematicians make universally the mistake of supposing themselves so too, it is impossible so to regard the university. It is the saint, not the saint's leg-bone, that is holy. It is the university, not the university's mathematics-bone, that is moral. The mathematician, considered with respect to the community of mathematicians, may be morally neutral: his partisanship counts for nothing. It matters nothing that it is he, and not another, who takes a sum, so long as each taker observes a common rule in taking it. Considered with respect to the university community, the mathematician is permitted no such license of anonymity; his partisanship as mathematician is all that counts. It matters everything that it is a mathematician who speaks, for there is no other who can speak competently in his place. This reflection will not, I devoutly hope, alter his mathematics. But it makes every difference to his conception of his role as member in the moral commonwealth of the university. The university could be absolved of its moral role, and he of his part in it, only if it had no relation to society beyond it. Of that external relation it is never, and can never in obedience seek to be, absolved, and so long as it sustains that relationship, its role is, for better or worse, a moral one.

It may therefore be well, lest this moral addiction be thought to have taken from us our distinctive virtue, to consider the idea of a university in its internal relations, to consider, that is, the sense in which, for the sake of performing its function in society, it must conceive itself an intellectual commonwealth.

49. The Intellectual Commonwealth

If, as obedient critic, in its relation to the society it serves, the university is a moral commonwealth, it is, in the relation of its parts to each other, an intellectual commonwealth as well. Ideas are its commodity, and there is no commodity so subject to fraudulence, so liable to misuse, so readily debased. That is why there can never be any question whether the *Communist Manifesto* should be taught in the university. It must be taught. Only it is necessary that, in the university which teaches it, there be taught beside it Aristotle's *Politics,* St. Augustine's *City of God,* and Locke's *Essay Concerning Civil Government.* You do not treat a cancer by concealing it: you cut it out. But ideas are your true atom, subject to no fission: they cannot be cut, they can only be analyzed. An idea is not killed by being insulated. The only way to kill an idea is to expose it, the only way to preserve an idea is to expose it. Good or bad, exposed it must be, at all events and at any peril. Against an idea which is insulated from open discussion society is left permanently undefended. It is capable of defending itself only against ideas which it understands, and is helpless to defend itself against ideas which it only fears. A free society's motive for erecting the institution of the university within it is nothing less than this vision of evil. Society will veto any idea which it does not understand, and its veto, uninformed, is indiscriminate. It will suppress truth no less than falsehood, sanctity no less than vileness, the idea which will emancipate it no less than the idea by which it will be enslaved. A free society therefore creates the university as its critic, in order that its ideas shall not be limited fortuitously by its understanding. That *it* dares to do. The university which dares not to discuss the ideas society fears, which so circumscribes its intellectual role as to conform only to the understanding which society is prepared at any time to give, is therefore in treasonable default against society. It has deserted its proper competency and vocation, forgotten a higher loyalty in the pusillanimous pursuit of a lower one, which, when it cancels the higher, is no loyalty at all.

The university can be a moral commonwealth only on condition that it is first an intellectual one. Its moral role has an intellectual justification, else has no justification whatever. Therefore its members, who are the agents of a moral commonwealth, must be such as they are, men who, in Max Weber's definition of an intellectual, live not by ideas but for their sake.

I should announce myself in this matter as no neutral. I profess to speak only for myself. But I suggest that the conception of a university must represent, whoever speaks, a philosophical act. There is no such thing as a university of botany, or of medicine, or of public service, or of business, or of fine arts, or of law. There are only departments of botany, and divisions of fine arts, and colleges of medicine. The idea of a university includes these, but is more than any one of them. It is more than any group of them. It is more than the aggregate of all of them together.

The concept of a university represents an affirmation. It affirms that the several disciplines which fall within its precinct are not merely juxtaposed avenues of pursuit, but constitute a real totality, a universe of inquiry, in which each separate study forms a part of a single grand enterprise.

The term "university" may have other meanings than this. It may mean, for example, the legal entity, the guild or corporation (*universitas*), which is a composition of members—of faculty, of students, of administrative officers. Legally, it is an artificial person; it can sue and be sued; it has rights enforceable at law; it has incumbent duties which can be legally exacted from it. But that is as others see it who are abroad from it. If you would know what a family is, you do not consult a bachelor. The counsel you want is the counsel not of a spectator, but of a participant. The bachelor can tell you only what you are equally free to observe; the participant can tell you what is not available for your observation, since the bond of obligation which unites a family is not observable by anyone who has not himself experienced it. The sociologists, who are bachelors by profession, virgins with empty lamps, will not like this, but I cannot help it. The matter which concerns me in forming the idea of a university is not how others see it, but how it sees itself. The university, as it sees itself, affirms the integrity of the intellectual domain.

The interrelatedness of scholarly disciplines is nothing invented. It exists, and has always existed, in institutions of higher learning wherever the sciences and humanities are taught. In the natural sciences this interrelatedness of disciplines is postulated as a basic assumption: to every physiological phenomenon there exists a biological condition; to every biological phenomenon there exists a chemical, and hence also a physical, basis.

Among the humanities or liberal arts affinities of this kind are less rigorously formulated but are, in fact, everywhere assumed. A historian undertakes his study of societies and civilizations upon the assumption that art, literature, and philosophy are related to politics and war, politics to social conditions, social conditions to economics, and so on.

The interrelatedness of humane and scientific studies lies at the basis of the concept of a university. These studies are practiced together because they belong together and are impoverished when they are held apart. Everywhere it has been assumed that this actual interrelatedness, because it exists, is therefore necessarily apparent. It is not. On the contrary, it requires to be discerned and by design to be made visible. To discern it and to make it visible is the burden of the agonized solitude of every scholar, out of his mute sense of the relatedness of things to pluck, as Hotspur plucked bright honor, understanding. To discern it and make it visible is one part of the work of education. Philosophically, this part of the work of education is the part which, in a strict formulation, is called "general."

The term "general" is misleading, for it is not intended to suggest an interest which is an interest in the merely generic. The general and the special are never, in a rightly conceived program of education, opposed to one another. On the contrary, in the system of the university they are always in fact complementary and in conception indivorcible.

Since about this matter so much confusion has been spoken, spoken both by Specialists and by Generalists, spoken invariably by Manichaeans, who neither say what they mean nor mean what they say, spoken sometimes by persons who have not taken care to have a meaning, it will be well to deal seriously with it. I shall say what I mean. Anyone is free to reject that meaning. But if he rejects it, I submit that he has rejected the idea of a university.

Ideally, a program of general studies is an attempt to restore the integrity of a university in an order of society in which universities had ceased either to enact or to communicate their philosophic function. It reappropriates the function of a university as an educational institution. That a university enacts other functions besides the function of education is not in question; that an educational function is in part performed by special studies is not in question. The sole matter requiring assent is simply this, that the relations among the sciences and arts constitute a subject-matter as positively defined as the content of any special discipline—mathematics, physics, French literature, or the history of the Tudors. The study of the interrelationships of the sciences and arts is an indispensable correlate of these special studies; it cannot be suspended without suspending their veritable consequence for society and man and their actual significance for each other.

General education, in the sense which I have defined, does not mean an education for the many; neither does it mean an education for the few. On the contrary, it stipulates the fundamental condition of any education whatever, that it shall be in its issue philosophic, that it shall represent such wisdom as in the concert of our little knowledge we are capable of. The ignorance which Socrates professed is the only true wisdom, the wisdom which knows its own limits. The wisdom which the Sophists professed is ignorance unassuaged, ignorance which acknowledges no limits except limits not its own. Ignorance may cancel learning, but there is no ignorance so contemptible as learned ignorance, as the ignorance of the learned, who would, in a sloth of intellect, leave the tasks of philosophy to infants still suckling. Out of the darkness that covers it and us, a suckling infant must at last decide its own destiny. You do not, therefore, to preserve its freedom, lock it in a closet. Nor do you permit it to lock itself there. On the contrary, from your poor bounty, such as it is, such as it cannot help being, you give it what you have, which is your best. To give it less than your best, to give it the immunity of a closet, is not an essay in freedom. It is an essay in theft. For you require of it what it is not prepared to give, and what even you are only in part prepared to offer, the decision of an informed desire as to where its good must lie. The freedom you have given it is empty, since it is a freedom which it can only defile. It has the freedom to which the poor of the earth are always committed, which is the freedom not to do, but only to suffer and to die.

Whether few or many shall be educated must be decided independently of the question what an education is. The two questions are distinct, and only to one of them is the university competent to supply an answer. The number who shall be permitted the opportunity of an education must be decided by the separate mandate of society itself. In American society we have that mandate. It is the mandate of a democratic society, that a democracy must make education available to all men, to the *generality* of its citizens.

We are therefore obliged to distinguish a second sense in which education may be said to be general. I for my part believe that most of the basic divisions on the matter of education in a free society are occasioned by an ambivalence of the term between this second meaning, the democratic meaning, and the first, which, for want of a better term, I call the philosophic. The concept of a general education may mean either an attempt to make the diffusion of education general, or an attempt to make the issue of education philosophic. Both meanings are legitimate; in a democratic society both are necessary. Ideally, in a democratic society the two meanings must be complementary. It is the presiding peril of a democratic society that the two meanings should ever be made inconsistent.

The single peril to which, in the conduct of a university, we stand exposed is that either of these meanings should ever be permitted to *substitute* for the other, to suspend the operation of the other.

For if in the interest of making the issue of education philosophic we make its virtue inaccessible even to serious men, we shall make it also ineffectual among them.

And if in the interest of making the diffusion of education general we compromise its rigor, we shall make even serious men defenseless before the very forces in the world which threaten our free society and would extinguish both philosophy and democracy together.

The education of a democracy inevitably exists in the tension between these two meanings. The task which is given to the fashioners of its programs is to respect both and preserve both.

I leave it to you to decide how well the actual commonwealth has been wrought. I confess to finding my world too heavily populated by Manichaeans who regard civilization as a datum, not a task. A university will not be made by Manichaeans. The idea of a university is a most perspicuous essay in the tasks of civilization, which must always discover balance by discovering elements of counterpoise. A democracy which is intellectually destitute will be led by scoundrels; an intellectuality which is unresponsive to the needs even of the qualified will wither and dry up. If the commonwealth of the university is all destitution or dryness, the fault is ours, for a university is bound by no law save as it gives laws to itself.

50. Science and Humanism

As it conduces to the advantage of society that there should be a division of its labors, that one should forge the ploughshare, that another should turn the soil, so in the university men's labors are divided. Though there be an acknowledged common good, such good as they achieve is the fruit of the labors of men who work solitary, and must inevitably work solitary, in all of their distinctively creative acts. That is why in all germinal scholarship and in all germinal science there is an ingredient of art, which the study of others has prepared, which the association with others has disciplined, but which no study or association has ever sufficed to guarantee. Fustel de Coulanges was wont to tell his students: "Do not applaud me: it is not I who addresses you, it is history that speaks through my mouth." Let it be allowed. Let it be allowed that the historian is a neutral conduit, and that history speaks French. It remains still that there are Frenchmen and drain-pipes through whom no reflective act of the historian is transmitted. What qualifies Fustel to be the mouth of history is the courage of his solitude, not the word he utters, but the word he impregnates. It is so with all of us. We labor best who labor silently and speak germinally when we speak at all.

Within the university the prime division of labor is the division between the systematic and the historical, between what are customarily called the sciences and humanities. There is nothing so unprofitable as the inquiry whether historical studies have the virtue of being scientific. It is quite certain that science has not the virtue of being historical. That is a matter of words, and one is free to use them as one pleases, provided only that one uses them to assist rather than to abort one's purposes. The important question is, What constitutes the difference between the one kind of inquiry and the other?

If you abhore frogs, you may be assured that you are no biologist. What you ought to abhor is not the frog, but the idiosyncrasy of a frog, which its brothers fail to share. A systematic inquiry seeks after general truths. The frog which the biologist dissects has no interest for him save as it exhibits the type of which it is a specimen. The specimen itself is expendable. Its uniqueness as an individual is not the object of systematic inquiry. It is a redundancy to which nature is typically and prodigally committed. Therefore, if it be spoiled, it may be discarded, and its place taken by another, which is equally fitted to fill its role as experimental beastie. The aspect which is grasped, the aspect which alone is permitted to solicit interest, is what it shares with others of its kind; and the kind of science which emerges from this interest is a science which consists of general truths, of truths which give information concerning *any* object of the kind in question.

But now consider the interest of the historian or humanist. He characteristically interests himself in unredundant singulars—in the giving of the tablets of the law to Moses, in Rembrandt's *Syndics of the Cloth Guild*, in the mind of Milton, in the Peloponnesian War, in the rise of capitalist economy, in the segregation of the negro in American society. If he would study Leonardo da Vinci or the Russian Revolution, he cannot find, outside the historical locus in which each of these particulars is set, the object of his reflections. It is all biography—the life-portrait of a man, or of a movement, or of a people, or of an epoch. The singularity of the man or of the movement or of the nation, which interests the historian, is precisely the aspect which the interest of the systematic thinker is content to omit. That is why, between the systematic and the historical disciplines in the university, the gulf seems to be so radical and so impassable. It is our reason for distinguishing the role of the scientist (narrowly so-called) from the role of the humanist, whose science is as real but of a different order.

Let the scientist of society and the historian define for themselves a common object, and let each proceed to grasp this object according to his special genius.

In the *Institutes of Justinian* there occurs the following definition of justice (I, 1): "Justice is the set and constant purpose of rendering unto each that which is his due (*Justitia est constans et perpetua voluntas suum cuique tribuendi*)." To each that which is his own—that is the sense of the definition. The scientist of society is least of all interested in the circumstance that Justinian's jurists spoke it. He may apprehend the definition simply as a phenomenon, as the jural postulate—the norm—of a society. But the definition will excite his systematic interest as an unusually lucid expression of the general circumstance, that in *any* society—in ours no less than in Justinian's, in Justinian's no more than in the society of the Hopi Indian—what is accounted just presupposes some normative distribution of rights among the members of the society, which it is the business of law to preserve, and if it be lost, the business of law to restore. This distribution, which the law is designed to define and protect, is the juristic equilibrium of society. It is what is meant by the justice of that society, that each should have preserved to him that which, in the juristic equilibrium, is his own. In one society and another the portions distributed by title among the members of society may vary. They may be in one society equal, unequal in another. But that is nothing to the principle. Its interest is certified under either of these contingencies. It is simply this, that the principle enables theory to grasp the common juristic lineament of *any* society whatever.

Very well. That is your scientist of society. What is the historian's distinctive reflection? He sees likewise in the definition its quite extraordinary power as an intellectual tool, which fits it to secure its place in the codification of Roman law, in the reflections of medieval canonists, and in the formation of every system of Continental law of modern times. But his interest is rather beyond than in it. He apprehends in the definition the form of human mentality which was capable of producing it. The definition, as it was the product of that form of mentality, is also its document, as an artist's painting is the document not of a landscape, but of a man. It is the definition in its documentary function that the historian distinctively grasps and interprets. For that form of mentality which was capable of producing the definition is, like all things excellent, a rarity among men, and deserves their attention no less than the definition itself. The form of mentality of the Hopi Indian is not competent to that act which Justinian's lawyers performed, and to know the conditions of that act, to seize upon the form of mentality which can generate this intellectual power, is to discover a lesson of humanity of which the sociologist has said not one word. That is why the scientist, who sees no science in history, so desperately needs the historian, that he may see himself. The history of ages and nations of men, whose biography the historian records, is not an idle pottering with things old. It is a conquest of discovery, which ranges before men's eyes the genius of all that is human, which discovers in a poor potsherd, as in the majestic fabric of the Roman Law, the possibilities of the human type, what it has done and what it is capable of. It discovers the Hopi Indian, it discovers the age of Justinian, it discovers the sociologist, it discovers you and me. By that discovery men make their final essay of self-awareness, of that self-knowledge in which alone is wisdom or dignity in their kind. Such self-knowledge is denied to the Hopi Indian for so long as he moves, like bee in hive, under the secret dominion of institutions and of laws which he inherits but has not, in the dignity of free choice, affirmed. The inheritance which is the sufferance of the bee is the task of the man. For the human type is what dust must labor to inherit, that so this dignity which dust claims may be by right its own.

chapter XI

Education and
the Moral Frontier

51. *Walden and the Village of Concord*

Henry David Thoreau kept on his writing table at Walden Pond, besides his Greek Homer, three pieces of Yankee limestone which had pleased his eye on one of his walks. He shortly observed that if they were to be kept, they had then to be dusted. Out of the window they went in a sublime renunciation, consigned to the elemental care, attentive enough, of wind and rain. The cost of their maintenance indoors so far outweighed the marginal advantage of having them there that the keeping of them was in the domestic economy of Walden quite unthinkable, and in the moral economy of Thoreau a treason against simplicity. What business had he, Thoreau, dusting such clutter of mere things so long as the living soul within him had dust upon itself, having still to be made pure in its proper element?

I never read that passage in *Walden* except with approval. That is the essential Thoreau, the intimate special character and clean seriousness of him, which I find in every way admirable. So perfectly educative is that act that I embrace it as my own and would to God I had thought of its first. Like all Americans I regard as most typically American in Thoreau the very trait which I find in no other, but in him only: the fluent consequence of act upon thought, the thought without hint of indecision, the act without hint of misgiving. Your typical American has no such trait. He is like me, filled with indecisions, plagued by misgivings. He wears his freedom like a stain. He would be caught dead before claiming infallibility for the least of his opinions on any matter. Therefore, before any matter which concerns his way of life, except it be the abstract right of forming it for himself, he hesitates. The thought trembles on the razor's edge ill at ease, decisions are sought in the village where respectability can be never questioned, and the act, if the village is itself in doubt, is permanently puzzled over and permanently withheld.

I hold the tolerance of privacy of opinion in America in a very sincere affection. For one thing, as an American, I share it. For another, I am securer in my idiosyncrasy that others cultivate and share it too. But its consequence is that in the matter of education, in the one matter in which an unerring firmness of decision is initially required, public opinion in America is perennially unbuttoned. It is perhaps well for our image of Thoreau that he desisted early from teaching school. For in that engagement, as I surmise, he must as signally have failed as at Walden he succeeded. It is quite impossible to have a Concord in which all the villagers regard civil disobedience as a duty; which is to say, that the image of Thoreau, which we justly elevate, is an image of the genius of our privacy. Image of citizen it does not afford. America would be irreparably poorer without the riches of Henry David Thoreau. But the sufficient education of a society is not to be gained from meditating the absolutions of a hermitage. I suspect that American education has nowhere failed so abjectly as in instructing men on the uses of their solitude. But that is only to have said that it has failed everywhere, outside the village as well as in it. For it has surely failed in instructing men on the uses of community.

I am content that every American should damn Concord. But an educator must somehow contrive, even in damning it, still to labor for its sake. The problem is to realize an education of men, to draw forth Thoreaus, in spite of Concord's complacency with its own image. Concord is every educator's world. Always in its own eyes it is irreproachable; always, in the eyes of an educator, it is partly fake, inauthentic, merely respectable. Concord is un-

impeachable only because no one has had the courage to impeach it. Immemorially the fault of Concord is that it will not license the Thoreau in each of its silent villagers. Silence is the price of the village, the petty fee which the villager exchanges for the civil guarantee of his freedom of speech. The village requires of each man that he become the desecrated effigy of the least part of his neighbor. That is why, if the truth were confessed, to labor for Concord's sake as an educator of its citizens is always to be, like Thoreau, a trifle treasonable to it. The education of a citizen cannot be drawn from a study of the pattern of a city's habit. For the task of education is at last to set free not the habit of a city, but the dumb aspiration implicit in its habit, the buried virtue which its habit has incompletely liberated.

As an educator I would shape men who are free to walk in the village as independently as Thoreau walked beyond it. If this be treason, I am guilty of it. An uncritical deference has no place in education. Your originality in taking the sum of two and two does not interest me. For originality is here out of place; deference to rule alone is in place. But if you ask me to educate your son, I would sooner see him unformed than stamp upon him the image of you or the image of me. He has a better and less anonymous calling. You would make of him a cipher? Then let him be what you are. You would make of him a man? Then let him be what he is capable of becoming, a critical intelligence abroad in the world, loyal to the only Concord to which you in fact are loyal, a Concord capable of sheltering his virtue as it shelters yours, so much the object of his care, so intimately a part of himself in intercourse and solitude, that to desert it is not to find Walden, but to wander with Cain.

I speak from the University, not for it. There was a time at which the University shared the absolutions of Walden Pond. It does so no longer. The academic grove was once a seclusion from society; today it is society's laboratory. It is consultant for the commonwealth. Of its learning all men make confession. Its ignorance no one confesses. It has acquired all of the thoughtless deference which Concord formerly reserved to itself. In that, if the University but knew the measure of its ignorance, there

would be some gain. But for so long as its ignorance remains un-
known, it is a peril to itself and to all men, striking flint where it
thinks itself only to be dusting stones.

52. *The Permanent Frontier*

There is, I suppose, an element of risk even in the circumstance
of our being in the world. What a man gets, what good he falls
heir to, is always in part owing to matters which fall beyond his
control, which owe nothing to his will or to his act.

Of those matters which fall beyond our capacity to change
—as that, to live, we must eat; or that, to have society at all, we
must be subject to some restraints—of these matters I propose to
take no account, not because they are not important (on the contrary, they are most fatefully important), but because they are
matters which nothing we do or say can in any wise affect. They
afford the bare stage within which all human decisions are taken,
and just as the actor on the stage is not free to suspend the conditions of the stage on which his part is cast, so neither are we
free to suspend the conditions of our stage, which is nature.

All that we can do, all that we can ever hope to do, is to make
use of those conditions which the neutral stage affords. For it is
possible, as the ancient Stoics saw, even given these conditions
which are unalterable, either to play our part well, or to play it
ill.[1] That alone is within our power, to envisage the role clearly,
to envisage the role within the limits by which nature hedges our
acts, and to determine what constitutes the proper enactment of
it.

That at last is what all statesmanship is, it is what all education
is, among men, a cultivation in them of a capacity to understand,
under given circumstances of nature and society, what are the
real possibilities, the authentic alternatives, that are available for
choice; to embrace, among those alternatives, that one of them in
which the human welfare is found most abundantly to lie; and
having embraced it, to draw forth, out of resources which the circumstances afford, the most efficient instruments for the having
of it.

[1] Epictetus, *The Enchiridion*, XVII.

In the making of a garden a man does but bring together soil and seed, and set each to a work which each was already fitted to perform before his act took place. The seed does not receive from him its capacity for growth; the soil does not receive from him its capacity to sustain growth. His act of gardening is simply an act of combination, drawing together capacities in things which are by nature fitted to complement each other. The combination alone is his; the elements combined are inevitably borrowed. They belonged to nature before his act, and belong still to nature after his act. The result of their combination would equally have ensued, had they been combined by an accidental gust of wind. They would have retained equally their fitness for combination, had their combination not in fact occurred—had seed remained still stored in pod, and soil unturned and fallow.

All human art—in matters of society, all statesmanship of any kind—is an art of combination. It is form-producing, not thing-producing. Its elements are given. It simply assembles, organizes these elements, introduces among them a pattern of its own, so that actually what art creates is not things, but only the forms of things.

That, very simply, is what men do, who enact the roles of educators in society. They institute forms in which the human community can be sheltered, and in which, if they do their part well, its better genius can be realized.

That is why the work of educators is so profoundly important in the comings and goings of the human community. For by the same freedom by which, out of decisions which we take, that community may be exalted, so equally, out of decisions which we take, that community can be abased. Make no mistake about it. Our capacity for doing evil is at least as large as our capacity for doing good. It is probably larger, for as men will follow when they are energetically led, it must be the appalling reflection of all energetic leaders, that there are more ways of going foul than of going pure.

What, then, is the responsible act of education in a society of free men?

Old Socrates had an answer for that question, and I still regard it as the only profitable and honest one in human terms.

The work of teaching, he thought, whether it be the teaching of the young or the teaching of the old, is after all a piece of midwifery. The teacher is an intellectual midwife. What does the midwife do? The midwife produces no child; she simply delivers one. Unless the mother produces the child, there shall be no child. For the midwife's virtue consists not in producing capacity in others, but only in delivering others of capacities which they already have.

It is so with education among men. You cannot make men better than they are capable of becoming. You are not competent to give them anything. But what you can do is to deliver them, by the services you perform, of the best that they are capable of.

Such is the sense of that strange imperative pronounced by the Existentialist philosophers in our own day. They say: "Become what you are!" Why should that be commanded of a man? Why should a man be commanded to *become* what already he *is*? You do not bid a child to gravitate or to grow. For a child gravitates and grows independently of your command, and will gravitate and grow still, even in the absence of your command. So much you may leave to nature, as the child in effect leaves it to nature, and adds not a cubit to its stature, or an ounce to its weight, by taking thought. Yet still it makes sense to say to a child, "Become what you are!" For one then speaks not to the child, but to the man in the child. That is the strange paradox of the human condition, which is shared by no other condition in nature, that a man is capable of being less than he is, and discovers himself, in any stage of the development of human society, less than he is capable, rightly nurtured, of becoming. He is nature's singular essay in tragedy, whose destiny nature has left undetermined, except as he shall determine it, gross Caliban, from the vision of Ariel in himself. As he shapes his society, as he fashions its institutions and frames its laws, so at last he shall become. It is for this reason that, of all animals, man alone requires to be educated. Mere training will suffice for an ordinary animal, since of an ordinary animal no choice concerning its own estate is ever demanded. But of a human animal that choice is precisely demanded. The taking of sides, the granting of allegiance, the exercise of loyalty to an image of himself, is what makes him human.

So therefore, to that task, we educate him to the freedom of the human act, and regard mere training as suited not to the art of making men, but to the art of lesser fishermen.

A man, as the educator or the statesman is bound to conceive him, is not merely a creature born promiscuously into the species *homo sapiens*. He is that. But he is also, besides that, a creature whose thought, whose reflection, whose conception of his own promise makes him what he is. He alone, in all of nature, is obliged to seek out his proper image, since nature in its careless dispensation has left it undetermined, and he alone can, for good or evil, determine it—for evil as for good, as he chooses; and for evil no less than for good, unless he chooses.

That is man's fate, as the old philosophers saw it, that he must choose his fate. That is man's fate, as your modern Existentialist sees it, that unless he chooses and responsibly allies himself, he shall suffer in the indifferent round of mere nature the despair of utter nakedness and desolation.

Therefore, for Concord's silent villagers, the vision of America has always creatively to be reworked. Therefore, for every generation of Americans, the task is original, generous, heroic, and unfinished. Man is himself, in the late President's phrase, the new frontier. He is the only frontier that is permanent. For the frontier did never lie in the unpeopled land. It lies in the peopled one. It lies in us.

53. *Education and the Human Covenant*

The one compelling and inescapable datum of the modern consciousness is its sense of crisis. Of crisis, of crisis alone, amid the corrosions of unbelief and moral incertitude which beset our world, is anyone perfectly persuaded. Men may differ on all other matters. They may differ in their opinion of the causes which have brought men and nations to their present posture; they may differ in their judgment of the remedies which can relieve the modern *malaise*. On the matter of crisis itself there are no differences of opinion or of judgment.

The crisis itself is certified. It is what no one doubts. But the nature of the crisis is very much a subject of dispute. For while men feel the exacerbations of the times, and experience, out of the conflicts of their institutions, an arrest of allegiance in their simplest acts, they all alike persist in believing that the present crisis is like any other, simply an exaggeration of every other, an incidental failure of efficiency or organization. So that each sees the ill in what he is most prepared to see, in what lies nearest to him and pinches first—a fault of economic distribution, a defect of political planning, a failure of communication or of design or of reverence.

It is the indomitable opinion of twentieth-century man that there is no ill which a better knowledge of utilities might not remove. It is presumed everywhere that the ills of mankind are the baneful effects of our too little knowledge, and that as knowledge is increased, those ills must be diminished, and at last must disappear.

That opinion, that trust, is the motive which underlies the study, and gives moral seriousness to the pursuit, of all of the descriptive sciences of human behavior—to the pursuit of psychology, of sociology, of economics, and political science.

I will say frankly that in my judgment that opinion is a delusion. I do not depreciate the descriptive sciences of human behavior. I do simply despair of the claims which are made in their behalf, which require of them answers they cannot give and set for them problems they cannot touch.

The dilemma of twentieth-century man is at his core, not at his surface. His dilemma is philosophical: it concerns his fundamental commitments, not his incidental acts, the quality of the ends he pursues, not the efficiency of the means he commands in pursuing them.

Knowledge is power, Francis Bacon once wrote, for if you would command nature, you must be content to obey her. That is the permanent challenge to the positive sciences at all times. Our sciences of nature and of human society are simply our studies in obedience. They have conferred upon mankind great powers of control, the technical powers which enable us to produce in nature and in society the effects which men have chosen.

The problem is in the choosing. For that knowledge which confers upon us the power of control says not a word concerning the ends to which it shall be committed. The power itself is, like a knife, neutral: it cuts for him who wields it. It will cut for a surgeon to save life, it will cut for a quack to cripple it, it will cut for a murderer to cancel it. It will cut equally to save or to mutilate. But who will tell us what is saving and what is mutilation?

You reflect upon the same circumstance when you observe of 2-4-D, which has utility for killing dandelions, that it has equal utility for killing the clover in your lawn. The knowledge is as neutral as the chemical. It produces good and evil indifferently, and stands mute before the question, whether any crop in nature shall be thought a weed, or any death in nature a benefit.

Plato used to say that the education of a society consists in leading human beings from childhood to feel pleasure and pain in the proper things. Erich Fromm has spoken to the same effect with a devastating modern lucidity. What a society does in educating its young is always one and the same: it teaches them to desire that which it is society's interest that they should desire.

If that shocks your moral sensibilities, it must nevertheless excite your admiration as a descriptive account of human social behavior. Men act not according to their interest, but always according to their opinion of their interest. Their opinions are therefore society's great concern, for by governing their opinions society governs them. Every dictatorship in the history of mankind has understood this principle. The most generous democracies have understood it. Dictatorship and democracy have made use of it, the one by suspending free discussion; the other by cultivating and requiring it, that the truth should set men free. Thomas Jefferson so fully believed the principle that he founded a university; Joseph McCarthy so fully believed it that he silenced the universities, Jefferson's university among them.

No one can be pleased with this issue of our argument, for it calls to our attention, out of the University itself, not the profession of its knowledge, but the admission of its ignorance.

Statesmen and educators must know that ignorance. They must know the reason for it, that the descriptive sciences of nature and of human society do not themselves decide to what ends they shall be committed. For unless we know, and be ready to confess, the ignorance of the University, we cannot be proper advocates of the knowledge it in fact can claim. Nor will we ever understand why the present generation, which commands greater knowledge than any of its predecessors, should also experience greater anxiety than any of its predecessors.

The weapon which a child can trigger is, in the hands of a child, the most dangerous of all weapons. Who is the child? It is we at last, you and I, human society at large. I wish I could say, as the degradation of political theory in our day has taught us to say, that my fear was fear of a bomb. A bomb is the least of my fears. I do not fear dying tomorrow. Let the cause be to me real enough, I shall consent to die today. No, the real fear is not that tomorrow I shall die, but that tomorrow I shall live, and in that morrow find both you and me and all society made victim of the instruments we have fashioned, captured by the communications which could in a better use have exalted us, driven by the dumb procedures which could in a better use have set us free.

Knowledge is not necessarily wisdom. Neither is the imparting of knowledge necessarily education. We have lost in the modern world our capacity for regarding the destiny of mankind as a problem. We view our humanity not as a problem, which demands reflection, but as a datum, which prohibits it.

Therefore, in the peril of our old habit, we look only to those ills of society which technology can be depended upon to remedy. Poverty is evil, therefore the absence of poverty must be good. War is evil, therefore the absence of war must be good. Disease is evil, therefore the absence of disease must be good. These are our invincible certitudes. It should follow from them that a major end of education is a teaching of men to die. For in death you have each of these things: in merciful death there is neither want, nor war, nor disease.

The physician who works at healing the body knows his task is done when an ill has been removed. But in the education of men the elimination of an ill does not suffice. The real problem for education is not in identifying society's ills, or even in assisting in the removal of them. The real problem is in determining, in society's interest and for its sake, in response to its dumb aspiration, what constitutes its health.

Yet where, if not in knowledge, shall men find wisdom? Where, if not in knowledge, shall one discover the proper education of a society and the uses of the human freedom?

The question is very justly raised. And the answer to it is: Nowhere, nowhere save in knowledge. But the knowledge in question, which affords wisdom and can guide education, shall not be had in our present exercise. "Whatsoever thy hand findeth to do, do it with thy might," says the writer of *Ecclesiastes*. It is an indecent and cruel precept. For shall it be thought to matter not at all what the blind hand has found to do? And shall it matter not at all what we become in following it, defining the soul's commission according to the accidents of touch? As the twentieth century has had tragically to learn, he who regards the hand as infallible will before long desert the head and the heart. The infallibility of the hand is the fierce dogma of a brute season, and we have all been party to it. That is why the knowledge needed, the essential knowledge, is a knowledge of the covenant which is man, of the civilizing covenant in which men will be content to abide permanently without constraint, since beyond it their humanity has no place and their dignity no warranty. Let men set for themselves the task of framing such a covenant, they shall know the education of their young and the conditions of their community. For in that covenant will be found the sources of the human dignity and the nature of the good society, in which, in the words of Micah, men love justice, and do mercy, and walk humbly with their God.

chapter XII

Politics and
the Human Covenant

54. Politics and Ecology

There is a species of mushroom, *Marasmius oreades,* which behaves in a fashion very satisfactory to geometers. It propagates
itself in circles. On green turf, in an open pasture land, it will en-
close a grassy space with a ring of yellow buds. You will run
upon it of a morning, a whole bed of tiny globes sprung up over-
night, distributed with prophylactic regularity about a common
ideal center, each at the end of a radius, busily engaged in regi-
mented but open array in setting spores astride the wind. I have
permitted myself to wonder at times whether that is how geometers make love. The visible order of these mushrooms is so tidy
and engaging that even Plato might have been induced to look a
second time at this womb-of-becoming. They are in fact, as the
curious have come to know, the organs of a single spawn, all
connected with that center by subterranean filaments—by the
mycelium, as the botanist calls it, so that their center is not in
fact ideal, but material enough, simply, like the loves of geometers, not visible on the surface. A little digging will discover it,
nor does it deserve less to be celebrated that its geometry is
realized, like yours and mine, out of clay. It is nevertheless, that
mycelium, the tangible emblem of what in reflection men call a
principle, that connection which, being known, gives understanding, and which, buried, requires in the interest of understanding
to be dug up.

Well, such a connection is the thing wanted when one asks, What is the principle, the mycelium, of a political order? One asks the same question in asking, What are the conditions of peace among men? But that latter question, which is the one more frequently heard, is answerable in either of two ways, according to the interpretation which men put upon it. It is answerable as a question of *politics;* it is answerable as a question of *ecology.* I do not diminish the importance of either answer. But it is our habit to identify the two, and to suppose that, having stated the ecological conditions of peace, one has stated its political conditions as well. There is, in the affairs of men, a political reality. There is also, in the affairs of men, a political illusion. A science of political relations should enable us to mark this distinction. Our habit effaces it.

If peace be order, then a concentration camp has peace without a flaw. There is peace in Dachau and Buchenwald, a peace mute and unarguable as the peace of the dead is mute and unarguable, except that these forlorn and desecrated ones, who suffer it, still somehow, after their fashion, live—eat, defecate, and feel pain. Emblematically, in Auschwitz, out of smokestacks, their peace colors the air. Theirs is the peace, this peace of prisoners and their captors, the negative peace, imperfectly annihilating, that belongs to any ecological phenomenon in nature, to the mutual tolerance of cat-reed and algae, of fly, frog, and watersnake, in the tepid equilibrium which issues, unwilled and unreflected on, from their commerce with each other. So, in the ecological community of Dachau, given that distribution of powers and their interplay, there results, mechanically, a condition of equilibrium. The equilibrium of Dachau is, like the equilibrium of the swamp, that state to which the system will mechanically gravitate, and in which, once gained, the system will exhibit no further tendency to change.

I would at all costs avoid sentimentality in this matter. It matters not at all that the terms related in an ecological system are beings born of men. Dachau is a machine for producing smoke, just as a dairy herd is a machine for producing milk; and it is ecologically a matter of perfect indifference that either of these issues has been designed or willed, or that men thrive or suffer, eat or starve, in the event. As the dairy herd, given these conditions, would produce milk still, even if the husbandman willed nothing, so, in Dachau, given its conditions, the willing does not qualify the result, either hasten it or alter it or make it more inevitable.

Why does the cat-reed not grow in the desert? Why does the cactus not grow in the swamp? Because, we say, in neither case are the conditions supplied which permit its growth. Because, on the contrary, the ecological conditions prohibit its growth. Such is the circumstance of any ecological community in nature: what it does not favor, it prohibits.

If in the fatigue of old habit we dignify that circumstance as "natural selection," we employ a metaphor, the most deceptive metaphor in the history of science, a metaphor which, even in biology, where it originated, confounds indifference with design. In desert as in swamp, nature selects nothing; it simply eliminates or absolves. The living and the dead alike are but fossils strewn in its path—the living as well as the dead, and the living no less than the dead. Enemy of nothing, partisan of nothing, the order of nature simply *is*, and we are as it would have us be, if we are permitted to be at all, in that sublimest and most impassive of all dispensations known to man. As by its default one dies, so equally, by the same default, another lives. Nor shall the living sing forth praises of its wisdom or benignancy, that they, the quick, are by grace of nature and right of inheritance the choirs of the elect. In that soundless equilibrium there is neither grace nor right, but only displacement. They too, the living, are, like the unreprieved and vanished dead, part only of the litter of the world, things amid things, in a common alley.

Such is the stage upon which our human act is cast, and there can be no question that, whatever our act may be, it is forbidden, ecologically, to transgress the limits of that stage which nature has laid down. A spectator in the theater can afford perhaps to forget, in attending to the exits and entrances of actors, that the stage has stipulated absolutely the conditions of their movement. The dramatist who forgets it cancels his art. For his art consists at last in realizing out of those conditions, out of their resources as well as their prohibitions, a play.

I am interested in this dramatist and his play. For he is, like the immemorial Caliban in us all, part of the world's litter, part of its refuse, but a resilient waking part, a creature of dreams and intricate surmise, filled with strange presentiments of which nature is innocent, that there is room still on that stage for a play, for a dozen different plays, which nature has not written, which therefore he shall write in an essay of free artifice. That is Caliban's divination of history, his vision, half-formed, of the wakened Ariel in himself. Estranged in nature, he domesticates himself in history, as a caterpillar weaves its chrysalis, and by a web spun from its own body shuts out the world, to immunize its sleep in preparation for its transformed waking act. That is what is meant by man's history, a new order of being, his proper act and dispensation, which not nature, but he, Caliban, has contrived, in the tragic liability which is man.

The human dramatist produces a covenant. By a shaping imagination he conceives a set of roles which draw together into a common purview the acts of those who walk within them, and are content, abiding there, as persons to the drama, to regard its demands as obligatory on themselves. What difference shall come of that in nature's imperturbable silence? This only, that those who stand together in such roles, as parties to a common covenant, acquire, with respect to each other, a status which none has who is not party to it. Beyond the covenant of the play, all are things; in the covenant of the play, all are persons.

In that simple image of human artifice is visible the difference between *positive* and *negative* peace, between the peace of a political community and the peace of an ecological one. An ecological community is a community without a covenant; which is to say, that it is properly a community not at all, but only a *de facto* equilibrium in nature. To every *I* in political community there is a *thou* which corresponds, and their community with each other lies in the circumstance that they stand related as persons, so that to diminish *thee* is to diminish *me* also. Of the privilege of status which a covenant confers mere nature knows nothing. It harbors no persons; it harbors only things. Nature flows carelessly, according to its monstrous insensate habit, impassive and undisturbed, whether or not men institute political relations among themselves.

The loss of political community among men may, for a time, produce no discriminable difference in the outward pattern of their behavior. But the transformation which attends that loss is, for those who suffer it (as the twentieth century is in course of suffering it), the profoundest transformation which we as humans know. Each party becomes stranger to the covenant of the community which formerly he kept. Each sees no *thou* in the other, and becomes himself a bare *it*, another poor parcel of mere nature, part only of its litter, in the other's neighborhood. We are all estranged, without love, without loyalty, without allegiance, like swamp-flies on still water, whose common habitat dissembles their actual solitude.

That community of persons is a fiction? Assuredly it is, if by fiction you mean that nature fails to afford it. Like all else that properly matters in the human story, it is the work of our artifice, a fiction we have instituted, not a condition we have found. That is why a naturalist theory of politics is a deception; that is why a Marxist theory of history is a fraud. Each is an essay in ecology; each deserts the topic it has professed to treat.

A political community is a community by covenant, a community of persons mutually allied by virtue of the obligations they are committed to preserving with respect to each other. Cancel those obligations which men in community acknowledge as real, as binding on themselves, in their intercourse and conduct, you have cancelled their community. I would not make such a dust about an old truth if it were not our habit, in describing "political reality," to forget it. Obligation *is* the political reality. Where there is no obligation, there can be no politics. That is the fault of Dachau, whose peace is an illusion, whose sole reality is the reality of the gun-butt and the lash across the face, of steel and hot grit and the ache in the body. For, let it be repeated, if you would have from a people not merely submission, but obedience, not merely the act constrained, but the belief that the act is necessary and justified even apart from constraint, you shall have it on the one condition that the law which binds is a law to which consent has been freely given. Law competent to bind a man gains its authority not from the barb of wire which confines his path, nor from the hand of a watchman who stretches it or relaxes

it, but from the man bound who is party to it, who chooses the
path, and consents to abide within it, since beyond it his proper
identity would be lost.

Nothing is so misleading, or in our world so dangerous, as the
assumption that men have peace wherever outwardly they have
no war, that men have community wherever, as the positivist
phrase has it, convergent patterns of behavior preponderate over
divergent ones. The outward conformity of men's acts may dis-
simulate the inward motive of their acts, nor shall one know, even
in the best conditions of outward harmony, as between Jack Sprat
who ate no fat and his wife who ate no lean, whether their peace
stems from love of each other or from an accident of appetite.
Their concord is the result either of a love affirmed at all times or
of a truce of the hate in their hearts at mealtimes. But which it is,
one cannot, on the bare evidence that each eats the leavings of
the other, say. For that reason, the division of labor, which discovers the complementarity of men's acts in society, is not equal
to explaining their society, and is never a sufficient evidence for
confirming that they stand as persons in each other's presence.

Such is the inevitable default of positivist description before
any normative circumstance whatever: it discovers no mycelium,
even after digging; therefore supposes there is none, though
mushrooms die on every hand for each other's sake.

55. Law and Covenant

The derangements of habit in modern life are so grievously multiplied that men no longer affect to conceal them. Formerly it was
necessary for a man to travel abroad to encounter aliens. Now, by
the progress of enlightenment and the advance of the behavioral
sciences, he need only remain at home. He will find alien enough
in himself and aliens all in others. Sensitive natures who become aware of this may after their fashion, without protest, stifle
the dim misgivings which they feel, and move still in that mute
animal passion for life, which equips them now, as it has
equipped them always, even in desolation, to endure the shock of
existence. But the derangements of habit remain nevertheless
visible, neither concealed nor concealable, in the stunned arrest

of faith which men of the twentieth century experience out of the conflicts of their institutions.

Now as always, it is task enough to preserve, in the solitude of one's private act, the integrity of a dedicated life. But what formerly appeared as the perspicuous moral problem, in the visible relation of man with man, is nowadays obscured in the relation of man with corporation, or in the relation of corporations with each other. The place of the Negro in American society is simply the example the moral implications of which, in the riot of our season, have been made most visible. But a sensitive eye will find illustrations as real, and of no less urgency, in the articles of tax-rates, in social security legislation, and in anti-trust acts. The taxation of a society is a redistribution of society's wealth; a social security law is a stipulation on the part of society that the share of society's wealth for any of its members shall in no case be zero; an anti-trust act is society's prohibition of any concentration of power which shall economically prevent other power from appearing. The moral implications of such laws are no less authentic than the love of Ruth for Naomi. But their positive feature is less readily seen. All men know what they forbid; few men reflect what they affirm.

In America the laws permit what they do not forbid. That is the proper feature, as it is the proper risk, of law in a free society. The role of law in human society has not always been so conceived. Calvin wrote: "Whatever is not a duty, is a sin." The law prohibits what it does not command. That is the stamp of law which risks nothing in men, which imputes no dignity because it believes in none. The difference is one of the broadest which civilized men know. In Calvin's society the letter of the law is paramount, in American society the responsibility of the citizen. The citizen in America is therefore, for better or worse, a moral agent, since the law which governs him lives rather beyond its letter than in it.

It may one day be seen in America that the dignity of man is not a natural endowment, which men have in being born. The dignity which rights protect in America belongs to men not because of what they can claim under the law, but because of what under the law they allow and disallow. For what the law of a free society protects is not dignity, but the effort after it.

Meditate, therefore, that law of Calvin, which is so different from our own. It is in principle a form of idolatry. In principle it forbids what it does not command: whatever is not a duty, is a sin. That conception of law in human affairs is, in an age which has lost confidence in its own capacity to direct itself, of all enticements to moral absolution the most seductive. It is at the root of every consent to authoritarianism in our world; nor is there any symptom of moral and intellectual decay so profoundly disturbing as the contemporary retreat to it. It affirms, as every idolatry affirms, a partial truth. It affirms the truth, that there is no dignity beyond law. But it affirms, besides, that because there is no dignity beyond law, there can be no freedom under it, that freedom is a stain, the pursuit of the human good an egotism, the unsurrendered conscience a depravity.

America, the America we inherit, was born of a sublime protest against that conception of law in human affairs. America will be dead if the spirit of that protest be ever forgotten. For such is the delicacy of the American inheritance, the simple affirmation of its spirit, that the law of a free society permits what it does not forbid. That is why a free society is permanently, in all places and in all times, for every generation of men, so precarious an adventure. For it must appear, in many of its acts, very like an ecological community. Its restraints are minimal by principle, and as the freedom of men appears greater as restraints are less, it is always apt to be supposed that if the restraints upon act and enterprise were extinguished, then freedom would be perfect.

The belief that law is bondage, that he alone is free whom no obligation touches, is the most persistent of all human delusions. Where men acknowledge no limits upon their actions, there can be no settled order of expectations among them; and where such an order is wanting, no man is significantly free. Such is the dissolute tragedy of modern nations in their relations to each other. Each nation protests a sovereignty unbound by any law. Each therefore purchases its lawless freedom at cost of a permanent bondage to those it fears, whom it cannot predict, and dares not trust. The bond of law which may effectively unite nations, and set men free, remains still, in the most momentous moral issue of the twentieth century, to be forged. The international order stands meantime, in its brute equilibrium, under a continuous threat of dissolution. Such peace as it has is ecological. It rests not upon the disciplined respect of nation for nation, or of man for man, but on an agonized and faithless distribution of power. It is secure only in the measure in which that distribution is stable, and is cancellable whenever that distribution may change. What is politics? In the harsh equation of Mao Tse-Tung, simply war that sheds no blood. And what is war? Simply politics that sheds it. Each nation must therefore dissemble an independence that enslaves, since, though bondage is everywhere, nowhere is there a political bond. As their community is a fraud, so also is their peace a fraud. The most powerful are the most stricken, for it is not the weak, but the strong, whose status is at any time in jeopardy. Therefore, morals are left to the care of the weak, who have only weakness to lose. To the strong, whose harsh neighborhood they endure as men endure the coming and going of cyclone and pestilence and holocaust, are reserved, as the perquisites of power, only fear and the tyranny of each other's presence.

Society, whether it be of men or of nations, cannot exist without imposing restraints upon its members. Society is an implicit equilibrium, and it is by restraints that its equilibrium is preserved. That is the ineffaceable condition even of Thomas Huxley's wolf-pack. The members of the wolf-pack, if they would eat of the hare, must be content not to eat of each other. Rescind that measure of restraint, let wolf eat of brother-wolf, there may still for a little time be wolves, but there can be no pack. The society lapses with the restraint which was its incorporating bond.

The natural ferocity of wolves is neither tempered nor assuaged by their social condition: it has simply been required to look beyond the society for the sphere of its legitimate exercise. That sphere is nature. The sphere of the wolf is society. Which is the paradox of society, that its members are in nature, but not of it.

The minimal condition of human society is not otherwise. That is why the segregation of the Negro in American society is so fundamental an index of its moral indecision. Society is itself an act of segregation. Wherever men associate themselves together under a common bond of alliance—as nation or municipality, as government or opposition, as capitalist or communist, as Christian or Moslem or Jew—they mark a distinction between those who belong within their covenant and those who do not. All partisanship is segregation, and society exists by partisanship. It must inevitably segregate those whom it acknowledges as its own from those whom it rejects. Whom does it acknowledge? The parties to its covenant, those only who act in obedience to a common rule and observe common restraints with respect to each other.

The American dilemma neither is, nor has it ever been, whether there shall be segregation. There must be segregation if there would be society. The only question of moral consequence is, Who shall be segregated? Who shall be wolf, and who shall be hare?

Such is the moral predicament of American society. It is simply a society uncertain where its boundaries shall be drawn, undecided what are the limits where society ends and nature begins. Its tragic perplexity has nothing to do with the restraints by which it is governed. It has always known, it has everywhere agreed, that its members shall be protected by its laws; the meaning of its Constitution had not to wait upon a decision of the Supreme Court, that the intention of the laws should be made clear. The decision of the Court has discovered nothing in the law which was not known before. For it is not the intent of the law, it is the membership of the society, which the Court has chosen to define.

Cain asked: "Am I my brother's keeper?" Alas, poor Cain, about that matter there is never any question. Each man in society is his brother's keeper as he would keep his brother's company. The only serious question is, Who is my brother? And that is the moral question of our world.

56. *"The Law of Nature and of Nature's God"*

An authentic science of politics is not, and can never become, a merely descriptive account of the redistributions of power in human affairs. For a political condition among men does not consist in the circumstance that power has been distributed, but in the circumstance that a law, commonly admitted, defines its exercise. It is as sentimental an addiction to suppose that armament can confer legality as to suppose that disarmament can confer it; and there is no crueler deception worked upon men than the belief which we permit ourselves to cultivate, that the one reality of politics is power, or that a political solution is to be found, for men or nations, in the study of any *de facto* distribution of it—by a balance of it or by a disbalance of it, by a concealment of it, or (in that last admission of moral infidelity) by the destruction of its instruments. If peace is in jeopardy where men have arms, it is equally in jeopardy where they have none, nor will any nice calculation of marginal utilities minister in either event to the civilization of our hate.

For the simple fact is, that whether we be armed with the munitions of modern warfare, or be stripped to the naked equality of fang and claw, peace is in our covenants, never in our tools. There are in fact some tools which, given the condition of peace, will be found quite useless; but there is no tool ever fashioned by men or destroyed by them, which, without the condition of peace, will serve to supply it.

It is the appalling reflection of every generation of men, that men may die politically, and physically still live. In our generation, in the affairs of nations, that is no mere reflection. It describes the actuality of our condition: physically we live, politically we are dead. We have discovered, by default, that peace is not of nature, but of man. Peace is our historical risk, the thing we institute in nature, not the thing we find there. Neither is war the infrangible terror to which nature commits us; it is our historical relapse, our decease from the human risk, to which we commit ourselves, surrendering back to nature the riskless dust, which, in a presentiment of history, had risen out of it, Caliban with Caliban's dream.

The poor in all times have a wisdom which is denied to the learned: they know their poverty as mere learning never does. Their poverty will not permit them to forget it. A poor scholar, all rags and bones, has cultivated in himself the disciplined capacity to conceal, even from himself, the moral destitution in which he and others float. That is the social advantage which learning confers upon him, that he is able to conceal, if not his nakedness, at least the full measure of it. But his physical poverty, the deprivations of his body, he can neither conceal nor forget, and in this he has a real advantage over his brothers of ampler cloth. They may be wholly naked and know it not at all. No moral destitution will announce itself except men be ready to see it. Therefore, a learned man well-fed may be a fool and never know it. That at last is what is so melancholy in the human condition, that even among men who enjoy by common consent "the highest standard of living" poverty may no less strike, like the democratic gentle rain. It simply strikes unfelt, neither seen nor heard, dampening no cheek, experienced only as a secret disquiet of the soul. When in this rough indecent season of the world men accuse the learned, and even sometimes (discipline failing) the learned accuse themselves, of treason, of being derelict to the duties of intellectuals, they speak only what society dumbly knows. If society but knew the dereliction sufficiently to name it, its wisdom would be equal to its poverty, and shortly it would be no longer poor. But that is unlikely. Ambergris is rot in a whale, and if men of the most refined and delicate sensibilities pronounce the smell of it exquisite, what presumption must it appear, in a person of duller and less polished taste, to say that rot, however delicate in the nostril, is in the whale still rot?

The fundamental problem of all political reflection is, to determine an order of law such that those party to it shall be content voluntarily to remain within it, since to desert it is to desert what they value most intimately in themselves.

I do not pretend that that problem is very seriously agitated in our day. It is not. Men are so fearful nowadays of surprising a deity in nature that they regard with profound distrust any affirmation that there are real conditions without which there can be no moral community among men. The only reality which they will admit is the reality of nature—an invincible proposition, except that, for four centuries, the whole exercise of Western intellect has been dedicated to extruding from the idea of nature any reference to the human realities which men have constituted, historically and creatively, in its precinct. Thomas Jefferson did not hesitate, in the great *Declaration,* to appeal to "the law of Nature and of Nature's God." That is a phrasing which, still in his day, serious men would have understood. Rights and duties among men are, as Jefferson perfectly well knew, matters of covenant, instituted of men and therefore cancellable by them. There are nevertheless some rights which must be guaranteed, and some duties which must be acknowledged, in any political community. They are the conditions of any community of persons, since to will community is necessarily to will these. What is the ground of their necessity? Simply this, that wherever they are denied, men have no covenant, but only the illusion of one. Any relation of men to each other, which falls beyond covenant, is a matter of ecology, not of politics at all. Therefore, since peace by covenant is the proper object of political reflection, as Jefferson and his contemporaries understood political reflection, they did not hesitate to pronounce those fundamental rights and their corresponding duties inalienable, to proclaim, for all the world to hear, the rights of man, and implicitly also the duties of man, as belonging to him by nature, according to the law of Nature and of Nature's God.

Our day does not understand that phrasing. It has preferred to oppose nature to human convention, fact to artifact, the moral silence of nature to the instituted peace of men. But, having exercised this preference concerning the use of terms, it has refused to draw the consequence to which it is then committed, that if nature is an order of indifference, then those conventions of our human world, so far from being trifling, must become our profoundest first concern. The reality which includes them must be wider than nature, since it includes, besides nature, history as well, besides Caliban, the Ariel who quickens him. History is a new order of being, as perfectly authentic as the order of being in which the denizens of nature live, suffer, eat, displace each other, and die.[1]

We are of all generations the most perverse, who suppose sanctity to lie in what nature has sanctified, which sanctifies nothing. We suppose that because in nature nothing matters, there-

[1] Compare Herbert Schneider's profoundly sensitive chapter, "Cultural Being," in his Woodbridge Lectures, *Ways of Being, Elements of Analytic Ontology* (New York: Columbia University Press, 1962), III, 44-75.

fore in history nothing matters, that the moral community, because it is our convention, is not therefore our real responsibility,
criticizable and momentous. That consequence is illicitly drawn.
For, properly, the only consequence which follows from our resolution to regard nature as the order of indifference is that the
order of human obligations cannot be understood on natural
grounds. It is doubtless true that you shall have no juice from a
squeezed lemon, but you are forbidden to assume, on ground of
that empty tautology, that there is no such thing as lemon juice.

The whole force of the naturalist position in the contemporary
world rests upon an equivocation, which it has been the study of
positivism to conceal and of moral indolence to permit. We have
denied to the historical sciences their proper object. We have
made of the sciences of nature a study in moral absolution, forgetting that, if morals are pretense, then science is demonstrably
a part of it. For the scientific community—the community of scientists with each other—has, no less than the political community,
its covenant, its rule of method, by obedience to which all scientists stand allied, sharing as persons in pursuit of a truth commonly divined. If the community of scientists has real conditions
without which it could not be, so also, for the same reasons and
with no less certitude, has the political one.

We men of the twentieth century must speak to our own community, and in that community I am content that we should disallow Jefferson's phrase, "the law of Nature and of Nature's God."
But it is inexcusable that we should disallow, with the phrase,
the motive which occasioned it. Natural law, *ius naturale*, there
cannot be, as we nowadays understand the term "nature"; covenant there must be, as we would understand ourselves. The fact
is, that law among men has never depended for its validity on
Nature or on Nature's God. I do not respect the law of Nature and
of Nature's God because God commands it, or Nature commands
it. If I denounce the tyranny of men, shall I any the less denounce
tyranny if it be God's? God's command is as little competent to
bind me as yours or another's, unless I bind myself, unless, by my
own act, I be party to the command, and make his will or yours
my own. God may give to the law its goodness; I alone can give
to it its authority, so far as it governs me. And that is Jefferson's

essential truth, that all government is by consent of the governed. When it was objected to Melancthon, who believed in the law of Nature and of Nature's God, that if the law were by nature, then it would be superfluous for men to make laws, he was, as you might suppose, enraged at the thought. But there is a truth in that objection, though not the truth he saw. The fault in him as in us is, that we both alike seek to have community without having the responsibility for it. Melancthon would have community by gift of God, and we by gift of nature, in the absolution of a simple inheritance, in which nothing is risked, because our partisanship is never exercised. And in this, as I believe, our Jefferson was wiser than Melancthon, and wiser than you and I.

I am as aware as another that the political condition of mankind, wherever mankind has a political condition, is discovered always in a context of struggle. Such peace as men have, or, as it would seem, are capable of, is a peace of factions competing for advantage within a common scene. Faction in human affairs is never to be avoided so long as men are free to associate according to their interests, as they see their interests. It appears wherever the interests of men conflict, and the possibilities of conflict are in a free society always open. You shall not legislate in a free society whether there shall be struggle. You can legislate only that the struggle which occurs shall be human. A struggle is a human struggle not because power is loosed in it, but because persons are party to it. Their alliance at last outweighs their division, and regulates it, as the stones of an arch are held aloft by the very forces which, unchannelled and untamed, would tumble them in loose débris upon the soil.

It is told of the elder Dionysius, the tyrant of ancient Syracuse, that when at a banquet Damocles, one of his courtiers, praised the lot of kings, he caused an unsheathed sword to be hung by a thread, suspended precariously above Damocles' head, that the courtier might prove at once his stomach for government as well as meat. It is not recorded, except by historians turned moralist, whether Damocles survived the test, either in appetite or in privacy. The sword of Damocles images nevertheless the condition of every man in a free society. For that sword poised thus tenuously aloft on a simple filament is the image not of tyranny but of government itself, of any government, whether government by the people or government in spite of them. If I were asked to state the first condition of a free society, I should state it thus simply: a society is free in the measure that every man who is party to it undertakes the honorable risk of sitting voluntarily, for all his suppers, in the place of Damocles.

An American poet once wrote: "What means the noise of the wind to the dust in the wind?"[2] That is of course the query only of a poet, of one who looked with too intimate a sympathy upon the agonies of America in the Civil War. Any historian will understand it. I despair in the modern scene of having it ever understood by any professor of politics. The modern positivism is at once too sentimental and too truculent to know the burden of it. We are that dust which requires a meaning, even in the wind that scatters us. For our humanity is not the name of the species which we inherit, passively and promiscuously, without ennoblement, in a germ. It is the name of our tragic liability, of the tragic task which belongs to historical creatures, and only to them, makers of history and made by it, who would not,

> . . . seizing the swift logic of a woman,
> Curse God and die.[3]

To run the risk of men may not be to be a hero, as to run a race may not be to be a victor. It may be, for all the valor of the effort, to be only ordinary thee and me, this perfection of ordinariness which I discover in myself, quick to stifle the regret that we are no better, quick to urge the defense that we are no worse. But to run the tragic risk is nevertheless, I say, to be human. For in that risk of abasement which belongs to heroes is also the premise of all freedom which belongs to men. In the exercise of that freedom lies whatever is human in ourselves, and if you are diffident of that freedom, that it is a delusion of the ignorant or a sentiment of the forum, then, whatever it is you discuss, you do not discuss the historical condition of men. Which is simply to have said, you do not discuss politics. You may reject the tragic risk which another has imposed, for then you reject only the tyranny of

[2] Stephen Vincent Benét, *John Brown's Body*, III, 101.
[3] Edward Arlington Robinson, *The Man against the Sky*, 135-136.

Dionysius. But if you reject the risk which you yourself impose, you do not secure your humanity; you desert it. The wind bloweth where it listeth, heavy with the tortured dust, and you in it, supinely hurried by it, faster than a man shall walk or run. But you cannot win the race, and neither can you lose it. For you have not entered it.

Index